Stock Split Secrets™

Other Books On This Topic
From Lighthouse Publishing Group, Inc.

Wall Street Money Machine, Volume 1
Wade B. Cook

Wall Street Money Machine, Volume 2
Stock Market Miracles
Wade B. Cook

Wall Street Money Machine, Volume 3
Bulls & Bears
(formerly titled Bear Market Baloney)
Wade B. Cook

Wall Street Money Machine, Volume 4
Safety 1st Investing
Wade B. Cook

On Track Investing
David R. Hebert

Rolling Stocks
Gregory Witt

Sleeping Like A Baby
John C. Hudelson

Making A Living In The Stock Market
Bob Eldridge

STOCK SPLIT SECRET$™

Profiting From A Powerful, Predictable, Price-Moving Event

Miles and Darlene Nelson

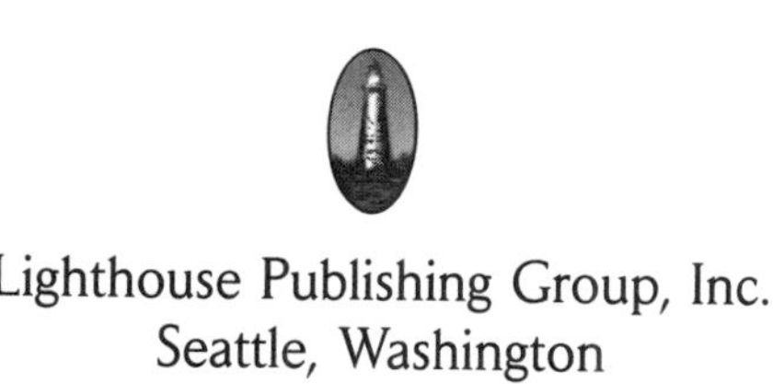

Lighthouse Publishing Group, Inc.
Seattle, Washington

Library of Congress Cataloging-in-Publication Data
Nelson, Miles, 1958-
Stock split secrets™ : profiting from a powerful, predictable, price-moving event/ Miles and Darlene Nelson.
p. cm.
Includes index.
ISBN: 1-892008-51-3
1. Stock splitting. 2. Stocks. 3. Speculation. I. Nelson, Darlene, 1958- II. Title.

HG4028.S75 N45 2000
332.63'22–dc21

00-031627

Source Code: SSS00

"This publication is designed to provide general information in regard to the subject matter covered. It is sold with the understanding that the publisher is not engaged in rendering legal, accounting, or other professional services. If legal, accounting, or other professional services are required, the services of an independent professional should be sought."

From a declaration of principles jointly adopted by a committee of the American Bar Association and the committee of the Publisher's Association."

Book design by Judy Burkhalter
Dust Jacket design by Angie Wilson and Judy Burkhalter

NASDAQ™ is trademark of NASDAQ-AMEX market, AMEX™ is trademark of American Stock Exchange, NYSE™ is trademark of the New York Stock Exchange. CBOE™ is a trademark of the Chicago Board Options Exchange Nasdaq®, Nasdaq-100®, Nasdaq-100 Index®, are registered service/trademarks of The Nasdaq Stock Market, Inc.

Charts produced by TeleChart 2000® which is a registered trademark of Worden Brothers, Inc., Five Oaks Office Park, 4905 Pine Cone Drive, Durham, NC 27707. (800) 766-4940 or (919) 408-0542. http://www.tc2000.com

Published by Lighthouse Publishing Group, Inc.
14675 Interurban Avenue South
Seattle, Washington 98168-4664
1-800-706-8657
206-901-3100 (fax)

Printed in the United States of America
10 9 8 7 6 5 4 3 2 1

In loving memory
of our son
Philip Dicecco Nelson
2/3/86 - 4/14/86
who died of
Sudden Infant Death Syndrome

And in loving memory
of Darlene's Father
Philip Barney Dicecco
6/19/29 – 7/30/93

Contents

Chapter Highlights .... *ix*
Preface .... *xiii*
Acknowledgments .... *xv*

Introduction to Stock Splits 1

1 The Power Of Stock Splits 11

2 Investing In Stock Splits 19

3 Finding Stock Splits 35

4 Stock Splits—The Mini-Play Book 47

5 Stock Split Patterns 73

6 Why Companies Do Stock Splits 85

7 The Stock Split Process 95

8 The Stock Market Is A Cash Cow! 123

9 Options For Stock Splits 143

10 Technical Concepts 159

11 The Five Power Profit Plays 185

12 Putting The Pieces Together 231

13 Bonus Plays And Tools **251**

Appendix 1 .... **267**

Appendix 2 .... **277**

Chapter Highlights

Introduction To Stock Splits
3 The "Clear Technologies" Parable
7 The Truth
8 What To Expect From This Book
9 Explanations And Terminology

1 The Power Of Stock Splits
13 Stock Splits Are Magic
14 Stock Splits Are Emotional
15 Stock Split Companies Regain Value
16 Stock Split Companies Perform
17 Explanations And Terminology

2 Investing In Stock Splits
20 Building A Stock Split Portfolio
30 A Review Of Your Holdings
31 The Buy And Hold Technique
34 Explanations And Terminology

3 Finding Stock Splits
36 Stock Split Timeline
37 The Road Map To Profits
37 Research Management
38 How To Identify Good Stock Split Companies
45 Explanations And Terminology

4 Stock Splits—The Mini-Play Book
48 Taking Aim
48 Rules Change When A Split Is Announced

49 Definitions
49 "Runup" And "Profit Taking" Defined
50 Support And Resistance Defined
51 Uptrend And Downtrend Defined
54 Up-Market/Down-Market Rules
55 How To Use Uptrends And Downtrends
55 Call Options
57 Limit Orders Versus Market Orders
58 Stop Losses
59 Short-Term Plays
60 Mid-Term Plays
60 Long-Terms Plays
61 The Five Phases And Five Plays Of A Stock Split
70 Review Of Formulas—The Mini-Play Book
71 Now On To More Detail

5 Stock Split Patterns
73 Looking At Stock Split Patterns
81 Don't Expect To Play All Five Phases
84 Explanations And Terminology

6 Why Companies Do Stock Splits
85 Increase Liquidity
86 Broaden Base of Stockholders
87 Increase Affordability
88 Pay Dividends Without Cash
91 Increase Shares To Qualify For Listing
91 Qualify For Options Market
91 Keep Up With The Joneses
92 The Greed Factor
92 It's Geometric, Wahoo

7 The Stock Split Process
95 It's A Secret!
97 Looking For Clues
98 Stock Split Requirements
99 The Typical Company That Splits Is:
99 Failing To Announce Can Hurt
101 Reasons Not To Split
101 The Rules
105 The Date is Set

108 SEC Filing Requirements And Forms
116 Running Numbers: Formulas
118 Knowing What To Look For
120 Making It Real

8 **The Stock Market Is A Cash Cow!**
123 How To Milk A Cow
124 The Development Of The Dairy Business
124 In Comes Technology
126 How To Milk The Stock Market
130 And The Survey Said…
130 Comparing With A Known Quantity
131 Playing The Stock Split
136 Using Options For Leverage
139 How To Beat The Market And The Money Managers
141 Explanations And Terminology

9 **Options For Stock Splits**
144 Feelings Change With More Knowledge
144 The Use Of Options Is Common
145 What Is An Option, Really?
146 Real Estate Options
148 Stock Options
149 Stock Option Terms
152 Stock Option Considerations

10 **Technical Concepts**
160 Support And Resistance
160 It's How We Started
162 Support And Resistance Defined
164 Breaking Through: A Strong Indicator
165 Resistance Can Become Support And Vice Versa
166 Moving Averages
171 Buy Low And Sell High
172 Know When To Get In
172 Know When To Get Out
173 Stop-Losses
179 Review Of Basic Trading Terms
180 Uptrends And Downtrends
180 Up-Market/Down-Market Rules

11 The Five Power Profit Plays

187 Phase 1 - Before The Announcement
189 Selecting Stock Split Candidates
190 Which Companies Merit Investigation?
197 Phase 2 - The Announcement
198 Stealing Home
199 The Fast Pitch
200 The Problem—Hitting The Fast Ball
201 The Double Play
203 The Triple Play
207 Phase 3 - Pre-Split Dip
208 Other Events To Play
209 How To Play The Shareholder Event
209 IBM Revisited
215 Phase 4 - Split Date Event
217 Split Date Versus Ex-Date
225 Phase 5 - Post-Split Dip

12 Putting The Pieces Together

231 Investor Psychology
232 Emotion Is A Powerful Force
233 Fear And Greed
234 The Prayer Meeting That Moved Markets
236 Analysts and Market Makers
237 Practice Trading (Paper Trading)
238 Step By Step Rules For Practice Trades
239 Practice Trading That Hurts
241 When To Do The Real Thing
241 Laws And Rules Of Engagement
250 Explanations And Terminology

13 Bonus Plays And Tools

251 Buy On Rumor, Sell Before Fact
253 The Sympathy Play
253 The Earnings Game
255 The Date Of Record Or Recording Date
256 Play The Shareholder Meeting
256 Self-Preservation Tools
262 Swimming Lessons
263 The Deep End
264 Experience Is A Great Teacher
265 Explanations And Terminology

Preface

This book is about making phenomenal money in the stock market! After many months of learning various strategies, we have fallen in love with stock splits. We despise losing money, love quick cash-flow plays, and are deeply fond of repetitive duplicable methods. Stock splits fit this pattern. We have been rich, and we have been flat broke. By experience, having money is so much more fun! After all, if good people can make phenomenal amounts of money they are the ones who can do a world of good with it.

We have found, after learning and making money from the 11 strategies we devoured at a Wall Street Workshop™ in July of 1997, that stock split companies and stock split strategies appear to be one of the sweetest deals of all. When you top this off with Einstein's greatest discovery (the law of compounding), earning a living in the stock market just couldn't get much better!

One day Darlene looked at Einstein's law of compounding and turned it into a real motivator. She took $2,000, and using a calculation of 20% per month for 36 months, generated some extremely exciting results. We started sharing this with other people. We even made them run the numbers themselves, because they would laugh and say we had made a mistake, that we had punched the wrong numbers into the calculator. We would say, "Okay. Let's do it together." And we would all sit there astonished as the numbers climbed past $1,000,000!

Some of you may be thinking, "But who can earn 20% a month on their money?" We think it is silly to expect that you can earn

20% per month on *all* of your money. However, we do expect to earn fantastic returns on that part of our investment capital allocated to stock split investing. We will show you, as we go through some of the strategies, how we have earned over 200% in just a few days using split plays.

Coming from absolutely no knowledge of the stock market two years ago, to earning significant money in the stock market, what we want you to know is that we are just ordinary people and you too can do this with knowledge and perfect practice.

Yes, we do have some college degrees, however we have found the school of hard knocks has been our favorite teacher. Darlene has a Bachelor of Science degree in accounting, and a second Bachelor of Science in business administration, specializing in International Business. She also won a national award for financial planning, and became a top entity specialist. I have a degree in Communications, owned a pre-licensing and continued education school for insurance agents, and have been a professional speaker for many years. Together, we owned and operated a very successful tax firm, where our specialty was IRS audits, tax collection cases, and small business. In 1995 we retired, and sold the firm.

The important point here is that neither of us, in spite of our backgrounds, had any significant knowledge of the stock market. We attended the Wall Street Workshop™, fell in love with a few strategies, and continued to gather specialized knowledge to make them work. This included taking valuable courses in Wealth U™, the best investment education series we have ever attended. Now, we live a lifestyle that many only dream about. Our goal is to help others realize that they can obtain similar results, so that together, we can all devote more of our time and talents to helping others.

Sincerely,
Miles Nelson

Note: This book is written in the first person, as if Darlene is the speaker. In reality, it is a compilation of the experiences of both of us. We felt it would be easier to read the book if it were written from Darlene's point of view.

Acknowledgments

This book could never have been completed done without the support, expertise and help of so many people. We are sincerely grateful to everyone who has aided our efforts. Among some of our greatest mentors in the stock market, to whom we are eternally grateful are Bob Eldridge, Steve Wirrick, Mike Coval, Gary Brecka, Dr. Patrick, and the one who changed it all for us, Wade Cook. In addition, we could not have gotten to this point without Richard Lowman. We will be forever grateful to our father, David Nelson, for harassing us to go to the Wall Street Workshop™, which gave us a life of time, freedom, and money. And our stepmother Ginny Nelson who took care of our children so we could attend the workshop. A huge thank you and gratitude to Lighthouse Publishing, Larry Keim, Dave Hebert, David McKinley, Cynthia Hyatt, Thomas and Kristine Keiser, Todd and Tracy Nelson, Patricia Powell, Kathryn Drinkard, Catherine Coval, Kathy Voorhees, and Jane Grinnell for their ongoing support, faith, and empowerment.

A loving thank you to those closest to our hearts, our three beautiful children, Hollie, Marin and Bryce and to our mothers, Colleen Dicecco and Margaret Sanchez, who put up with us daily and have been there from the start cheering us on with their never-ending belief and love in all that we have set out to do!

Last, and of eternal nature, we thank our Heavenly Father every day for the blessing we have been given, and we pray that this book will reach the hands of those who will take the profits they earn and make a difference in this world.

Stock Split Secrets™

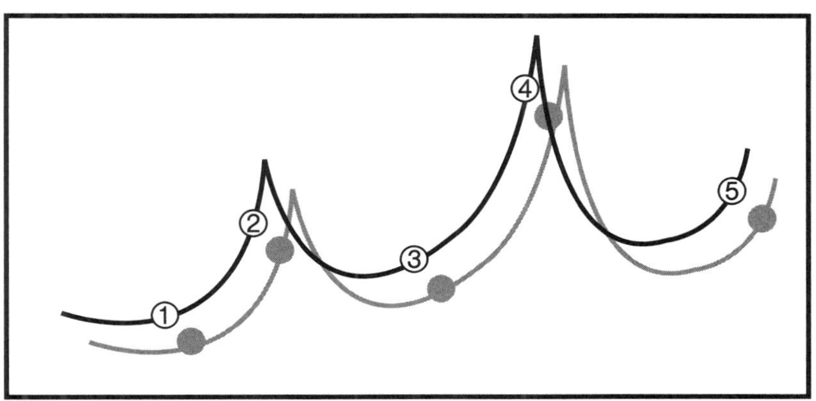

Introduction To Stock Splits

You might have grabbed this book off the shelf while waiting for a connecting flight, or possibly a friend told you about stock splits and you wanted to learn how to profit from them. However you picked it up, by the time you finish this book you will feel very much like a family bird waiting to be roasted—totally stuffed with information, techniques, and answers. You will know why splits are such powerful, predictable, price-moving events, and how to play them for outstanding profits.

Before we get knee deep in technical jargon, I want to tell you a story. I love the power of stories on the human psyche. With your permission I'll start this book off with a short parable. This story is fiction, but it's not a waste of time. It's actually a valuable teaching tool that will set the stage for this book. Mixed throughout the story are important concepts that illustrate the power of splits, the reasons for splits, and the results of splits. This fable is a method of creating value and bringing every reader to the same basic understanding. Consider the following narrative as Act One in the play "Stock Splits."

The "Clear Technologies" Parable

In the distance, I heard a wild rooster announce the start of a new day. The bittersweet taste of salt lingered in my throat as I inhaled. Each breath filled my lungs with the essence of the Kauai surf. Beneath my feet, the smooth planking of our private third-story deck was still damp from the morning dew.

My husband and I were flying up to Namalokama Falls in a few hours. The helicopter pilot had said if we arrived early, we would catch the morning sun breaking through the mist for a breathtaking display of rainbows. I looked out over our ocean-side swimming pool to see the ocean tide ripple under an early breeze. The Princeville Resort in Hawaii was the perfect place to hold our November board of directors meeting.

Again, the rooster celebrated the 5:00AM sunrise. It was early, but I couldn't sleep anyway. I was too excited about the previous night's board meeting, a meeting that meant my husband and I would never have to worry about money again. I could actually quit working and we could live like royalty for the next 100 years. Let me tell you what happened, but first, a little history.

In 1996, a large corporation named MT&T wanted to spin off part of its non-core business. They created Clear Technologies and promised the newly formed board of directors, of which I was a member, cash, support and an edge on the market. Part of the compensation package they used to attract quality officers was an aggressive stock incentive plan. As officers, we would receive stock and options to purchase stock as a reward for company performance.

Clear Technologies did very well during the first year of operations and MT&T kept its promise. I had received more than 200,000 shares as a signing bonus when I joined the Clear Tech management team, and the February 1997 bonus provided me with an option to purchase another 600,000 shares.

In January of 1997 my 200,000 shares were worth $51 each, meaning I could sell my shares and raise a cool $10.2 million. In addition to the 200,000 shares I owned, I had the right to purchase 600,000 more shares at $50 each. But at a market price of only $51, even if I raised the cash to exercise my options and purchase all 600,000 shares I would only net $1 per share.

Now $10.8 million is a great deal of money, but I knew I could do better. A lot better! So I decided to stick with the company for two more years to take advantage of the bonus programs and incentives.

I made the right decision because a year later, things really started moving. We had our 1998 Board of Directors meeting the first week of January. At that meeting, Garth Sacket, president of Clear Technologies, told us about an idea he had. He said that the company stock had done well, but that it had stalled around $75 in June of 1997. It would go up, then fall, go up, then fall. We had everything going for us–growing revenues, increasing market share, *and higher profits–yet investors just didn't seem to understand how well our business was doing. The stock just could not seem to break $75.*

Then Garth told us about a friend of his, Mike Sand, president of Sand Compuware. It seems Mike's company had done a stock split in the middle of 1997. Within 15 days of the announcement the stock had really jumped, and by the time the stock split was finished, shares had almost doubled in price. Then Garth told us his idea. "Why don't we have Clear Technologies do a two-for-one stock split? If investors catch on to the idea, we could have a very good 1998."

The decision of the board was unanimous. We would announce a stock split at the 1998 annual shareholders meeting on February 18th. Still, we needed a way to get the stock price moving right away, or a large chunk of our incentive options would expire at the end of February, worthless. We tossed a few ideas around, but nothing came of it.

Garth said that we had to be careful to avoid trouble for tampering with the share price. He suggested we get a good night's sleep and finish the board of directors meeting during breakfast. Maybe someone would have a idea by then.

That next day, as we gathered over breakfast, Garth stood up and said, "I think we need to discuss the upcoming Clear Technologies stock split." He had spoken casually, but I noticed that his voice carried well, which seemed strange since we were in a public restaurant. What I didn't know was that this particular restaurant was a favorite of local stockbrokers and high-flying investors. After Garth mentioned the stock split, about half the tables went dead silent. It reminded me of the 1970s commercial where someone says, "My broker is _______, and he says..." and everyone in the room freezes, waiting to hear what he says.

All eyes were on Garth as he raised his glass of orange juice to catch a shaft of sunlight. "We don't need shareholder approval," he continued in a clear voice, "because we already have enough unissued, authorized stock. We have three billion shares authorized and only 750,000 issued, so we have plenty of shares to do a two-for-one split. All we need is the approval of the board of directors. I propose that we vote right now on splitting the company stock two-for-one. All in favor say, 'Aye.'" Everyone at our table responded "Aye!"

"Now," he went on, "I propose we let our stockholders be the first ones to know about the split, since they will be affected by Clear Technologies issuing more stock. I think we can make the formal announcement at the shareholder meeting on February 18th. We'll make the split effective in April, on the anniversary of our creation. I'll have our accounting firm take care of the paperwork

and SEC filings." Then Garth sat down. We all looked at each other. We didn't have long to wait.

The next moment was a scene right out of a Charlie Chan movie. The room erupted. Diners from the surrounding tables hastily excused themselves and rushed for the phones to call their brokerage houses, or if they were brokers, to let their best clients know about the pending Clear Technologies stock split. I looked at the smiles on the faces at my table and knew my own was just as broad.

Now, some brokers think a stock split can be bad for shareholders, since the company is issuing part of the authorized shares. Some people say that a split causes a dilution of the stock, but actually, when a stock split occurs there is no change in net value. At any rate, the stockholders would be the ones receiving the stock, so I didn't see any problem.

Garth said he wanted to make the announcement at the annual stockholder meeting in February. Then, to avoid any insider trading issues or misunderstandings with the SEC, he put us on "scouts honor" to keep the news quiet, to say nothing to family or friends until the shareholders meeting. We were instructed to refer any questions about a stock split to the company's public relations office. "That about wraps it up," Garth said. "I move we adjourn. Do I hear a second?"

Things started hopping quickly, the wrong way! The stock went down and kept falling for a couple of days. Not a real collapse or anything, just a few dollars. Within the week, we mailed out the annual reports and shareholder meeting announcements.

The very next day, magic happened. As shareholders began getting their notices, the stock price started moving up. By February 1st the stock had climbed $15 per share. Rumors in stock market magazines and investor publications claimed that something was happening at Clear Technologies. As the rumors increased, so did the price of our stock.

At the February meeting, the stockholders were excited about the rising price of their stock and were more than happy to approve the new options bonus package for officers. After the meeting, we received hundreds of letters from shareholders excited about the stock split. On February 28th, I arranged acquisition of all 600,000 shares listed in my options package, and by the time the split was over, my shares had jumped from $50 to $128 a share!

That was eight months ago. At last night's board of directors meeting, Garth announced that he felt it was time for another two-for-one stock split, however, we were short on authorized shares. "We have 3 billion authorized shares and have already issued 1.6 billion, which leaves us a little short. That means we need to get shareholder authorization to issue additional shares. I want to increase Clear Technologies' authorized shares from 3 billion to 6 billion. That will provide enough shares for a two-for-one split, plus officer incentive packages and other possible transactions such as mergers, acquisitions or raising cash."

No wonder I was having trouble sleeping! I had started out with 200,000 shares in 1996. With the April 1998 split my ownership had doubled to 400,000 shares. In addition, my options to purchase 600,000 shares had doubled to 1,200,000. After exercising those options, I now owned 1,600,000 shares of Clear Technologies, each one worth $87. I would have almost 140 million dollars! If things went as well as they did last time, my 1.6 million shares would become 3.2 million shares, each worth about $60! The only thing we needed was another rumor to shoot the price of the stock up again.

I take a bite of my Caramac bar and swallow. The morning sea breeze ruffled my hair as the thought formed. Then I turned and walked back into the room to rouse my sleepy husband. "Honey," I called out. "Time to get up. I want to eat before we fly to the falls. A local broker told me about this great restaurant nearby. It's a favorite breakfast spot for all his business associates, plus they have a killer omelet. While we eat I'll tell you about the February shareholders meeting–I have great news!"

The Truth

The story you have just read is fiction. As far as I know there is no company called Clear Technologies, nor is there a Garth, Mike, Sand Compuware, or Caramac Bars. Any similarity to actual people, places, things, or companies are purely coincidental.

The purpose of this story is to illustrate the power and potential profits in companies that split their stock. It also provides a peek into the psychology of the people who control major corporations. Some top executives love their work, others love the power, and others want to make a statement, and if we are honest, money is the driving force behind the existence of nearly every public company. Stock splits are a source of rumor and excitement. Fortunes can be increased geometrically and companies can go from blah to blazing in moments.

> *"Money is not happiness. But, with enough cash, you can have a key made."*
>
> *–Aesop's Rich Uncle*

What To Expect From This Book

When Miles and I started writing this book, we initially intended it as a support tool for active traders. We mentioned to people that we were writing a book on stock splits and everyone expressed interest, whether they were actively trading or not. Even my 13-year-old son is excited—he can't wait to get his hands on one of the first books off the press! In those conversations, we discovered that for many readers this book will be their first exposure to the stock market.

If you are an experienced trader, you might be tempted to jump ahead and read the chapters on actual trading formulas. Then you might back up and read other sections of interest to you. Keep in mind that I will introduce new concepts in every chapter, and some will be new or radically different even to experienced investors. I suggest that you take the risk and read the whole book front to back.

In order that you might gain as much as possible from this book I have incorporated a few special elements to aid you. Throughout the book I have included icons to alert you to new information, tips to assist you in your decision making, as well as situations where I feel you might want to observe a little caution. Also, an "Explanations And Terminology" page at the end of each chapter will furnish you with definitions, explanations, and reviews of important concepts.

We invite you to read on and begin to build what you dream.

Explanations And Terminology

Authorized Shares. Authorized shares are used for many purposes, including stock splits, pension plans, employee incentives, mergers, public offerings, debt restructuring, et cetera. There needs to be a surplus of shares to cover these eventualities, in addition to the stock split.

Dilution of Value. Dilution of Value can occur when a company issues additional stock; when more shares are placed in the market, it waters down the value of each share. Dilution usually occurs when shares are given to corporate officers, employees, or via public offerings. Stock splits are not dilutive because the share prices are adjusted, assuring that the stock split is like giving change for a ten dollar bill (2 x $5 = $10).

1

The Power of Stock Splits

When we first started trading stock splits Miles asked our broker if many people used this strategy. The broker replied,"There is no reason to buy a stock just because it was splitting. In fact," he went on, "the split actually dilutes the stock and can reduce the perceived value of the stock."

Many stockbrokers may tell you that a stock split has no real impact on the value of a company. You might hear someone say, "When a stock splits, the share values are adjusted with no actual change in shareholder equity. A stock split is no reason to buy that stock."

Brokers have to pass a licensing examination on SEC rules, stock market basics, and legal definitions. As a result, most brokers learn what a stock split is, but not how to profit from one.

When a company splits their stock they simply issue more shares of stock and distribute them to current shareholders. In a two-for-one stock split, a stockholder with 100 shares of stock would receive an additional 100 shares. Before the split, if 100 shares of ABC stock are worth $10 each, the value of this holding would be $1,000. After a two-for one stock split, ABC issues 100 more shares of stock to the shareholder and the value of all shares is reduced to $5.

Multiply 200 shares by $5 it's still $1,000—the result is no change in shareholder equity.

Although there is technically no change in value, there can be a substantial change in perceived value in the market. If a company splits their stock they are usually doing very well; business is growing and profits are improving. Because of the great news, share prices are climbing. Stock splits are often done to increase affordability by lowering the share price, to increase the number of shares on the market, and to reward shareholders. Some companies pay dividends of stock rather than cash.

After well-known stocks have split, they tend to continue increasing in value until they have returned to the pre-split stock price. If you purchase shares in a strong company that has just split, you have the law of averages on your side. Chances are, if you purchase today and it splits two-for-one tomorrow, that stock will probably increase in value. Eventually it could be selling at a price equal to the pre-split price.

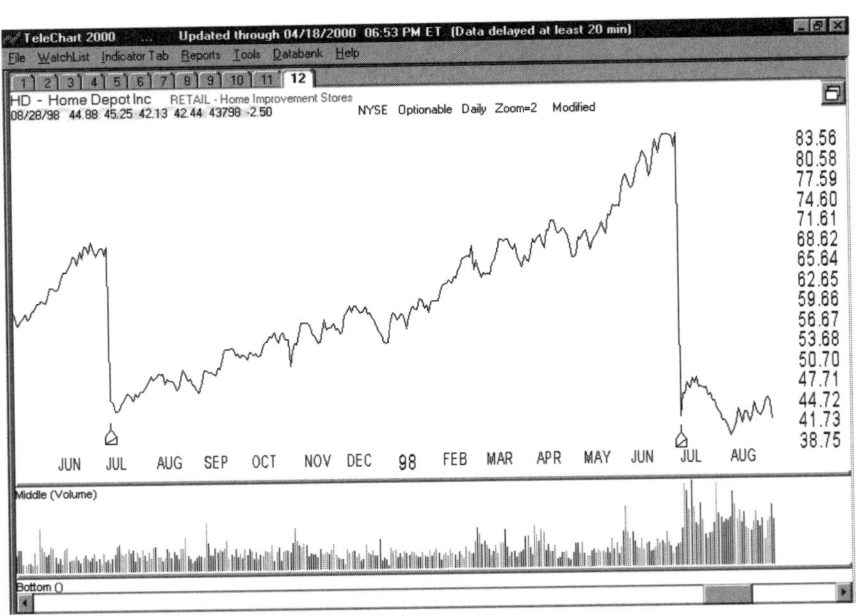

Whenever you see this symbol "⌂" in a chart, it represents the ex-date, or the day after a stock splits.

Let me give you an example: If you own 300 shares of Home Depot, Inc. (ticker symbol HD), selling at $70 today, and the stock is split two-for-one tomorrow, you would end up with 600 shares worth $35 each. Wait for a year or so and as Home Depot continues growing, expanding, and profiting, your shares will probably have increased in value until they're worth close to $70 again!

For a basic description of line charts see Appendix 1.

Stock Splits Are Magic

There is something magical about a stock split. Investors get excited and stock prices jump. In many cases this jump in price is based not on fundamental data, but on pure emotion.

This kind of emotion can create high demand: more buyers than sellers. The law of supply and demand says that if you have people buying more than selling, the price must go up. How far? How long? Who knows? However, if you know that it is going to happen, you have the ability to make a profit from it. Applied knowledge is money!

If you knew the future, you could use that knowledge to make millions of dollars in the stock market. Imagine knowing about the crash of 1929 a month early. You could sell everything and have cash under your pillow. Then, in the months after the crash, you could buy stocks in big companies for pennies on the dollar.

You may not be able to tell the future, but you can predict the likely performance of stocks based on scheduled events. A perfect example is what happens to a stock when it is being added to the Standard and Poor's 500™ (S&P 500™). In order to match the movement of the S&P 500, index funds need to purchase shares of any stock added to the list. As a result, within a few days of an announcement that a stock is being added it becomes a hot target for index fund managers.

This creates a situation where there is more buying pressure on the stock than owners willing to sell. With this pressure the stock price goes up and it can become like a feeding frenzy. If you knew beforehand which stocks would be added to the S&P 500, you could purchase before the buying delirium, then sell when the stock price is pushed up.

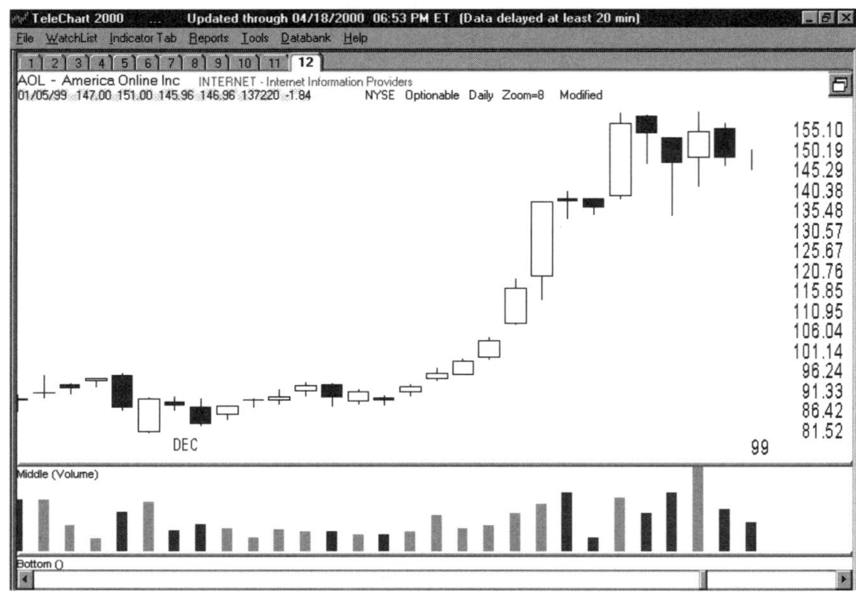

You can apply the same concept to companies that are splitting their stock. These companies tend to behave in a very predictable manner. It's almost as if the stocks are handed a script. Knowing this is like being able to see the future, and you can profit from it. If you are one of the people with a copy of the script you can read between the lines—making a profit whenever you want!

For a basic description of candlestick charts please refer to Appendix 1.

Stock Splits Are Emotional

Stock splits are emotion-based, and so is the stock market. Each business morning when the bell rings, people are faced with another day of trading. One day the market is shooting up and the bulls are taking no prisoners. The next morning, bears are in control and news anchors are declaring the end of the world. It's amazing how a bean-processing plant failure in some Third World country can signal a rash of sell orders and send the market into a tailspin. Then some analyst makes a public statement and the emotional climate changes again, with massive price shifts within moments.

Do these up and down swings really happen because of facts and figures? Could huge corporations really be so unstable that the stock price merits a 5% adjustment one day, only to turn the other direction the next morning? Not very likely! The market usually changes because emotional tides sweep through the trading floors, causing wave after wave of intense buying and selling. Of course, there are things that start the emotion, but the market seems to overreact to everything.

There are times when massive price adjustments do need to be made in a stock. Perhaps a news announcement declares that the company will increase profits by 50% the following year, or that their biggest market has been eliminated and they will have an 80% reduction in earnings. When big news announcements occur, the stock price is usually adjusted very quickly. But the emotion of the market can cause up and down swings, driven by pure speculation and rumor, not fact.

By understanding the psychology of this game you can reap massive rewards. Professionals look for specific events that can be used to predict the direction a stock will take. Stock splits are one such event—a tremendous indicator to help you predict the direction and timing of stock movement.

Professional investors use pre-defined formulas to profit from these specific events. This book will discuss many such formulas, time-tested recipes that have been refined and proven successful in stock splits scenarios. In order for these formulas to work, you need to have all of the ingredients, which is where this book comes in. By following these recipes, you can have your cake and eat it, too!

Stock Split Companies Regain Value

Experience has shown me that after a quality company has split, the stock tends to keep increasing in value. This trend continues until the price per share is nearly equal to the pre-split price. If a company were to split its stock two-for-one when it was selling for $146 per share, after the split the adjusted price would be $73. Top companies may continue growing and the stock price will slowly climb until it approaches $146 per share again. This price recovery may take anywhere from six months to three years, but the stronger companies usually reach their pre-split price within 2½ years or less.

If a company grows at an annual rate of 24% it will be able to split two-for-one every three years. The S&P 500 has grown at approximately 20% per year (not considering dividends). In order for a company to grow at 24% it will have to be a little better than average.

Stock Split Companies Perform

Some time ago I learned about a professional study that looked at two-for-one stock splits. This study, "What Do Stock Splits Really Signal?" by David L. Ikenberry, Graeme Rankine, and Earl K. Stice, discovered that these companies tend to grow at an annual rate of 54.24% faster than the general market—prior to the split. After splitting, they continue their explosion, growing another 7.93% faster than the market, for an entire year. If you look closely at the top splitters, you'll see their growth rate is even better.

When you look at the history of strong, profitable companies, you will discover that their stock price performs, on average, much better than other companies. You'll also find that most of these powerful companies split their stock on a regular basis—usually every one to five years. Stock split companies are usually the top performers in their sector and industry. This observation can become powerful when looking for stocks to add to your investment program. In the next chapter you will get to experience the excitement of developing a stock split portfolio.

Explanations And Terminology

Bears. Bears are those who believe stock prices will fall.

Bulls. Bulls are those who believe prices, either of a stock or the market overall, will go up.

Use the Formulas. In order for the formulas to work, you need to have all of the ingredients. By following the recipe, you can have your cake and eat it, too!

2

Investing In Stock Splits

In this and future chapters, I will be discussing real companies. If I discuss a particular company, stock, or market, it is for the purposes of illustration only. I am not making any specific investment suggestions or recommendations; I am only discussing techniques and formulas. Although I have done my best to assure accuracy, my stories are created using the market conditions that existed on the day the page was typed. Tomorrow, everything could be different; stock and financial markets change in a millisecond. These examples are presented so that you can learn stock split concepts, not to provide investment advice. Please—Don't buy or sell any stock or option because you read about it in this book. Before you make any stock split investment decisions please do the following:

1. Finish this book.
2. Do practice trades until you have consistent success.
3. Consult your broker or investment professional.

The only way to select an appropriate investment is to do your homework. Nothing in this book is to be considered a recommendation to buy or sell anything. Do not purchase or sell anything because you see it mentioned in this book. By the time this book is printed, conditions may have changed and every company mentioned could have gone out of business or become insurance companies selling freezer coverage to Siberian polar bears.

Building A Stock Split Portfolio

I find that people learn in a number of different ways. Remembering what we learn is the real challenge. The most effective educators are ones that make learning enjoyable. Personally, I like the teachers who use stories.

Based on this, I want to teach you by telling a few stories. In these stories are powerful concepts that I will use as I discuss techniques to profit from stock splits. Using these stories I'll build a "stock split portfolio," so you can see how it performs compared to the market as a whole. As our baseline for a minimum rate of return, I'll use the performance of the S&P 100 index, which tracks the performance of 100 of the top companies.

Clear Channel Communications, Inc (CCU)

CCU traded in a range between $4 and $6 (split adjusted) for more than five years. By 1990, communications technology was changing rapidly. The FCC began removing regulations at a feverish pace. Recreational broadcasting was exploding. In the midst of this, CCU was making the right choices—including taking a risk by using programming services from Fox. This was a wise move because Fox's network affiliates seemed to have a license to print money.

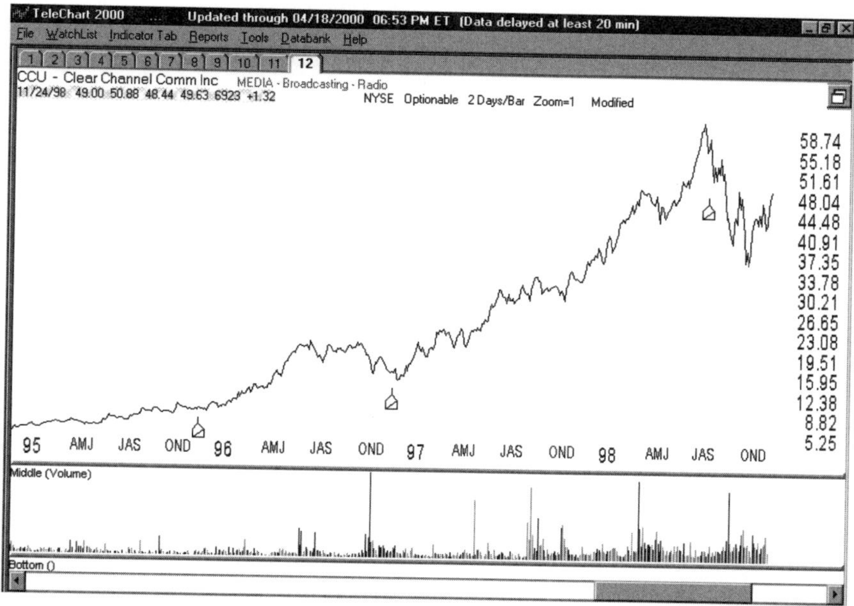

Business was electrifying and CCU's stock climbed from $6 to $15. In December of 1992, CCU declared a five-for-four stock split (dividend in the form of a split). The stock soared as high as $22 before splitting. After the split things kept hopping; the stock price continued to climb. By July 1995, the share price was over $60. At that price some investors considered it an accident waiting to happen. But CCU continued growing and improving, resulting in continued positive earnings surprises and exciting announcements.

If you had purchased 100 shares of CCU in October of 1995, you would have paid $77 per share. Your investment would have cost $7,700, plus broker commissions. That stock split two-for-one in December of 1995, again in December of 1996, and yet again in July of 1998. By November 1998, your 100 shares would have increased 800 shares worth $44 each. Your holdings in CCU would have gone from $7,700 to $35,200! That's over 100% rate of return each year, for four years' effort.

Now CCU is stalled and doesn't seem to be growing as fast as it did. That's okay. You've already made plenty of money--on paper. It's time to take your profits and move on. You can sell your CCU holdings and move to another company that is growing, or you can afford to keep 100 shares, sell the rest, and put the money to work for diversification.

Lucent Technologies (LU)

In 1996, AT&T did a spin off and created Lucent Technologies (LU). LU is a company sitting on the edge of the technological world, providing products and services to key technological organizations. LU has very positive plans and business is clicking.

On April 8, 1996, LU was worth $31 a share. They had to get the world to remember their name and prove they were worthy of their blue chip heritage. Most companies that spin off from AT&T are solid, profitable, and powerful. LU wanted to become another worthy child of this powerful parent.

At their February 18, 1998 meeting, shareholders were told that LU was going to execute a two-for-one stock split on the anniversary of their creation—April 2, 1998. (Isn't nostalgia great?) LU had three billion shares authorized and about 750,000,000 shares issued. Since the company already had enough shares authorized to do a split, they did not need to have shareholder approval.

If you had purchased 100 shares of LU on February 18, 1998, after the shareholder meeting, you would have paid $92.88 per share. Your total investment would have been $9,288, plus broker commissions. The split was completed as scheduled on April 2, 1998. Just before the split your 100 shares would have been worth $134 each ($13,400 total value).

That night you would have called your favorite person, the broker who has your 100 shares of LU, and learned that after the split, your account had received a deposit of 100 more shares of LU, compliments of Lucent's CEO, Henry B. Schacht. Your 200 shares would have been adjusted to reflect the post-split price, so they are now worth $67 a share ($134 ÷ 2 = $67). Your 200 shares are still worth $13,400 ($67 x 200 = $13,400).

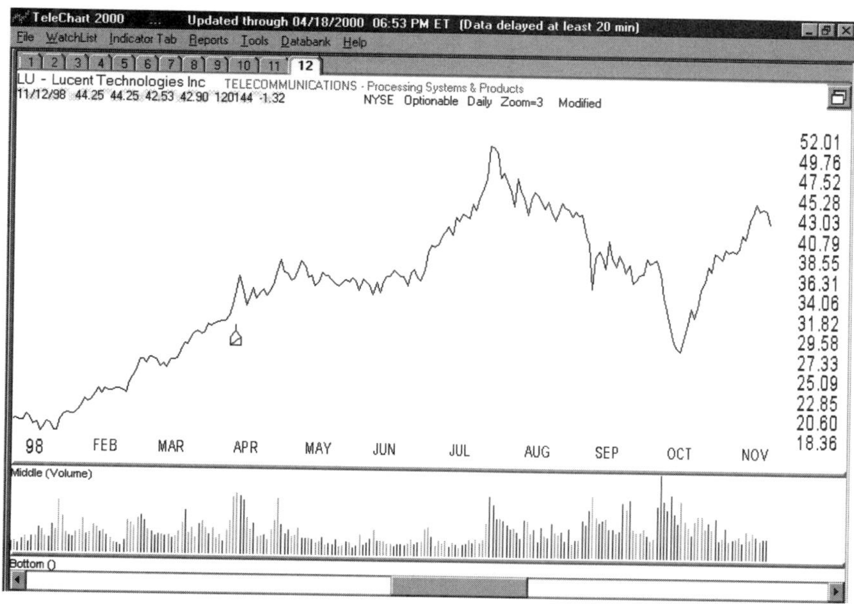

Now, you really like Lucent and feel that the stock has more room to grow, so you hold on to the 200 shares to wait and see what the future will bring. By July 1998, they are worth $105 each. Things are exciting, but only a few months later, the world is in the middle of a meltdown. Since you were in a coma and you forgot to tell your broker to place a $10 trailing stop-loss on LU, you watch the stock fall. By the first week of October, the stock has collapsed to $55 a share. But the great thing about the stock market is it loves to climb up! By November 1998, your stock has returned to $88 a share. Your Lucent holdings are worth $88 x 200 = $17,600. Wow! Your investment has grown 163% in less than nine months for a 217% annual return.

Stop-loss is a technique that limits your loss if a play moves against you. I'll cover this in detail later in the book.

In November, your broker tells you that Lucent has just filed an SEC proxy form in preparation for the February 1999 annual shareholder meeting. The form has a wonderful item to vote on—Lucent is asking shareholders for permission to increase the number of authorized shares of common stock from three to six billion shares. It looks like another stock split is set to happen between February 1999 and April 1999. The board of directors will probably get nostalgic again and make the split effective near the anniversary of the company's birth in April.

Microsoft Corporation (MSFT)

Can anyone talk about stock splits without mentioning Microsoft (MSFT)? Miles's brother Cole went to high school with Bill Gates. Cole had some amazing stories to tell, but I think I'll keep them secret. Perhaps they'll come in handy when the *National Examiner* gets tired of running the "Bat Boy Found Living in Cave" article.

I can remember my mom telling me that she had an opportunity to purchase 1,000 shares of MSFT in the early years. She couldn't really afford to invest the money ($10,000) and had no idea what the future would bring. Had Mom bought those shares, she would now be worth more than ten million dollars! Oh well, we all have similar sad stories to share—"I cudda been great, if'n I had only taken the risk!"

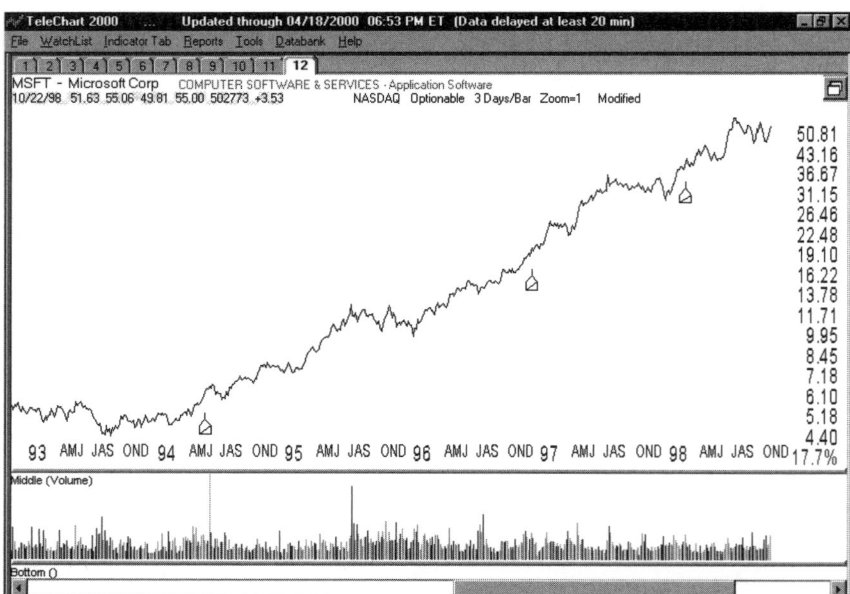

MSFT is probably the best-known stock split story in the world. Prior to the last Microsoft split, rumor used to be that Bill Gates only needed to split MSFT's stock one more time and he'd become the richest man that ever lived! Unless, of course, you include Solomon from the Bible, who owned most of the known world.

I will not go back to the start of Microsoft—if I did that my calculator would run out of zeros. Let's start with May 20, 1994. MSFT is going to split tomorrow and you decide to take the plunge even after the stock has already run up tons. You purchase 100 shares at $88 a share ($8,800 plus commissions). The stock splits two-for-one on May 23, 1994, again on December 9, 1996; then it splits again on February 23, 1998. Your 100 shares grow to 800.

Action	Date	Shares
Purchase	*May 1994*	*100*
Split 2:1	*May 1994*	*200 (100 x 2)*
Split 2:1	*December 1996*	*400 (200 x 2)*
Split 2:1	*February 1998*	*800 (400 x 2)*

You notice that Microsoft seems to climb back up to the pre-split price within two years of the split. You also notice that the stock split announcements have been almost progressive. The first one happened when the stock was above $100 a share, the second above $110, and the third above $120 a share. Could that mean the next announcement might happen when the stock hits the $130 to $140 range?

Your original investment was $8,800, and you held the stock from 1994 through November 1998. Now you have 800 shares worth $109 each, for a total value of $87,200. Do you hang on or take your profits? The stock price is close to an all-time high and not far from the $120 to $140 target. However, you take a closer look at the charts, and see that MSFT is stuck in a trading range. There is a good chance that the stock will not have a split announcement until it breaks out of the trading range and continues its climb to the sky.

Of course, some companies have used split announcements to get the stock price moving again. A split announcement can actually cause a stock to jump out of its trading range and head for the stratosphere. You also notice that Microsoft is in the middle of a big Federal Trade Commission (FTC) anti-trust lawsuit. Some people believe the FTC case affects only 4% of Microsoft's total business.

It also appears that Microsoft will come out shining, no matter what happens. The case could have far reaching implications for Microsoft and its future is looking a little uncertain, which might be the reason the stock is stalled.

Dell Computer Corporation (DELL)

In a moment, you'll discover that Dell Computer Corporation has actually performed better than the other stocks in your portfolio, including Microsoft, and you'll learn why. It begins with Michael Dell.

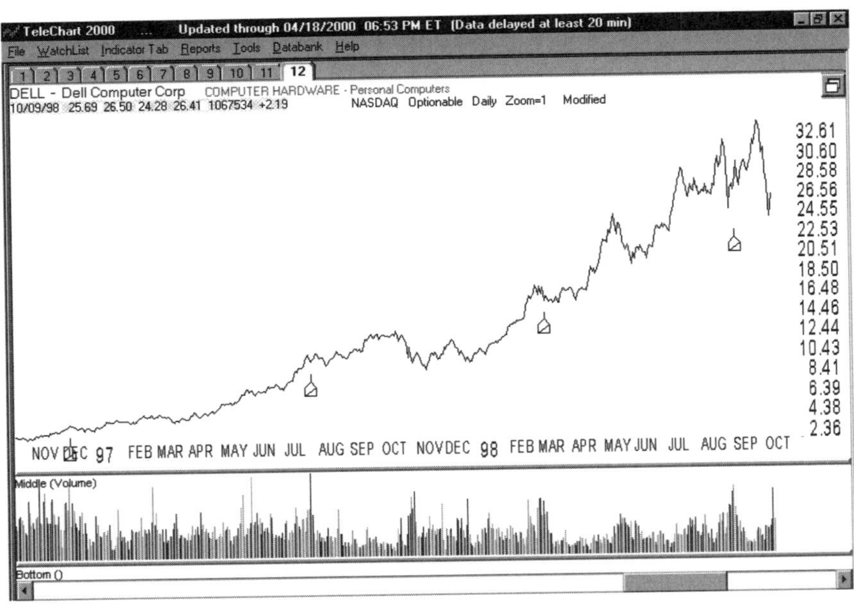

Michael Dell was probably one of those pocket-protector guys in science class. I don't mean that as a slur; he reminds me of Einstein. In my imagination, I can just see Michael in the early days of Dell Computer, his kitchen table covered with computer components as he assembled homemade computer systems for his family and friends. I bet he still loves the smell of solder in the morning.

It was this genius, coupled with remarkable business skill that transformed the small business into a worldwide enterprise. Operating on a shoestring budget, DELL Computer quickly became a powerhouse in direct marketing. It didn't take long before the company needed more manufacturing space and better equipment in order to keep up with the constantly increasing orders.

Even then, DELL seemed to have a crystal ball that told management what changes would decimate the industry, allowing them to step aside or make adjustments, leaving them virtually unaffected when bad news broke out. Since its simple beginnings, DELL has become one of the most influential technology companies of the 1990s. *Fortune Magazine* listed DELL as #1 in total return to investors in 1998 in its April 26, 1999 issue.

But let's get back to your portfolio. Late in1996, Dell Computer announced a two-for-one stock split. Knowing that DELL was on the leading edge, you decided to jump in. On October 1, 1996, you purchased 100 shares at a price of $41.20 each. Your total investment was $4,120, plus commissions. DELL performs as expected and completes the two-for-one split on December 9, 1996. Your 100 shares had babies and you now own 200 shares. Split adjusted, each share is worth $30.24. Your 200 shares are now worth $6,048. That's a great return for a two-month investment.

Being a "buy and hold" kind of person, you decide to stick around and see what happens. Dell Computer Corporation lives up to your expectations and over the next 18 months it splits three more times! Two-for-one on July 28, 1997, March 9, 1998, and September 8, 1998.

Unfortunately, after the third split the markets almost roll up the carpet because of Russian financial collapse, Brazilian international loan defaults, and Japanese banking failures. World markets plunge, ticker tapes are a sea of red, and news announcers are declaring the end of the world. By the end of September 1998, you almost pull the plug, but you think that if anyone can survive, DELL can. Sure enough, DELL recovers a few weeks later and continues its upward climb.

In a press release a big name computer manufacturer stated that they planned to take away some of DELL's market share. This type of press release is a common tactic in the corporate world, where a competitor will use the fast growth of a rival to show their own potential.

Looking at your notes you see that DELL has split four times in two years—every six months! Will they continue their growth? A clue is presented in November 1998. Dell Computer announces fantastic earnings and the following morning Michael Dell gives CNBC a phenomenal interview. He states that a competitor's recent announcement will probably not hurt their bottom line. In addition, he reports that DELL is going to grow at better than average rates, five times faster than the sector as a whole. It looks like DELL will continue to be a great contender, and you decide to hang around for the party. At the end of November 1998 you check your financial progress. Your modest investment of $4,120 has multiplied.

Action	Date	Shares	
Purchase	*October 1996*	*100*	
Split 2:1	*December 1996*	*200*	*(100 x 2)*
Split 2:1	*July 1997*	*400*	*(200 x 2)*
Split 2:1	*March 1998*	*800*	*(400 x 2)*
Split 2:1	*September 1998*	*1,600*	*(800 x 2)*

Take your 1,600 shares at a value of $61.56 each and your investment is worth $98,496—that's better than 1,000% a year! Compare this with the growth of mutual funds.

The S&P 100™

The S&P 100™ is a list of 100 of the strongest public companies, maintained by Standard and Poors. The companies listed in the S&P 100 meet basic minimum standards of size, stability, and security. It is beyond the scope of this book to discuss how companies are selected and scored. A few seconds ago I pulled up TeleChart 2000® (TC-2000®) and did a scan of the S&P 100. It is amazing that the top 20 to 30 names are companies you see in the news almost every day, like Exxon, McDonalds, et cetera. Add to that a handful of companies in other indexes like: S&P 500, NASDAQ 100, DJ-30, DJ-20, and DJ-10 and you have the cream of the stock market. The S&P 100 is kind of the upper crust and the S&P 500 is the next best. There is a small group of companies that create most of the movement in the S&P 500. Look for yourself—you'll see that they also happen to be great stock split examples.

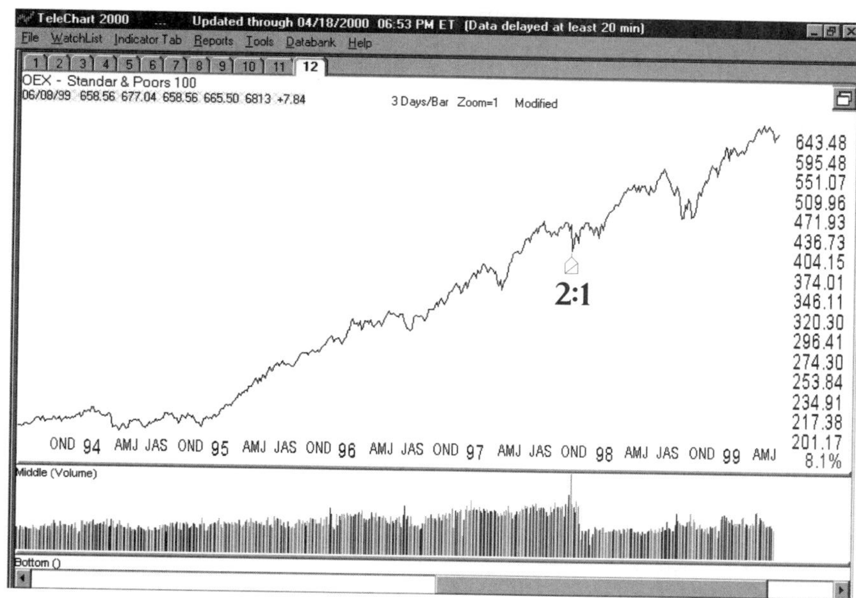

Your portfolio already includes CCU, LU, MSFT, and DELL. If you had enough cash you would love to purchase interest in every company listed in the S&P 100. Unfortunately, you don't have that kind of money, so you invest what's left in the OEX. (When you purchase shares of OEX you get tiny portions of the 100 companies listed in the S&P 100.) You are doing this to spread your risk through participation in a wide range of companies and sectors.

You purchase 10 units on May 20, 1994 at a price of $210.79 each. The investment costs $2,108 ($210.79 x 10 = $2,107.90) plus commissions. You sell your units on November 1, 1998 and end up with $536.97 x 10 = $5,370 (rounded up).

When you looked at the chart did you notice that OEX did a two-for-one split? Sorry–the split indicated was just a technical adjustment in the listed price of the index; there was no "stock split" play or change in value because of the split. In the case of the S&P 100, think of an OEX split like getting change for a $10 bill–you end up with two $5s, nothing more.

A Review of Your Holdings

It's November 1, 1998, and you have decided to sell everything and settle up with the IRS. You review the technology part of your portfolio. Look at the chart of your purchases and the annualized rates of return for each stock you purchased. Compare this to your typical mutual fund, money market fund, or index fund: which performs the best?

Company	Bought	Sold	Invested	Returned	Annual %
CCU	*10/1/95*	*11/1/98*	*$7,700*	*$35,200*	*116%*
LU	*2/18/98*	*11/1/98*	*$9,288*	*$17,600*	*128%*
MSFT	*5/20/94*	*11/1/98*	*$8,800*	*$87,200*	*200%*
DELL	*10/1/96*	*11/1/98*	*$4,120*	*$98,496*	*1099%*
S&P100	*5/20/94*	*11/1/98*	*$2,108*	*$5,370*	*35%*

Looking at the stocks, they performed better than the S&P 100. I'll admit that 35% a year is a good return. That's why indexed funds exist; they try to perform close to the index that they follow. The key word here is "try" because few indexed funds perform as well as the real thing, but they try. Let's face it, the list you have just examined represents some of the better performing stock split records.

If your figures turn out different than what I show in the chart, see the section called "Calculating your monthly rate of return." It's a simple formula that provides a quick way for comparing the success of your various investments.

The good old 20/80 rule still rings true, even in the stock market. Most stock splits will perform differently than the ones outlined here. Some will do better and others will do worse. So, if you are going to invest in the market, you might as well look at the best stocks available, right?

Reviewing this chart, I originally expected Microsoft to be the best performer, but MSFT has been superceded by DELL. And by next year DELL will be a slowpoke compared to a new "market miracle"—there will always be new companies with advanced methods that outshine the competition. This makes the stock market a constantly changing, very exciting resource for investment and opportunity.

The Buy And Hold Technique

What I have discussed so far is only one stock market investing technique—buy and hold. I think any person purchasing stock to hold it for many years must look at far more than great charts and a few reports—fundamental and technical analysis are both critical. This book is written to discuss how to profit from stock splits, which occur in short defined slices of time, comprising only a few months or less.

Miles and I find that every time we attend another investment class or seminar, we improve our technique and our profits are intensified. We actually spent our last anniversary at a fantastic course that discussed fundamental and technical analysis. We find that many of these classes review and reinforce what we already know, and there are always a few "a-ha's" that give us totally new trading ideas.

The truth is, most investors are ill equipped to purchase stocks for the long haul. Their potential for success is limited to their ability to guess well or follow the advice of a qualified advisor. Who has the time or resources to digest a 100-page financial statement for each company they want to consider? There has to be some work put into the verification of the company operations and the accuracy of their financials.

When it comes to the stock market, the only thing cast in stone is the fact that the market is constantly changing. Today the entire world can be headed for financial collapse and tomorrow it can be filled with opportunity.

Even large companies get caught with their pants down. Do you remember the horrifying news about Columbia Healthcare (COL) in April 1997? It shocked the Managed Care Sector. It was alleged that some of the financial departments in the organization were fudging on their books, stealing from Medicare, and cheating insurance carriers. As a result of the investigations, these facilities had to restate earnings for 3 to 10 years. After the restatements, there were further allegations of wrongdoing, fraud, theft, and so forth. Managed Care stocks took a nose-dive and COL lost 60% of its value. I knew people who were using a buy and hold investment technique to manage their retirement funds. They unknowingly had large chunks of COL in their pension funds. Right before their eyes they saw their life savings wiped out.

Another example is the Sunbeam (SOC) debacle. After early 1998 news releases, the company had round after round of termination notices and pink slips. The process reminded me of the management techniques used during the French Revolution, which I nicknamed "guillotine management." Unfortunately it was too little too late—in less than six months the stock collapsed from $50 to as low as $4.50—a 90% drop.

Sure, these companies might move back to their old highs—eventually. But I want to earn and spend my money while I am alive, not wait for my great-great grandchildren to finally see the profits from a stock investment disaster.

The reason I illustrated the buy and hold concept for the last four companies is to provide a point of reference when I talk about other investment formulas. Before I discuss those formulas, we need to talk about what companies to invest in and how to find them.

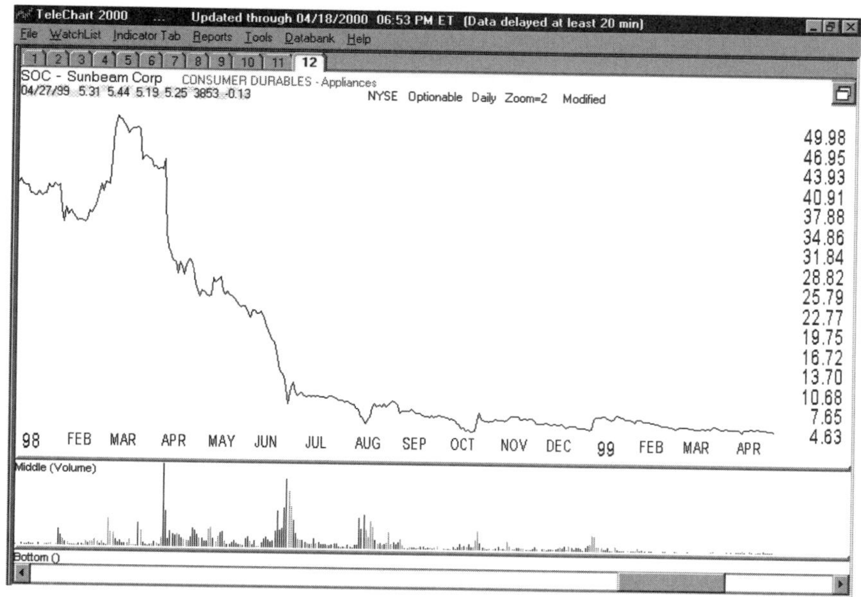
TeleChart 2000 ... Updated through 04/18/2000 06:53 PM ET (Data delayed at least 20 min)
File WatchList Indicator Tab Reports Tools Databank Help
SOC - Sunbeam Corp CONSUMER DURABLES - Appliances
04/27/99 5.31 5.44 5.19 5.25 3853 -0.13
NYSE Optionable Daily Zoom=2 Modified
49.98
46.95
43.93
40.91
37.88
34.86
31.84
28.82
25.79
22.77
19.75
16.72
13.70
10.68
7.65
4.63
98 FEB MAR APR MAY JUN JUL AUG SEP OCT NOV DEC 99 FEB MAR APR
Middle (Volume)
Bottom ()

Explanations And Terminology

Authorized Shares versus Issued Shares. "Authorized" means the ability to issue. "Issued" means placed into service (sold).

In order to authorize additional shares, a corporation must make an amendment to its articles of incorporation. This requires shareholder approval. The company has to ask the shareholders to vote on increasing the number of authorized shares.

Fundamental Analysis. The study of financial and historical operations of a company.

Split Adjusted. In a chart adjusted for a stock split, all the dollars prior to the split are reconciled to have the value they would have had after the split. An adjusted chart is necessary for indicators to be meaningful.

Technical Analysis. The study of the historical price changes of the stock, using such indicators as candlesticks, moving averages, et cetera.

Guillotine Management. A phrase coined by the author to describe the process of doing massive layoffs in middle and upper management—"Off with their heads" is the motto of the day—and bringing in new talent and trying to run a company with a team of new people who have no clue what's happening.

3

Finding Stock Splits

Shortly before a split is announced there is usually an increase in the price of the stock. When the split is announced there is instant excitement that causes a sudden, short-term surge in the stock price. After the announcement, investors take profits and the stock tends to calm back down a little. When the stock price moves down it gives investors an opportunity to jump into the stock at sale prices and capture profits as it later rises. I call this temporary drop in stock prices a "dip."

The stock price tends to move up and down a few times. Then shortly before the actual split, there is a strong increase in volume and the price of the stock. Shortly after the split occurs, investors take profits, lose interest, and the stock price falls down, creating another buying opportunity (dip). After the profit-takers have sold and the stock calms down, good news or other events will occur, which cause the stock price to start climbing again.

Stock Split Timeline

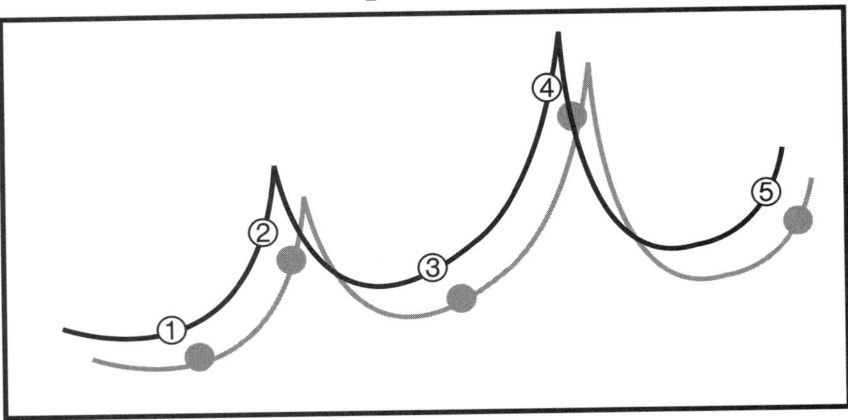

I can break this common timeline into five sections, called the five phases of a stock split:

- ***Phase 1***—Before the Announcement. A short-term increase in stock price before an expected or rumored announcement date.
- ***Phase 2***—On the Announcement. Within seconds of the announcement the stock price jumps up, and then usually falls back down—quickly.
- ***Phase 3***—Pre-Split Dip. After the announcement, the stock calms down, because of profit taking, and the price falls. Depending on the length of time between the announcement and the actual split, the stock may move up and down more than once.
- ***Phase 4***—Split Date. One to five days before the split the price runs up—the greatest price increase tends to be the day before and the day of the split event.
- ***Phase 5***—Post-Split Dip. Within hours or days of the split, the stock dips down because of profit taking. The stock may enter a sideways channel for 30 to 45 days before it levels out and starts climbing again.

This book will discuss the five common events that occur in the life of a stock split. There are specific formulas for earning money on each of these five phases. You have to understand the unique characteristics of each event or you could find yourself selling when you should be buying, or using techniques that could limit your success. Take it one step at a time, there is no hurry to master all concepts right away.

The Road Map To Profits

With a little practice, you can use the five phases as a road map to profits. You can get into a stock when you expect upward movement. Then exit the trade profitably, when the stock is starting to move down. Keep in mind that predicting how a stock will behave cannot be learned by just reading a book; it takes in-the-trenches practice. Use this book as a guideline for your success, but before you use real money, practice on paper first.

Practice Trading or Paper Trading is a defensive process where you pretend to invest your money and keep a record of your transactions until you have a track record of successful "pretend" deals. Later in this book I will cover practice trading techniques in greater detail.

These are small time frames. Some plays last a few hours, others a few days, and some a few weeks. It is rare that I see a stock split play last longer than a month. Knowing that I will have my money at risk for a short time, I can take advantage of techniques that return greater profits. In most cases, I use stock options instead of purchasing the actual stock, because they can return a much larger profit percentage than buying the stock.

Options are risky, but I manage that risk in many ways. With the correct techniques, options can actually help control your risk and allow you to conserve most of your capital for other investment purposes. I have found options provide me with more safety and control. When doing short-term trades, options allow me to leverage my money by controlling large blocks of stock with a small amount of money, leaving the rest safe. Later in this book I'll discuss options and techniques for using options to profit from stock splits.

Research Management

How can you identify good or exceptional companies to invest in? How do you determine what sectors are going to be the most profitable, and which companies are the most powerful in that sector or category?

I can think of two ways to get this information. The easiest is to subscribe to a qualified, top-quality research service that will ferret out top market contenders and provide a list of potential stock split plays. I use a service called Wealth Information Network™—W.I.N.™. (For more information, see Appendix 2.) The second method is using good old research and review. If you want to do your own research, the rest of this section will discuss a few basics.

Take a look at the current business and financial environment and see if you can predict the future. If you review current social and financial conditions, you can find some sectors in the market that are growing faster than others. If you know who has money and where it's being spent, you have a great indication of where to invest.

Each year, there are industries drying up because progress has passed them by. Others are in their prime on the forefront of development. Wise investing is a matter of identifying what companies have the greatest likelihood of growth. You will find stock splits clustered in sectors with a high number of fast-growing companies. The greater the growth, the faster the change in stock prices, and splits become frequent events.

If you read major business publications, you will often see consistencies between the magazines; there will be many similar articles written. What sectors are the subject of discussion? Which ones seem to have increasing growth? A 20-minute scan of three or four investment publications can provide a pretty good view of the hot industries. Once I have found the sectors that look promising, it takes only a few more minutes to bring up the charts of the companies in that sector. Since Worden Brothers research software is my favorite, I fire up TC-2000® and look at the sectors that spark my interest. Then it's a simple matter to scan the charts of the companies in that sector.

How To Identify Good Stock Split Companies

There are anywhere from 200 to 600 stock splits each year. Some of these companies are unreliable investment opportunities and other are fantastic cash-flow generators. Since I value my investment money, I want to be selective where I place my trust. There are several characteristics that lead to a predictable opportunity for investment. Today investors have an overwhelming amount of information available, I have found that it is imperative to check: Size, Direction, Volume, Open Interest, History, Environment, News, Volatility and Float. Using this research I apply a set of minimum rules for the companies that I consider valid stock split plays. (Please keep in mind that for every rule, there are six exceptions—usually.) Here is how I convert my research into rules:

Size

Stick with the big companies. They usually perform well and their movements seem to be more predictable. When I say "big," I mean a well-known company that has a respected presence in the financial media.

Direction

Is the stock in an uptrend? This concept is very simple. Grab a chart for the company you are considering and look at a one-year chart for the stock. Does the stock price seem to be trending up or down over time? If the stock seems to be moving down, take a walk—it's a loser. If the stock is generally increasing in value over time, it's in an uptrend. There might be a short one- or two-week downward move, which is acceptable, but if the stock has moved down for the last six months, give it a wide berth or you might find yourself on the Titanic with the decks full of ice cold water.

Volume

Share volume is extremely important. As I said earlier, when it comes to stock splits, company size is important. I prefer to play with the big money, so I look at how many shares are bought and sold in an average day. I usually prefer companies that have at least one million shares traded per day. If they have more than ten million per day, it's even better. If the company has less than 500,000 I get nervous; if the average daily volume is under 250,000 I don't even think about it. The thinner the average daily trading volume, the smaller my interest. Why risk money on a long shot when you can find winners by being patient?

Open Interest

If I am making a trade where I am purchasing options, I want to see a minimum of 100 or more contracts of open interest for the option that I am buying. "Open Interest" (OI) is an "accumulated volume indicator" in the options market. The higher the OI, the more liquidity there is for the particular option. When the OI is high, there are more options contracts being traded in the open market.

If there are less than 100 contracts of OI, volume is dangerously low. If you purchase options when OI is low, you could be the only person playing the option. That will make selling your options for a profit more difficult. Would you be frustrated if you think you have tripled your money but end up having to sell at a reduced price? How about having the contract expire worthless because you are the only person who purchased options and no one wanted to buy them from you? If you are the only retail customer doing a deal, you end up dancing with market makers, who can set their own price.

I love to find stocks with options that have open interest of 1,000+ contracts. With that much interest you can be confident there are plenty of buyers and sellers ready to play. It's easy to sell when someone else wants to buy. I sleep better at night knowing that I can sell my option contracts at a moment's notice.

The Open Interest rule is not as important when opening trades by selling options, unless you need to buy them back to close a position.

In the following example, you can see that some strike prices have far fewer contracts than others. This is a mini-snapshot of part of a printout that can be obtained from the Chicago Board of Exchange (CBOE) (www.cboe.com). The range is an OI of 695 to 12,449, but all have at least 100 contracts.

Dell Computer Corporation (DELL)			37 11/16		−2 9/16 Calls	
Last	Sale	Net	Bid	Ask	Volume	**Open Int.**
APR 32.5	*5 5/8*	*−3 1/2*	*5 5/8*	*6 1/8*	*150*	***695***
APR 35	*3 3/4*	*−2 5/8*	*4*	*4 1/4*	*464*	***1,036***
APR 37.5	*2 9/16*	*−1 13/16*	*2 7/16*	*2 3/4*	*2,409*	***1,601***
APR 40	*1 1/2*	*−1 3/8*	*1 9/16*	*1 5/8*	*9,014*	***9,171***
APR 42.5	*13/16*	*−1*	*13/16*	*1*	*4,919*	***12,449***

 Dell Computer, March 22, 1999, 3:16 PM PST

History

Has the company ever done a stock split? Has it split in the last three years? How did the stock perform—was it a big mover or did it have lousy performance? If the company has a history of splitting, look for patterns. You can also see if the stock has a track record of being a good performer. Some stocks may split every three to five years, but their performance is not worth the effort, others are far superior in performance and consistency during a split. You can use history to give you clues for the company's possible future actions.

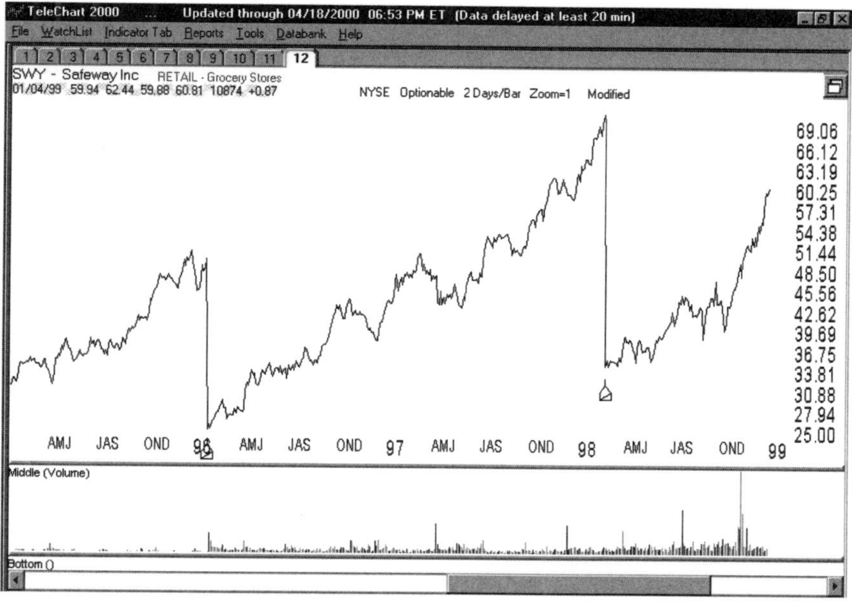

Environment

Have others companies within the industry split within the last year? How many? How did they perform? Make a comparison between the company you are considering and the other companies in the group. Is one of the top performers your target company?

Look at the industry group and compare it to other industry groups in the sector. Is the industry as a whole growing and expanding? Is the group among the top performers in the entire sector?

If the company you are investigating is in the top 20% of a top performing industry, you are looking at a stock that will have a better-than-average chance of profit compared to a low performing company in a poor industry group. If the company is not a good performer, the fact that a stock split is in the works will do little to improve your chance of making a profit.

News

Does the company sound familiar? After I look at the technical stuff like size, trend, and open interest, I look for news. If the company is unknown to the public, rumor will not travel fast. If rumor doesn't spread, who will know when good things are going to happen, like a stock split? If you are the only person who knows about a stock split, guess who earns the money: you, the market makers, or me? The market makers! When a no-name company starts getting ready to split their stock, it may remain a well-kept secret, because the rumor mill won't notice. If few people know about the event there will be little emotion to whip up a buying frenzy, and the stock isn't likely to move.

Here's my rule of thumb. If I don't recognize the company, I figure no one else will either. I double check anyway. Is the stock in a big index like the S&P 500, S&P 100, or the Dow Jones Indexes, et cetera? I'm talking about the "blue bloods," the top companies of major stock indexes. Don't get me wrong. I am sure that there are tons of great companies that are up and coming. Plenty of them will announce a stock split, and many will be very profitable. However, I like to keep my money as safe as possible. I find that big companies have fewer earth-shaking surprises. By sticking with big, well-established, highly visible companies, you can earn healthy returns. You have "safety in numbers." Sticking with the big guys will give you a better chance for safer and predictable stock split plays.

Is there any bad news? Look at the recent news reports for the company. Are there recent earnings disappointments, loss of market, or internal problems? If there are any news events that indicate the company is having problems, tread very softly. Bad news can drive a stock down fast, split or no split.

Look at the last one to two weeks of news announcements. Is there anything that could have a current effect on the stock? Has the stock changed direction and headed down since the announcement? How many bad news items are there? Does the company have a history of bad news?

As you research, you will see that stock split companies usually have few bad news announcements. If there is too much bad news the stock would be in a downtrend, and the chance of a split announcement is small. Or if there *is* a stock split announcement for a company that is in a nosedive, you can be pretty confident that the stock split announcement is an attempt to manipulate investors into buying the stock. If the company is losing ground, a stock split will not turn it around.

Is the stock a newsy company? If there is little or no news about a company, Murphy's Law states that there will be less news after *you* get into the deal. Without news, there will be less opportunity for rumor and public excitement to drive the stock price up. So in this case, no news is bad news.

Volatility

Is the stock too wild? Checking volatility is a combination of fact and personal evaluation. I check the chart to see if the stock moves in a calm and predictable manner or like a roller coaster moving fast and furious with sudden sharp changes. If the stock is a fast mover there may be an opportunity for fantastic returns, but there is also the potential for overwhelming losses. Does the stock seem to move in a consistent manner or is it wild and crazy? Are you comfortable with that type of movement?

Over time you can develop an instinct for volatility by looking at the chart. You need to look at the average daily movement (high of day versus low of the day). Also look at how far it moves between support and resistance. Then compare that movement with your accepted risk tolerance. If the stock moves more than you are comfortable with, pass.

Check The Float

In some cases you can look at the "float" and compare that with the average daily share volume. ("Float" is the number of shares available for individual trading in the open market.) If the stock float is one million shares and there is an average of five million shares transacted each day, the stock will be extremely volatile because the available stock is being turned over five times every day—a 500% turnover. On the other hand if the stock float is one hundred million shares and there are five million shares transacted each day, only 5% of the stock is being purchased or sold each day — a 5% turnover. Too much float will cause small price movements, resulting in low profitability. Too little float will cause excessive volatility and magnified potential of profits and losses

Explanations And Terminology

Industry and Sector. A sector is the major grouping of companies: basic materials, energy, technology, et cetera. The Industry Groups are within the sector. For example the Technology Sector includes industries like computer hardware, networking equipment, storage devices, semiconductor manufacturers, et cetera.

Liquidity. "Liquidity" is a term used to indicate the ease of converting an investment to cash. If something is very liquid, it's like having cash in the bank. The opposite of liquid is illiquid, which means you're stuck with it, because no one else wants it, or you have to sell it at an undesired price.

Float. Float is calculated by taking total issued shares, subtracting those held by officers and locked shares, also taking out institutional holdings, which are usually long term. The remaining shares are the float of available shares that could trade each day.

4

Stock Splits— The Mini-Play Book

In the beginning of Chapter 3 I showed the stock split timeline. This chapter will give a more detailed picture of the five phases of a stock split, including how to do the plays. I'll show you again what stock splits look like, how to take advantage of them, and what kinds of things can be done to increase your profits. And best of all, I'll provide a mini-play book to briefly show the most profitable way to play each of the five phases. Then in the rest of the book, I'll break down stock splits to discuss each element in great detail. So by the time you are done, you will have a firm grasp on the techniques to use for profiting from stock splits.

This chapter is like finding out "who did it" in a mystery novel. It's also just enough information to be dangerous. Please, please read the rest of the book and do practice trading before you start applying the concepts.

Taking Aim

Miles says that I used to be a "ready, FIRE, aim" kind of person. He's right, I was, and it was painful. I'm still a take-charge person. I hate standing in line, being put on hold drives me crazy, and people who don't get to the point send me to the moon. I like to make quick decisions. Why wait? I prefer to finish today, providing my actions are accurate and lead to success.

This drive is important, however, taking action before having all of the facts is unwise. It's easy to earn money in the stock market, but it is even easier to lose it. When investing, I've learned that *taking aim* is a terrifically important part of the game. You can't hit your target unless you aim at it. And you cannot possibly take aim unless you know what you are trying to shoot. The same thing goes for this book. Please read it first, *then* act on it.

Rules Change When A Split Is Announced

When stock splits are announced all of the rules of regular investing change. Volatility becomes common and swift movements are fast, sharp and exciting. In the last section, I talked about taking aim, and learning before acting. When you understand how stock splits affect the movements of a stock, you will be able to take accurate aim and turn your investment portfolio into a cash-flow machine.

Why am I stressing taking aim? Why am I constantly mentioning practice trading, and learning before leaping? Because, while stock split investing is an unbelievable cash-flow generator, predictable and powerful, it is full of volatility and presents numerous opportunities to make money, or lose it. It is by knowing the rules and using the formulas correctly that I have been able to create a stock split money-making machine.

In a few pages there will be a review of the five phases of a stock split and how to play each one. But first, I'll define a few terms and concepts so that everyone will be speaking the same language. These are rules that apply to the market as a whole, and they are of special importance when profiting from stock splits.

Definition of Terms

What follows are brief definitions of selected terms.

"Run-up" And "Profit Taking" Defined

"Run-up" means that the stock price has increased. If the market is expecting good news, like a positive earnings announcement, a big sales report, a new product, et cetera, investors and traders get excited. As this excitement grows, demand for the stock increases, causing the stock price to surge. This surge in volume and stock price creates a momentum that becomes self-feeding, causing even higher stock prices and volumes. This movement is called a run-up because the stock is running up in price.

This run-up happens because traders are expecting the price to go up and they manifest their own expectations. In addition, as a particular event gets closer people talk, excitement increases, and more investors want to get in on the action.

Profit taking is also a natural result of a run-up in stock prices. When the event occurs, or immediately before the event, investors decide they are happy with their results and they sell to reap their profits. After the run-up there is usually a period of "profit taking." Some traders take their profits to use in another opportunity, either selling their entire position, or just lightening their exposure. Some people will just take their original investment out of the stock and let their profits ride.

"Buy on rumor and sell before the fact" is a phrase used to describe how to profit from the run-up and profit taking cycle that happens because of rumor and pending events. Take a look at any stock chart. You can see the up and down movements in the stock prices. Often the up and down movements have no visible reason behind them. Many stocks run up and have profit taking even without news or events—it's part of the natural movement of the stock market.

*Many people use the phrase "Buy on Rumor, Sell on Fact." This phrase encourages people to stay in deals too long, so I've changed it to "**BUY ON RUMOR, SELL BEFORE THE FACT.**"*

How to play: Enter when rumor is pushing the price higher. Get out before the anticipated news is released. There will be no warning when the market decides to sell on fact–it will be swift, hard, and painful. In many cases, the stock is halted, it gaps down, and when it reopens–wham!

Support And Resistance Defined

Support and resistance are critical basic concepts for investing. You must be able to identify support and resistance points in order to determine entry and exit points for your trades.

Look at a chart and you can see a pattern where a stock price falls to a low point that tends to be the lower price limit. This bottom point is called "support" or "the support line." The stock will linger at this point, gathering energy for a while, then move up.

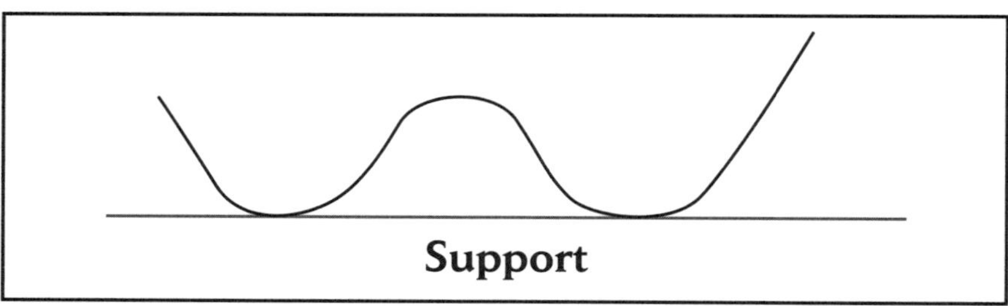

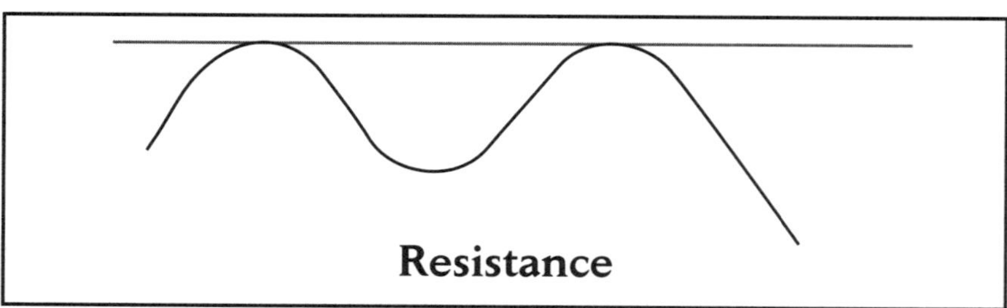

Eventually it reaches a higher limit where the buyers disappear and the stock price starts falling again. This upper point is called "resistance" or the "resistance line."

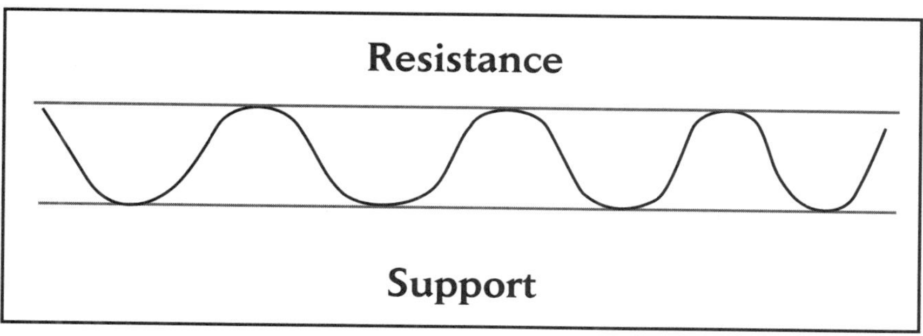

Professional brokers know how to identify support and resistance points. If you need help while you practice trading, ask your broker. If they do not know how to figure out the support and resistance lines, it's time to get a new broker.

Trading Point: You can use the stock's support line for a clue as to when you may safely enter into a trade. The resistance points tell you when you need to be ready to jump out.

Uptrend And Downtrend Defined

A stock is said to be "trending" if the price has been moving in the same general direction for a period of time. Look at your prospect's performance for the last year. If the stock price seems to be reaching higher each time it peaks, it's in an uptrend. A downtrend is indicated if the stock reaches lower levels each time it falls.

Uptrend

If a stock price climbs for a few days, then falls back, hits support, climbs a little higher, falls back, climbs a little higher, falls back, et cetera, then the stock is in an uptrend. This means the highs are a little higher each time, and the lows are also a little higher each time.

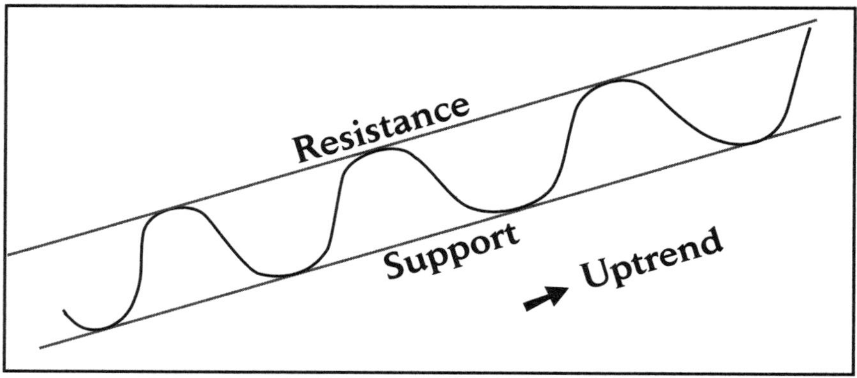

If the stock is in an uptrend, you can predict its likely future upward movements using a ruler and performance chart. In many cases, future support and resistance points can be projected by looking at a computer chart that draws a line showing the stock's "moving averages." When moving down, many uptrending stocks fall until they hit their 18 day or 40 day moving average. Once they hit support, stocks will usually stop falling and then begin climbing back up.

The 18 and 40 day moving averages are not always the best for every situation. Some stocks move on 15/30, 20/50, et cetera. You need to find the moving averages that match the general trend of your stocks. The 18 and 40 day moving averages work for me, for the stocks I play.

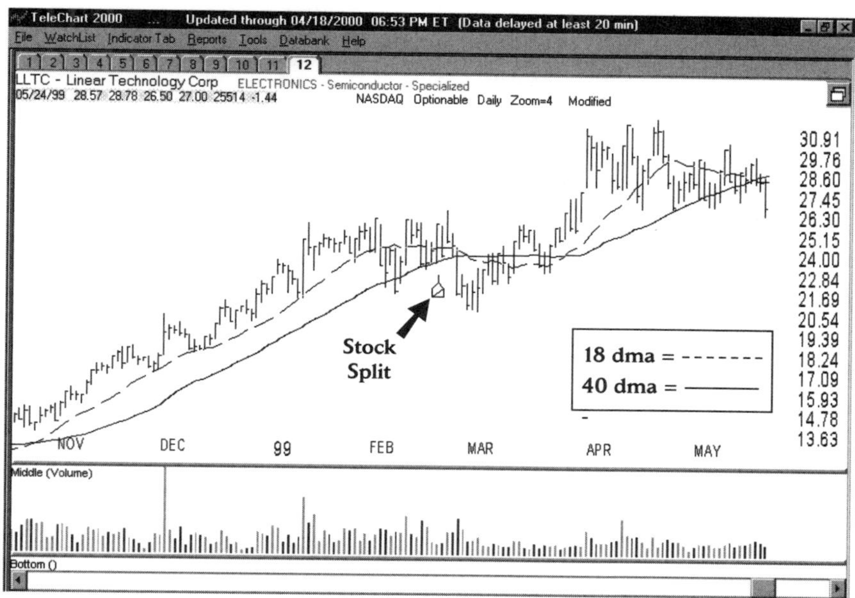

LLTC—Linear Technology Corp. October 98–May 99. From October 98 to February 99, LLTC was in a general uptrend. Support was the 18 day moving average (dotted line). Each time support was reached, the stock rebounded and reached a progressively higher resistance point. In February 99, LLTC executed a stock split, causing increased volatility and unpredictably. Then in April 99 (non-dotted line), LLTC resumed its uptrend, using the 40 day moving average as support. If LLTC violates support, the trend might change.

The upper limit (resistance) is a little more vague, but if you grab a pencil and ruler, you can draw a line using the resistance points from the last few swings. If you extend the line further, you can locate a possible upper price limit. Some charting programs will plot these theoretical support and resistance points for you.

Downtrend

If a stock is in a downtrend, the lows are a little lower each time and the highs are also lower each cycle. This time use the 18 day moving average and the 40 day moving average to predict the *resistance* or upper price limit, and use the ruler to determine the support lines. Once again, draw a line and allow it to extend beyond the current stock price, projecting possible future stock prices.

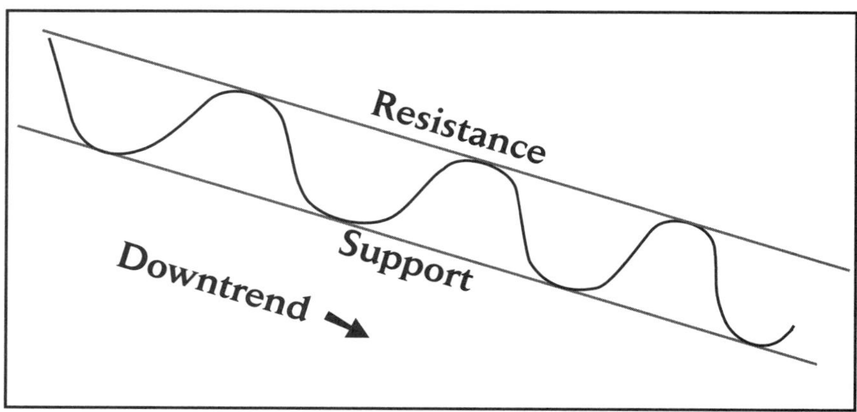

Can I give you a hint? If a stock is in a strong downtrend for months don't take a stock split announcement seriously. Someone is probably playing a sick game. Stock splits are generally used by successful companies, not losers headed to the undertaker. If a downtrending stock makes a split announcement, any investor excitement will be very short lived because the downtrend will take over and disappoint the gamblers. Why did I use the term "gamblers?" Who else bets on a loser, but a gambler looking for a long shot? If they want a long shot they could buy lottery tickets instead—it would save broker commissions!

Up-Market/Down-Market Rules

When anticipating a stock's reaction to an event, you also need to look at the market as a whole. If the general market trend is up, then investors are excited and money is flowing into the market (up-market or uptrend). If the trend is down, investors are nervous and money is flowing out of the market (down-market or downtrend). You need to modify your entrances or exits based on how you see the market is behaving.

Expect to spend more time in an uptrend play. In an uptrending market (up-market) enter the play earlier and stay in longer. Sell indicators are usually clear and you can take profits as expected.

Expect to invest less time in a downtrend play. In a downtrending market (down-market) get into the deal later and get out earlier, capturing a small amount of profits. Stop-losses must be tight and rules for play are based on the higher possibility of sudden sharp downturns in share values.

How To Use Uptrends And Downtrends

The reason for these different rules is that investors and day traders look at these two market trends very differently. Day traders are very excitable and nervous in a downtrending market. They look at price increases as an opportunity to sell stocks.

If the market is in a general uptrend, investors are the excited ones. They are looking for reasons to buy. They do not have as much concern with selling and dips are seen as buying opportunities.

Trading Point: You need to be aware of these trends and use them to your advantage. Uptrending markets look at dips as buying opportunities, and downtrending markets see price increases as selling opportunities.

Call Options

What follows is an extremely short introduction into "call options." If you need more information, refer to the Chapter 9, Options for Stock Splits.

Call Options Defined

A call option gives you the choice to purchase stock at a guaranteed price, or "strike price." You can purchase the underlying stock or sell the call option at any time before the expiration date of the option. Stock options for our purposes expire on the third Friday of the month. Once an option expires, there is no value or refund.

A Contract

A stock option contract usually represents a block of 100 shares. Thus if you purchase one call option, you are actually controlling 100 shares of stock. If you have five contracts, you are controlling 500 shares.

The essential elements of a call option are:

Strike Price	=	Guaranteed price
Expiration	=	Third Friday of the month
Premium	=	Price you pay/receive for an option, includes cash value and time value
Contract Size	=	Usually 100 shares

A contract is usually 100 shares, but there are circumstances when the contract will control 50 shares, 33 shares, or other odd numbers. These situations are rare.

Is The Option In The Money?

If the option is in the money, it will have a cash value. Meaning that you could buy the stock and immediately sell it for a profit, not considering the option premium.

An "in-the-money" call option is when the option strike price is below the current stock price. If a stock were currently selling for $40 per share, a call option with a strike price of $35 or lower would be considered in the money.

An "at-the-money" call option is when the option strike price is equal to the current stock price. If a stock were currently selling for $40 per share, a call option with a strike price of $40 would be considered at the money.

An "out-of-the-money" call option is when the option strike price is above the current stock price. If a stock were currently selling for $40 per share, a call option with a strike price of $45 or higher would be considered out of the money.

Is the Strike Price in the money?

Stock	Strike	In $	In, Out, At
$40	*$35*	*$5*	*In the money*
$40	*$40*	–	*At the money*
$40	*$45*	–	*Out of the money*

Limit Orders Versus Market Orders

By using a limit order, you set in advance the price that you are willing to purchase or sell your stock or option. If your price is not met or improved on, you don't have a deal. If you use a market order, you are letting the market choose the price for you. When purchasing and selling stocks or options, it is best to do so with a limit order.

The problem with using a market order is that you are allowing someone else to decide at what price you will buy or sell. This someone else is the market maker, and letting them decide the price is extremely dangerous. I remember a recent news report about a woman who entered a market order to buy 50 shares of a fast moving stock. She thought the purchase price was going to be less than $20 a share. When she finally got a fill confirmation, the broker had purchased her 50 shares at a cost of more than $100 per share—the highest price of the day!

The problem with using a limit order is that you are establishing the highest price you will pay for the stock option (or the lowest sales price if you are selling). If no one is willing to meet your price, you will not be filled on your offer. When you use a limit order you control the price, but you may not get the deal.

I prefer to use a limit order and miss a few deals. Using a market order may guarantee a fill, but the price could be much higher than I am willing or expecting to pay. By using market orders I would expose my investments to the whims of market makers—and that scares me too much. Using a market order is like walking into a used car dealership and saying, "I want to buy that car. Here's my VISA card. Send me a receipt telling me how much I paid." No one in their right mind would give a salesperson a blank check, but that is exactly what happens every day when people place market orders.

This is so important I need to repeat it—***Use A Limit Order***!

On rare occasions, like really bad news, I may sell using a market order to exit fast.

Stop-Losses

Stop-losses prevent you from staying in a trade longer than wisdom dictates.Without stop-loss controls people tend to let their losses run deeper than necessary. A stop-loss can cut off the loss and help retain capital.

Stop-losses can also be used to determine when to get out of a profitable trade. Stop-loss techniques can help you know when to take your profits, selling close to the top of a run.

You can set stop-losses many ways. Including tight stops, loose stops, and even trailing stops.

It is important to use closing prices for the establishment of your stop-loss and other investment controls. The professionals rule the closing prices and the amateurs set the opening prices.

Tight Stop-Losses

Determine the current value of an option and set a stop-loss $1 to $2 below the current option price. If the option goes below that limit, a sell order is automatically triggered and the option is sold. This type of stop-loss is common for short-term trades.

Be careful not to set your stop-loss too close to the current price or the market will swoop down and stop you out. You also need to allow for the typical daily ups and downs for the stock. You might use a mental stop-loss rather than an actual one, but only if you can watch the market, or have your broker set an alarm to call you if you hit your stop-loss target, so you can exit.

Loose Stop-Loss

This is set at one-half the purchase price of the option. As the option increases in value you might use a different stop-loss formula rather than keep 50% of your capital at risk. This stop-loss might be used when beginning a long-term trade.

Trailing Stop-Loss

Trailing stop-losses are usually set at 1.5 to 2 times the average daily movement of the option. A broker can tell you how far the particular option moves in an average day, based on the last 14 to

28 days. Then multiply the average daily movement by 1.5 or 2 and set your stop-loss using that figure.

Each day as the option price increases, raise the stop-loss an equal amount. This adjustment is done by looking at the closing price for the previous day and setting the new stop-loss limits before the market opens in the morning. For example: If the option is $3 and the stop-loss is $2, the next day, before the market opens, look at the option. If it increased in value to $5, that's a $2 increase, so move the stop-loss up $2 to $4.

When the stock stops increasing in value, the stop-loss is not changed. If the stock backs down off its high, the stop-loss is activated, and the option is sold. A trailing stop-loss is a good tool when you do not know how high a stock or option will climb, and it is very useful in long-term trades.

Short-Term Plays

A short-term play is one that you expect to complete within a few minutes to a few days. If you expect a play to last longer than a few days, you need to use the rules for mid-term or long-term plays.

For short-term plays:

1. Purchase in-the-money options.
2. Use expiration dates of at least one to three *full* months. (Current month options are very dangerous.)
3. Use tight stop-losses, a few dollars below the option price. You don't want to lose more money than you can earn. To avoid getting stopped out in the normal swing of the day, please read more details on stop losses later in Chapter 10.
4. Expect to capture $1 to $2 or less in profits.

Be careful—be sure you understand the use of stop-losses.

The use of current-month options may provide the biggest bang for the buck, but it also carries the biggest risk of loss. Time is not on your side and premiums can evaporate right before your eyes. My suggestion is to save this type of trade for throwaway money. Only use current-month options if you will be in and out of the deal in a few hours!

Mid-Term Plays

A mid-term play is a mixture of short-term and long-term concepts. A conservative, medium-term play provides you with the opportunity of capturing profits from a smaller move than is required for long-term plays. It is perfect for plays that you expect to last longer than a few days, but end within a few weeks. In other words, you have a specific sell date because of a fixed event like earnings, an upcoming stock split, et cetera.

For mid-term plays:

1. Purchase at-the-money options.
2. Use options that have an expiration of one to four full months (or longer).
3. Use trailing stop-losses that follow the stock as it increases in value.
4. Your exit point is determined by:
   a. the stop-loss,
   b. the target event or date,
   c. volume slows or technical indicators tell you to get out, or
   d. you are happy with the profits.

Long-Term Plays

A long-term play is one that you expect to last more than a few days. If you expect a play to last less than a few days, consider using the rules for the short-term plays.

For long-term plays:

1. Purchase out-of-the-money options.
2. Use options that have an expiration of four *full* months or longer.
3. Expect to capture profits until the stock changes direction.
4. Use trailing stop-losses that follow the stock as it increases in value.

5. Your exit point is determined by:
   a. the stop-loss,
   b. the target event or date,
   c. volume slows or technical indicators tell you to get out, or
   d. you are happy with your profits.

FYI: If you are expecting to capture only $1 to $2 in profit, you need to look at the rules for short-term plays.

The Five Phases And Five Plays Of A Stock Split

As I have said earlier, there are five different phases that a stock split frequently passes through. Think of each one of these phases as an opportunity to earn money; five different times to profit. Each phase has a specific behavior. Each presents a buying and selling opportunity. All it takes to turn a typical investment portfolio into a money-making machine is to master any one of the five phases. That's right—you only need to master one of these techniques to create fantastic returns.

The five phases to watch:

1. Before the announcement.
2. Split announcement.
3. Pre-split dip(s).
4. Split date.
5. Post-split dip and price recovery.

What follows is a brief description of the five phases and the most common play formulas. For a more detailed explanation of each of these, please go to Chapter 11, Five Power Profit Plays. In that chapter I devoted a separate section for each phase, examining in great detail all aspects of profiting from the five phases of a stock split.

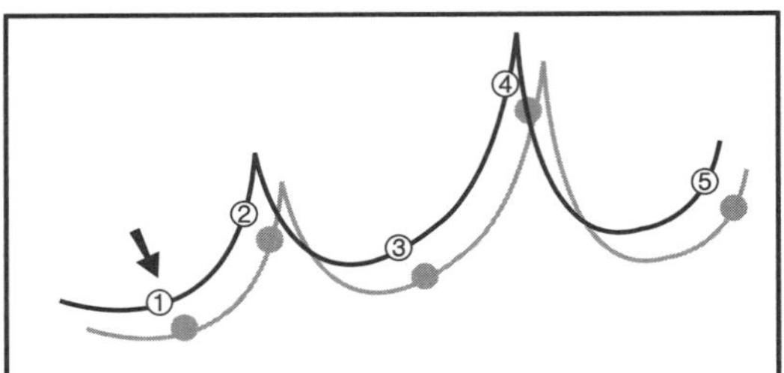

Before The Announcement

This is a long-term option play, using out-of-the-money options that have an expiration date of four or more full months. The reason this play is long-term is because we are guessing, and, if wrong, we need time on our side. We usually enter the play seven to ten days before the anticipated announcement. We exit just prior to the announcement, or the day of the announcement, depending on market conditions. We protect our investment using trailing stop-losses.

In the period just before the company announces a stock split, there is often a few weeks where rumor is running wild and excitement is in the air. The bigger the company, the more rumors will spread. It is this rumor and excitement that causes the stock price to climb faster than normal.This is probably my favorite stock split play, because there is an element of mystery and excitement. Since the company has not officially declared a stock split, there is no guarantee that the announcement will be forthcoming. However, you do not need an announcement to earn money; all you need is to be positioned in the stock and for rumor to move prices higher. If it happens, the stock split announcement will be a bonus. You should have already earned most of your money before the announcement, and be out already.

Handled correctly, Play #1 is very profitable, but it can also be a challenge because of the research involved. Let's face it: how in the world can you predict that a company is going to declare a stock split? The answer is actually a matter of experience. The answer to these few questions can give you an indication:

1. Has the stock split before?

2. What was the stock price when it split the last time?

3. Does the stock split at regular intervals (annually, every two years, et cetera)?

4. Have other companies in the industry declared a split recently?

5. Are there rumors of a stock split?

6. Is the company included on a list of potential stock splits?

7. Is there a board of directors meeting coming up?

If you think that the company is a stock split candidate, you can look for concrete evidence to give you a solid indication of a possible date. Look for an upcoming meeting or a scheduled reporting event. You can also look to see if there are any indications that the company might *not* declare a stock split.

1. Has there been any bad news recently?

2. Are they having big legal or financial problems?

3. Has the stock price been falling for a while, creating a downtrend for the stock?

If you think there is a possibility of a stock split, look for a potential announcement at one of the following events:

1. Board of directors meeting.

2. Annual shareholders meeting.

3. Meeting with analysts.

4. Scheduled earnings announcement.

5. Special industry convention, et cetera.

Once you have set your "target" date, start looking for an opportunity to get into the game. A highly profitable time to play is generally seven to 14 days before the target date. It is not uncommon for a stock to run-up 5% to 25% in the weeks prior to an announcement. Protect your investment by setting an exit point based on the target date, and use a stop-loss in case the stock does not perform as you expect.

Bonus Features: Here are a few "bonus" reasons why the Phase 1 play is so powerful:

1) there is a large run-up in stock values in the pre-announcement period;

2) the market makers have not beefed up option premiums, so you get to purchase your call options at a potential discount; and

3) you get in before the market makers even know what's happening.

2

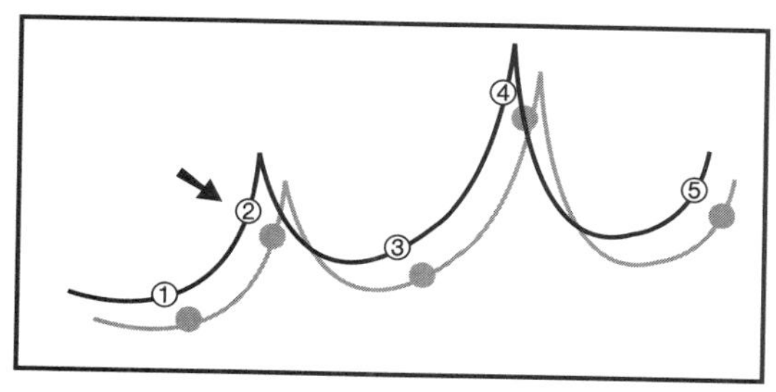

The Announcement

A selling opportunity! Within moments of the announcement the stock price makes a temporary jump up. I use the split announcement to tighten up my profits earned from the pre-announcement play, if I have not exited yet. If the announcement is made before the market opens, or if the stock was officially halted when the announcement was made this play may have less value.

This is a short-term opportunity. You should be in position already because you were playing Phase 1—Before the Announcement! That's right—this play is not to start a new position, it is to finish a play already started before the announcement.

When the stock split announcement is made you need to jump on the news and make a quick decision to either:

1. Sell.
2. Hold.
3. Tighten your stop-loss.

Be sure that you use limit orders and not market orders. This is a time when you do not want to let someone else choose your prices or you can get wiped out royally!

If you want to sell, give the split announcement a few minutes to do its magic. The stock price should surge and the option premiums should get a boost from the market makers. Then you can contact your broker and sell your position. It is important to use a limit order, not a market order. However, this is one time that you want to get filled. I choose to give the option or stock room to move, so I compare the bid and ask prices and tell my broker to sell at one-quarter to one-half a point below the bid. That's right, I am actually offering to sell the position below the current fair market price, so I am willing to give away 25¢ to 50¢ of my profits. What will happen is the order will get processed and I will probably get filled at a better price than I expect.

The only reliable way to make this play work is to have the broker coached on the exact play desired. When a call is made to the broker, the conversation is very brief: "Broker Joe, this is Darlene. AT&T just announced a two-for-one." The broker responds, "I'm on it already, do you want to sell X-options, or Y-options?" That way no time is wasted and the play can be executed profitably.

By now you will have noticed that I am not going to tell you how to jump on the announcement by trying to open a new position. I have found that the old fashioned split announcement play is unprofitable for the average person. So, instead of using the split announcement as a buying opportunity, use it to sell.

There are other ways to play stock split announcements. I have covered many of these formulas in Chapter 11, Five Power Profit Plays.

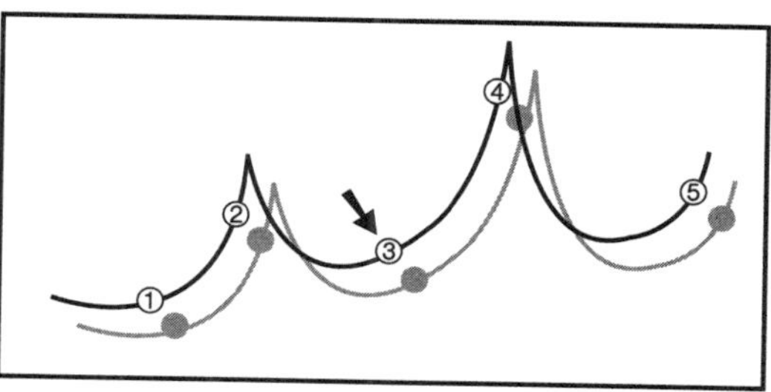

Pre-Split Dip

This is a mid-term play, using in- or at-the-money options that have an expiration date of one to four full months. Enter the play when the stock has bounced off of the support line and is starting to climb back up. Use trailing stops to ride the upward movement. As the stock nears resistance, tighten your stops or consider exiting the play.

After the initial excitement over the stock split announcement, there will usually be a period of profit taking. As once excited investors close their positions, the stock price will fall until it reaches a support level. It will usually take a breather and then resume its climb. When it reaches resistance it will generally see profit taking again, and the price may fall back to the support level again. Once again, it will climb up. This up and down movement can happen one or more times prior to the split *depending* on how long the period is between the announcement and the split.

When the stock hits its support line the price may stabilize. At this point a dip play can be started. Once the stock begins climbing back up, look for a one-day uptick in price, then jump in and ride as it climbs up to resistance. As the stock nears resistance watch it closely because it will probably bounce off the resistance line and stop climbing. At that point you should get out or tighten your stops—the stock may move back down to its support.

In some cases you can catch two or three cycles of excitement and profit taking until the stock splits. This phase is the workhorse for stock split investors, because they can watch the stock and make their decisions at night, when the house is quiet.

In order to handle this play effectively, you need to understand how to identify the support and resistance lines for a stock. A top quality charting service can be a very valuable tool to assist you in tracking stocks, locating support and resistance lines, and analyzing trends. A picture does say a thousand words.

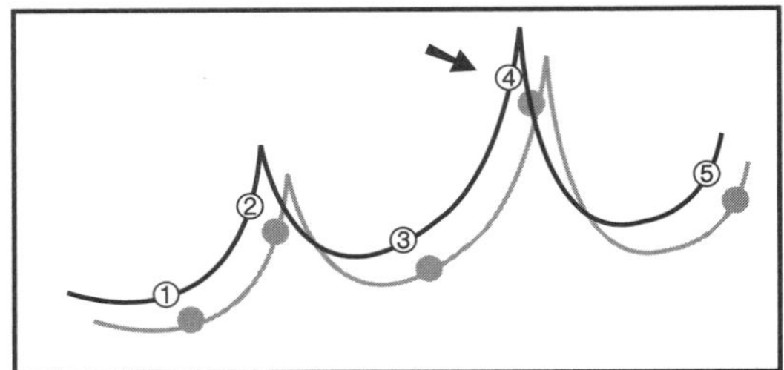

Split Date

Enter the play one to seven days before the split. This is a short-term play, using in-the-money options that have an expiration date of one to three full months. Exit the play after capturing $1 to $2, using tight stop losses. Or, if the market conditions permit, use trailing stop losses to let the profits ride until after the split. This is an emotion driven event, with quick movements.

This is a short-term play lasting anywhere from a few hours to a few days. Look for an entry point one to seven days before the split (usually one to five days), or even a few hours before the close of market on the eve of the stock split. In some cases you can enter the trade a few days before the split and take your profits before the actual split itself. If the stock price is falling prior to the split, wait for it to stabilize and start climbing before you open a position. If it does not start to recover, forget it—there's something wrong. Pass on the play and look to get profits from another stock.

Play #4 is a quick in-and-out trade, taking just a few dollars of profit. It is very important to use a tight stop-loss to limit your downside. Since you are only looking for a few dollars of profit, you do not want to lose more than you can earn.

The exit point on this play can actually happen on the eve of the split. If there has been enough run-up and you are happy with the profits get out! In addition, if the stock starts to show some weakness, it's time to walk away. The rule of thumb is to take $1 or $2 and sell! The only time to stick in any longer is if you can watch the "moment-by-moment" movements of the stock and get out very quickly.

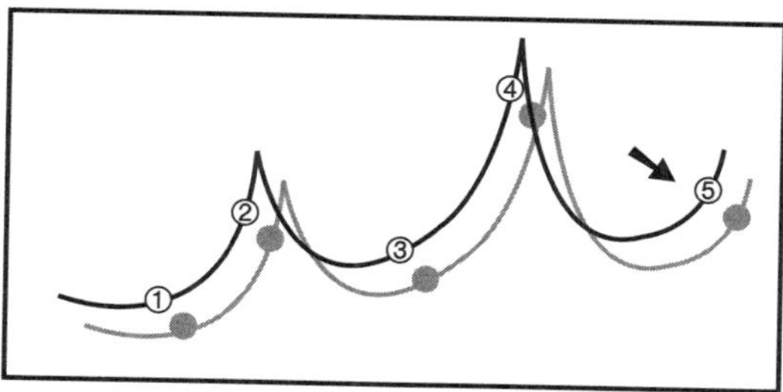

Post-Split Dip

This is a long-term option play, using out-of-the money options that have an expiration date of four or more *full* months. We usually enter when the stock starts its upward movement, using trailing stop-losses to determine our exit point.

This is a long-term play. After the stock splits, there is usually a short run-up in the stock price. Then, within a few hours or days of the split, profit taking kicks in. The stock will usually take a short break, dip in value, and collect strength as it sits near the support line. There may be an extended period of consolidation before the stock resumes an upward climb, anywhere from a few hours to 45 or more days. Jump into the play when the stock starts to show life and starts moving up in price. The exit point might be when it reaches resistance, when a better deal comes along, or when other sell indicators occur. We'll discuss those as this book continues.

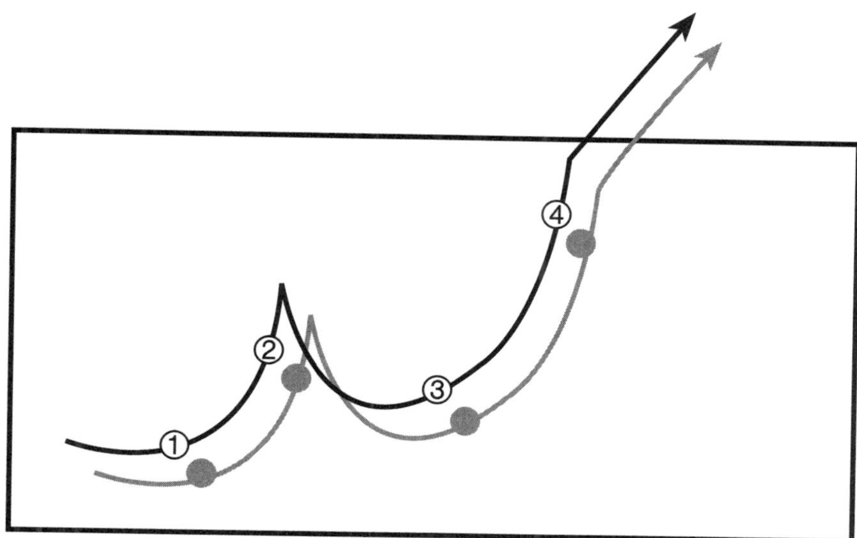

Review of Formulas—The Mini-Play Book

This section provides an abbreviated review of the critical elements of the plays I have just discussed.

Play #1—Before The Announcement

A short-term increase in stock price before the expected (rumored) announcement date. This is a long-term option play, using out-of-the-money options that have an expiration date four or more full months. Enter the play seven to fourteen days before the anticipated announcement. Exit just prior to the announcement, or on the day of the announcement depending on market conditions. Protect your investment using trailing stop-losses.

Play #2—The Announcement

Within seconds of the announcement, the stock price jumps up. Use the announcement as an opportunity to exit a play that was opened during the pre-announcement run-up. Give the announcement a few minutes to do its magic. Because of the announcement, the stock price should surge and the option premiums should get a boost from the market makers. Then you contact your broker and sell your position. Since this is a time-critical play, arrangements need to be worked out in advance with your broker.

Play #3—Pre-Split Dip

After the announcement, the stock calms down, due to profit taking, and the price falls. It collects strength and makes another effort to climb up. This is a mid-term play, using in-the-money or at-the-money options that have an expiration date out one to four full months. Enter the play when the stock has bounced off the support line and is starting to climb back up. Use trailing stops to ride the upward movement. When the stock nears resistance, tighten your stops, or consider exiting the play.

Play #4—Split Date

One to seven days before the split, the price usually runs up. The greatest price increase tends to be the day before and the day of the split. Enter the play one to five days before the split is effective (four days before the ex-date is common). This is a short-term play, using in-the-money options that have an expiration date of one to three full months. Exit the play after capturing $1 to $2 in profits using tight stop-losses. If market conditions permit, use trailing stop-losses to let the profits ride until the split date. This is an emotion-driven event with quick movements.

Play #5—Post-Split Dip

Within hours or days of the split, the stock often dips down because of profit taking. It then levels out, collects energy, and starts climbing again. This is a long-term option play, using out-of-the-money options that have an expiration date of four or more *full* months. You usually enter when the stock starts upward, using trailing stop-losses to determine your exit point. This can also make a great rolling stock or rolling option play.

Now On To More Detail

I have presented you with an overview of the basic concepts of stock splits. You should now have a picture of some of the motivations for companies to do splits, and how you as an investor can profit from these events.

Unfortunately, I have given you just enough information to be dangerous. The next step is to dissect each element of the stock split process. By the time you finish this book, you will understand the forces behind stock splits, the patterns, which companies split their stock, how to identify stock split candidates, which splits to play, and how to profit from these events using very specific techniques and formulas. What I have covered so far is just enough to whet your appetite. Next, I'll share the meat and potatoes of stock split investing.

When it comes to the stock market, the only thing cast in stone is the fact that the market is constantly changing. Today the entire world can be headed for financial collapse and tomorrow it can be filled with opportunity.

5

Stock Split Patterns

In this chapter I'll take a closer look at patterns and discuss many of the forces that control a stock split. These forces can change stock prices before, during, and after the split, and understanding them will let you profit while protecting your capital. People who don't understand these driving forces and critical elements can make poor decisions and end up believing that stock splits are not a viable investment opportunity.

Looking At Stock Split Patterns

I'll show you a few charts and discuss the patterns that emerge. By studying these patterns you will be able to see when each of the five phases occur. Of course, few companies will follow a "picture perfect" chart pattern, but they will be close enough to provide you with wonderful opportunities to earn money.

If I were to show you 100 charts, you would find that every company is different. That doesn't really matter, because you should treat each phase as a separate investment opportunity, taking advantage of the winners and discarding the losers.

Keep in mind these five stock split phases as you look at these sample charts.

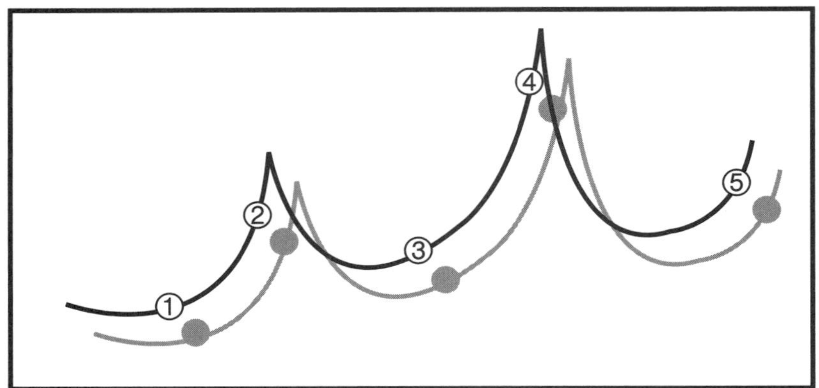

1. Before the Announcement. A short-term increase in stock price before the expected (rumored) announcement date.
2. Announcement. Within seconds of the announcement the stock price jumps up, and then falls back down.
3. Pre-Split Dip. After the announcement, the stock calms down due to profit taking, and the price falls. Depending on the length of time between the announcement and the actual split, the stock may move up and down more than once in this period.
4. Split Date. One to seven days before the split the price runs up. The greatest price increase tends to be the day before and the day of the split.
5. Post-Split Dip. Within hours or days of the split, the stock dips down because of profit taking. The stock may enter a sideways channel for 30 to 45 days before it levels out and starts climbing again.

Note: The split date is the day that ownership is required. After the market closes, the stock split will become effective. The next morning at market open, the split adjustment is made–this is the ex-date. For more information, see "The Date is Set" in Chapter 7.

Schering-Plough (SGP)

SGP is one of those companies that is huge and yet many people claim they have never heard of it. With a name like Schering-Plough, it's no wonder. Perhaps you have heard of Claritin™, the non-drowsy antihistamine. Or how about Proventil™, Vancenase™, Dr. Scholl's™, or Coppertone™. You might not recognize the company name, but these products speak loudly in the retail market.

On August 21, 1998, rumors circulated that SGP was going to announce a stock split any day. The stock gapped up the next two mornings. On September 23rd, the company announced a two-for-one stock split to take effect on December 3rd. Take a look at the chart. SGP provides a textbook example of all five phases

Do you see the five different phases? Go ahead and look on the next page. I've written them down and provided a chart that shows each phase.

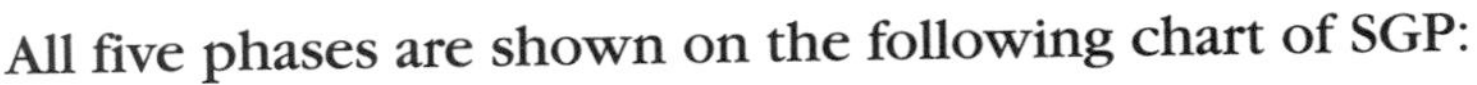

All five phases are shown on the following chart of SGP:

Phase 1. There is a run-up prior to the split announcement on September 23rd.

Phase 2. SGP announces and the stock price jumps.

Phase 3. The stock starts moving down on the 24th. Support is reached on October 7th, and the stock turns upward on the 8th. (There is a second dip in mid-November.)

Phase 4. The split date run-up starts December 1st. The stock splits on December 3rd.

Phase 5. On December 12th the excitement is over and the stock heads down in a post-split dip.

Charles Schwab Corp (SCH)

SCH is a discount investment broker with a fantastic growth rate. There is a good price run-up in October 1998 and SCH announces on October 22nd with the split effective December 14th. Looking at the chart, can you see a pre-split run-up and a small break after the announcement? How about the climb until the second week of November, when it takes the customary dip before splitting? If you look closely, the day before the split there is a surge in the stock price, which provides a great Play #4, then the stock takes a two-day breather and resumes its exciting climb. All five phases are present.

Can you see the five phases in this chart? Go ahead and identify the five phases.

This was especially fun because there were two opportunities to use Play #3.

I realize that the dates are not shown, but the key here is to see the general entry and exit points for trades. Of course, looking at a chart and doing it for real are two different animals. However, in order to learn the formulas, it is important to look at historical charts and practice identifying the different phases.

You can now check your notes by looking at this chart:

SCH does have a consistent pattern of executing a stock split every year. Look at the following table and see if you notice anything:

Schwab Split History

Month/Year	Type
12/91	*3:2*
6/93	*3:2*
3/95	*3:2*
9/95	*2:1*
9/97	*3:2*
12/98	*3:2*

Looking at the chart, SCH seems to like having splits effective in the 3rd, 6th, 9th, and 12th months. This type of observation can germinate the seeds of a great rumor that could be highly profitable.

Yahoo! Inc. (YHOO)

YHOO is a high flying Internet stock. When I was writing this book, the Internet stocks were probably the most powerful and scary stocks in the entire industry.

When it comes to valuation and performance, the Internet stocks broke every rule ever written. Many of these companies survive in the market purely on the speculation of traders expecting someone else to buy from them at a higher price. Some professionals claim that there is a speculative bubble developing and that it will eventually burst, leaving the Internet stocks worth less than penny stocks—others maintain that the prices are fair and will eventually be supported by income and net profits. I don't know who is right. What I do know is that YHOO has made plenty of millionaires in the last few years.

YHOO was stuck in a trading range in May of 1998 until a rumor started the first week of June that a stock split announcement was nearing. Sure enough, on July 8th the company made the split announcement, to be effective on July 31st. This chart shows the true power of stock split rumors. YHOO climbed sharply in June. When you look at the chart, you can see the run-up before the announcement.

I have also provided a second YHOO chart below, showing a 1997 stock split. By comparing the two, it becomes clear that each stock split takes on a life of its own, each acting very differently.

In this second chart, there are two or three "dip" plays prior to the split. Then a run-up two days before the split, and after the split the run-up is still very strong. You can see a few dips between the announcement and split date. These provided healthy opportunities for profit. What is especially interesting is the continued growth after the split. YHOO kept climbing for two weeks, nearly recovering its pre-split price. This type of quick price recovery is very unusual. Do you see that after the split, the stock actually shot back up from $39 to $57 (split adjusted) in less than a month? This was caused by pure excitement and speculation. The big risk is that inexperienced investors will put all of their money into a play like this and when it backs off, they may sell in a panic. Fortunes are won—and lost—in days, sometimes hours.

Don't Expect To Play All Five Phases

Not all companies will perform as you expect or want. If you pull charts for the last 100 companies that split, you would see that every chart has patterns of its own. Few companies have charts that conform exactly to my example showing the five phases. However, since you can treat each phase as a separate event, you can take advantage of stocks that perform the way you expect. The stocks that violate the established pattern can be set aside, because tomorrow will bring another company and new opportunities.

Here are a few example charts illustrating companies that failed to follow the typical stock split pattern. Keep in mind that you are looking for particular events and not step-by-step chart development.

Norfolk Southern Corp. (NSC)

When I have allocated my funds to the plays I want, other opportunities always present themselves. If I don't have cash left, I do a practice trade. NSC was one of my practice trade plays, because I had already allocated my money, and the volume is a little low for my taste. If you were to look closely, you'd see they average 250,000 to 500,000 shares traded each day. Do you remember the rule to look for stocks that have an average of one million shares in trading volume each day?

NSC made a three-for-one split announcement on July 24th (Miles's birthday), and investor excitement created one of NSC's biggest single day price jumps ever. The stock split was set for October 9th. As you can see, the pre-announcement run-up was magnificent, and the split announcement play was great. But after the initial investor excitement ran out, ouch! Reality set in and the stock started falling. Adding to that was bad news in the sector, and NSC barely recovered. Can you see the damage that can happen when a stock or other stocks in that sector have bad news? Once bad news breaks, even strong companies have problems. Can you see how stop-losses would have protected you with this stock?

Why am I showing you this chart? It demonstrates that you need to compare the actual stock behavior with the movements that you expect. If the stock is not moving the way you need, run—don't walk, to the nearest exit! It also illustrates the damage-saving power of stop-loss controls. Without using a stop-loss, you could find yourself riding a one way elevator into the financial basement. Remember, you can learn a great deal from a practice trade.

Dell Computer (DELL)

DELL has become a favorite among investors. Each quarter, founder and CEO Michael Dell amazes the analysts. The company has had intense growth, which continues to blow away doomsayers. What I find interesting is that DELL has been an incredible split play and it has been just as profitable between splits! The technology industry has been an exciting investment resource—the volatility creates ongoing entry and exit opportunities.

In many cases, playing DELL as a traditional split play can be frustrating. It is extremely volatile and the up and down movements are quick, sharp, and come without warning. All it takes is a negative comment from a heavyweight analyst and DELL can fall apart faster than anyone expects.

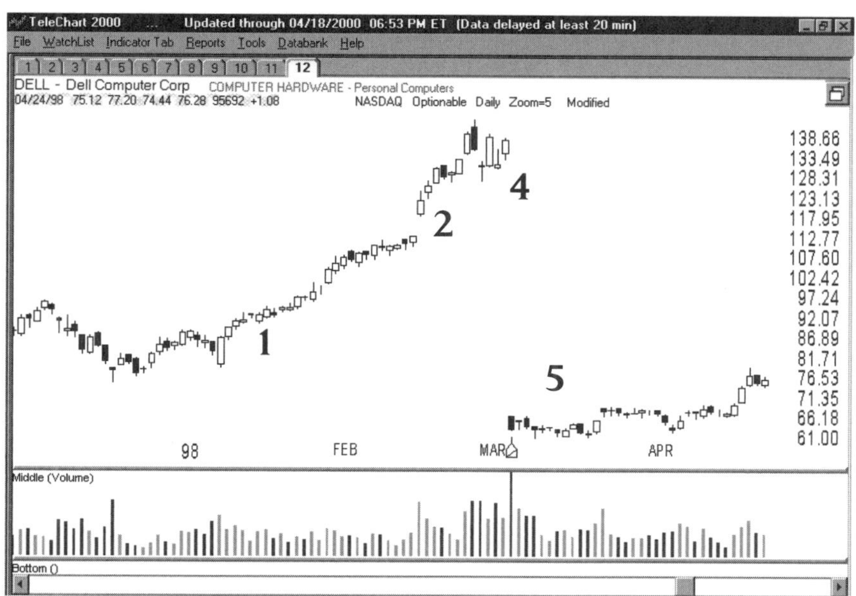

In this example, DELL announced a stock split on February 18th, 1998, with the split to take effect March 9th. The moment the stock opened on the 18th it gapped up and never looked back. The pre-announcement run-up was a two-month straight line, with only one dip four days before the split "announcement" (a perfect opportunity). After the announcement, the stock continued its sharp climb. Suddenly, on March 2nd the excitement was over. Some analyst (I don't remember who) pulled out his axe and slashed away and DELL's uptrend stopped cold and the stock went flat.

Looking at the chart, there is a great Phase 1, Phase 2, and then the stock headed into a dip and the split happened. There was no Phase 3. For Phase 4, many people got into DELL the day before the split, expecting a big gain the next morning. There was a little jump, but anyone that held on was hit the next morning; the stock actually went down. Remember, even great companies have problems. Don't invest only because of a company name, do it if the formula fits!

As of the printing of this book, Dell has actually become a phenomenal Play #5 for rolling options. The spread for the options is often only 25¢ and it rolls about $5 from support to resistance.

Note: Remember that circumstances change and by the time this book is published, DELL may or may not be a viable investment target.

Explanations And Terminology

Practice Trades. Practice trades are used to learn on paper, before using real money, or when your real money is fully invested in several trades.

Axeman. To denote outspoken person of influence that can chop a stock's price with their own opinion. See "Analysts and Market Makers" in Chapter 12.

6

Why Companies Do Stock Splits

Understanding why companies do stock splits helps give us the power to profit from them. This section is a collection of my own experiences. You may notice that some things have been oversimplified or, heaven forbid, overlooked. Overall, I have selected subjects for this book that I wish I had known when I started investing in stock split companies.

When a company goes public, it is authorized to issue shares for sale on the open market. The shares of some companies are sold over the counter, on the NASDAQ, on the NYSE, and so forth. Over time, successful companies have a growing demand for their stock. The greater the demand, the higher the price per share. At times the demand far exceeds the supply and there is a shortage of available shares. This can cause very large and volatile swings in the price of the stocks. Eventually the company reaches a success point where they decide to do a stock split.

What follows are (in no particular order) some of the most common reasons that companies declare stock splits.

Increase Liquidity

In some cases investment funds, pension funds or other institutions want to own large blocks of shares in companies that they like. Let's say ABC mutual fund wants to purchase 5% of a particular company's shares. QZZ fund also wants 5%, RBM fund wants 10%, and so forth. Once these funds acquire the shares, they tend to hang onto the stocks for several years or even decades. Eventually the publicly held company might find that 40% of its shares are owned by institutions and management has 55%: that leaves only 5% in the open market, also called the "float." If the company has 1 million shares issued, there would only be 50,000 shares of float available to trade on a daily basis.

When this happens the stock price can become artificially inflated or deflated when shares are traded. This makes it difficult for institutions to increase and decrease holdings. As a result, institutions tend to steer away from companies that have too few shares available.

Increasing the total number of shares tends to attract institution attention and investment. Public companies love institutions because they purchase large amounts of stock, have few complaints, and cause a lower turnover of stocks. Large institution investment also tends to lower the administrative costs for the public company. There is also an interesting correlation between the number of institutions investing in a stock and the price stability/growth of that stock.

Broaden Base Of Stockholders

Increasing the number of shares in the market can lead to a greater number of shareholders. Because of the human tendency to seek safety in numbers (in the market, this is called following the herd), having more shareholders creates greater confidence among investors. More confidence means greater stability, lowering volatility. More stability makes more people want the stock. When more people want the stock, the price increases, making it more attractive and boosting confidence.

You can see the self-fulfilling cycle starting here. Having a broad base of stockholders also means that there are usually more shares traded per day, increasing interest from institutions. The more institutional interest there is, the higher the value of the stock, and here we go again.

Increase Affordability

As a stock increases in price, the average number of shares per purchase decreases. Eventually the stock can get so expensive per share that investors get uncomfortable. In most cases, there are more buyers for a stock priced at $30 than one that sells for $300. As a stock increases in value, it becomes harder for investors to acquire. Companies use a stock split to drop the price per share to a more accessible purchase level.

After a stock splits, the lower price per share can increase the number of investors who will purchase the stock. Another side effect is that within months, the daily price swings tend to be the same as before the split.

For example, Amazon.com did a three-for-one stock split on January 1, 1999. Unless you've been under a rock, you know Amazon.com is an Internet stock and prices were really crazy. At the time I wrote this page Amazon typically varied in price about $10 to $20 per share each day. After the split, the price still varied about $10 to $20 per day. But that's $60 in pre-split prices ($20 x 3 = $60). Today a $60 move would be unusual, but a $20 move is considered acceptable to most investors.

This accessibility is a psychological illusion and a stock market reality. It's also a game. Amazon has split twice in the last 12 months (June 2, 1998 and January 5, 1999), two-for-one and three-for-one, which is like a six-for-one ratio. So a $1 move today is the same as a $6 move twelve months ago ($1 x 2 for the first split is $2, x 3 again for the second split is $6). A $20 move today is actually $120 in last year's price. Do you see how splitting the stock can allow investors to stay in their comfort zone, even though the stock price is increasing in ever greater dollar amounts?

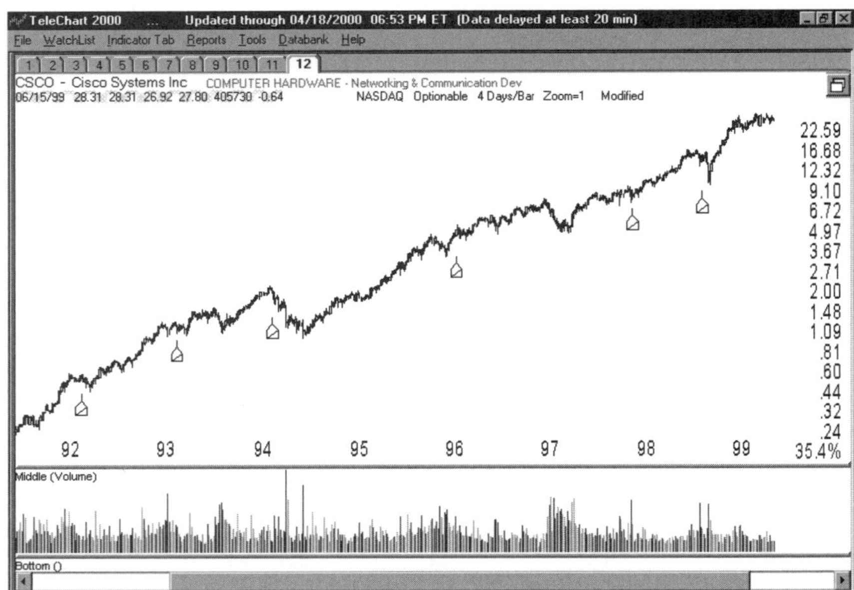

Want to look at an even bigger comparison? Cisco Systems (CSCO) has split seven times in ten years. Every dollar the stock moves today is equal to $72 of 1990 money. That means when CSCO moves up $7 it is technically a $504 movement, if you've held the stock that long!

Pay Dividends Without Cash

Some companies want to use their capital for expansion, development, or research. Others prefer to re-invest profits to expand market share. In either case, if the company returns profits to shareholders in the form of cash dividends, the money is gone.

As a solution the company can declare a dividend in the form of stock—essentially a stock split. For example, a 10% stock dividend is paid by issuing one additional share for each 10 shares an investor owns. The price per share is adjusted so that the 11 shares have the same value as the 10 shares did before the split. In so doing, the company distributes stock instead of cash, and retains capital for expansion, development, marketing, et cetera.

This may seem like a disadvantage to shareholders who get no cash income from holding the stock. In decades past, investors evaluated companies based on the cash dividends issued until the higher interest rates of the 1980s and global competition made dividend-paying companies harder to find. Even today, some investors ask what the point is of owning a stock that doesn't pay dividends: where is the return on investment?

The answer is simple. Even though a stock split or stock dividend makes no direct change in shareholder value, the return on investment comes from the increase in share values that often follows. Watch what happens if a stock is worth $10 and the company pays a 10% stock dividend.

1. If we assume the shareholder has 10 shares, the math will be easy. They have a total value of $100 in stock (10 shares at $10 each). The company declares a 10% stock dividend. After the split, the shareholder has 11 shares, with an adjusted price of $9.10 per share. The shareholder still has an investment worth: $100 = $9.10 x 11 shares (figures are rounded).
2. Within weeks the stock usually moves up in price, continuing until each share is worth $10 (the pre-split price) again. That will result in a shareholder value of $110: 11 shares x $10 = $110. Not bad—you get the dividend and the value, too.

Microsoft is a terrific example. From the company's beginning until 1997, MSFT never paid a dividend. Did the market care that Microsoft had not "shared the wealth" with shareholders? Not at all—instead, Microsoft has grown at unbelievable speed since they went public. Because the stock itself tends to increase in value over time, this is an indirect return on investment to the shareholder.

Before I move on, I need to provide a little warning about stock dividends in a kind of good news/bad news format:

The good news is that if a company is paying a 10% dividend in the form of a stock split, the price will be adjusted. Then within a certain time frame (days, weeks, or months), the price per share will often climb up to the pre-split price, resulting in a tidy profit for the shareholders.

Now the bad news: in many cases, the price of the stock then takes a nose-dive! This can happen when the company is paying a regular dividend, perhaps every 12 months. Investors know well in advance that the company is going to pay the dividend, and they also know that the stock price will climb, so there can be a short-term increase in the stock price before the split. After the split, the stock backs off and tends to stay in the doldrums for six to ten months. When the company is ready to do another dividend/split, the stock price will climb up again.

Analysis of COFI 21-for-20 (5%) Dividend Split

Look at the chart of COFI, which did a 21-for-20 split (a 5% dividend). You can see the small run-up before the split/dividend date. The price recovery after the split took only two months! Sure enough, shortly after the recovery is a dip in share value.

The arrows indicated each of the following:

A. 21-for-20 split (a 5% dividend).

B. The price recovery.

C. After the recovery is a dip in share value.

Increase Shares To Qualify For Listing

In order for a stock to qualify for listing on most exchanges, a company has to meet minimum requirements of size, outstanding shares, capitalization, et cetera. Some companies declare stock splits to increase the total number of outstanding shares so they can meet these minimum requirements. When you look at a listing of pending stock splits, you will see these companies—unknown names, with low volume and low prices. A look at the chart will usually show that the split is not because of growth, because there will usually not be a long-term uptrend. In fact, you might not even be able to get a six-month chart because many of these small companies are overlooked by the research and charting services.

Warning: This is not a good split play because the stocks have low prices, very low volume, and usually no uptrend. You will usually not get the expected upward surge in share values.

Qualify For Options Market

The same sorts of minimum requirements have to be met in order for a stock to qualify for inclusion in the options market—outstanding shares, size, et cetera. Options qualification *is* a price-moving event, because the investment community usually sees optionable stocks as stronger and safer. When a company announces that their stock will become optionable, you will usually see an upward movement in the stock price as the options listing date nears (seven to 10 days before).

Keep Up With The Joneses

When a company announces a stock split, share prices can soar. Other stocks in the same sector can also have rising share values, because of what is called a "sympathy" move. As company after company within the group declares a stock split, the entire industry group starts to increase in value (except for the non-performers, who get left behind). In some cases a feeding frenzy develops and stock prices soar with little or no reason other than the sector-based excitement. This can become a strong force, creating even more emotional buying. The lagging companies can actually begin to feel pressure to declare a stock split so that they can keep up with their competition and to maintain investor attention.

I remember a company a few years ago that was on the edge of disaster. The CEO was considering taking the company into Chapter 11 bankruptcy. At the last moment a white knight rode into the picture—the sector was simmering with multiple stock split announcements, prices were climbing, and investors were getting exuberant. Even this near-bankrupt company had a burst in its stock price. With growing demand for the stock, the financial picture changed. The company acquired new financing based on the newfound confidence, and disaster was avoided. I wish I could remember the name of the company, and show you a chart. Unfortunately I can't recall which company or even the sector, so I'll have to call this story a legend.

The Greed Factor

Greed is my favorite reason for a company to declare a stock split. There are many rational reasons to have a company perform a stock split, but I believe the most frequent motivating reason is greed. I am not making any kind of value judgment; I am simply saying that money is a very powerful force. CEOs will discuss terms like share liquidity, institution participation, turn-over rate, and payment of dividends, but the underlying motivation is dollars. Money is the reason the company went public in the first place, and each day management has to think about the bottom line. With experience, it becomes clear that a stock split is a powerful tool to increase investor excitement, resulting in a better price per share, more volume, and satisfied shareholders.

It's Geometric–Wahoo!

Now that you know the reasons companies declare stock splits, let's look at the results. Each time a stock split is completed the total number of shares increases—within a few years 100 shares can multiply into 1,600 or even more. Over time, those shares increase in value, another stock split is announced, and the excitement continues.

If your original investment in a stock was $50 per share and you purchased 100 shares, your total value is $5,000. Over time with a few stock splits, your 100 shares expand to 1,600. It's like owning a rabbit farm with golden rabbits—you could become the beneficiary of a rabbit-mating windfall!

Do the numbers. It's staggering.

- Assume your company does a two-for-one stock split each year for four years in a row.
- 100 shares x 2 = 200, x 2 = 400, x 2 = 800, x 2 = 1,600.
- After four stock splits, 100 shares have grown into 1,600 shares. That's in only four years!
- Assume that the stock price climbs back up to $50 after each split.
- Do the math—1,600 shares times $50 = $80,000.
- That is a 1,600% increase.

Can you imagine a company doing a two-for-one stock split eight times in a 10-year period? How many shares would you have starting with only 100? The answer is 100 x 2 x 2 x 2 x 2 x 2 x 2 x 2 x 2 = 25,600 shares (100 x 2^8). What is the total value of the investment if the stock returns to $50? It would be 25,600 shares times $50 = $1,280,000. That is $1.2 million after eight stock splits. *If rabbits do it, why not stocks?*

Now imagine what can happen to an investment account devoted to stock splits. With planning, patience, and persistence, it doesn't have to take 10 years to amass substantial holdings.

Think of the shareholders who invested in a newer company, purchasing 1,000 shares for a song. After a few successful years, the shareholders end up with millions of dollars, just because the company kept splitting its stock. Take 1,000 shares and complete four two-for-one splits; you end up with 16,000 shares of stock. Then watch that stock climb to $50 and the holdings are worth nearly a million dollars.

Of course, for every single success story from an upstart company, there are numerous losers. Investing in a company just because it's new is not what I am suggesting. What I am illustrating is the positive financial impact of investing in strong companies with a history of splitting their stock on a consistent basis.

Don't forget that key employees also benefit from stock splits. It is very common for key people to hold stock and options. They would benefit greatly from a stock split, which means their focus will be doing everything they can to assure the company continues growing and improving year after year.

7

The Stock Split Process

This chapter will clear up tons of confusion about the stock split process and how to profit from it. I'll discuss behind-the-scenes requirements and technical elements of a stock split. You'll learn about authorized shares versus issued shares, where to find Securities and Exchange Commission (SEC) filings, how to read quarterly reports, and even more secrets to make you look like a stock split guru to your family and friends.

It's A Secret!

When I first started investing in the market I felt like there was this big secret that everyone knew but me. I know that sounds paranoid, but don't you sometimes feel that way? I would hear things that seemed to conflict with each other and I didn't have any idea what was going on, especially when it came to stock splits. There were many issues that had me completely mystified.

I can remember being in a seminar listening to a few investors talking about an upcoming shareholder meeting. They said the shareholder meeting would be a big money maker, because the company was going to announce a stock split. That night I checked the news releases. I saw the announcement setting the date for the shareholder meeting, but there was no mention of a stock split. I had no clue how those investors knew a split was going to be announced and even if I did, I had no clue how to make it profitable.

Since there is a lot of excitement when a big company declares a stock split, companies tend to keep upcoming announcements a secret. If corporate management were to share that secret too soon, they could be accused of violating insider-trading laws. Stock splits must be kept confidential until there is a public announcement. This public announcement may be in the form of a press release, an announcement at a shareholder meeting, or at another public meeting.

I looked at the news reports again and there was no clue, or so I thought. Look at this sample press release called "Notice of Annual Meeting of Shareowners."

NOTICE OF ANNUAL MEETING OF SHAREOWNERS

TIME: 10 a.m. E.S.T., on Wed, Feb 17
PLACE: The Arco Arena
Main Hall
Sacramento, California

ITEMS OF BUSINESS

1. To elect members of the Board of Directors, whose terms are described in the Proxy Statement.
2. To approve an amendment to the Certificate of Incorporation to increase the number of authorized Common Shares.
3. To transact such other business, including consideration of Shareowner proposals, as may properly come before the Meeting and any adjournment thereof.

This announcement is similar to the news that I had found. When you find something like this you are in luck, it's one of the biggest clues you can find. The company was waving a 500 foot flag saying "Look at me, I am getting ready to split my stock!" Of course there are other reasons that a company may need to obtain an authorization to issue additional shares, but it usually means the company is planning a stock split. (I will share more about needing authorized shares in a few pages.)

Sure enough, a few days later the shareholder meeting was held and a stock split was announced. I was stunned, wondering how those investors knew that the stock split announcement was going to happen at the shareholder meeting. I figured that they must have had insider knowledge and they were cheating the system somehow.

Most companies want to tell their shareholders first, which explains why a large number of stock split announcements are made at the annual shareholder meeting. Other companies like to make the split announcement in association with a fantastic earnings report. When good financials and a split are expected to be announced at the same time, it can create a lot of investor excitement and the stock can skyrocket—in advance of the announcement.

Looking For Clues

You might also look for clues that could indicate a stock split will *not* be announced. When you know what clues to look for, you too will be able to make an "educated guess" when a company is getting ready to split their stock.

As you look for clues, keep in mind that they present themselves in a haphazard order. It would be nice if all companies did the exact same thing, because it would make our job as investors easier. But if the job was easy, everyone would do it and the profit opportunities would go away. When you understand the stock split process, you will begin to see many opportunities to generate cash flow.

For a unique perspective, take a look behind the scenes and see what happens inside the mind of a CEO. Let's say that you are the CEO of Super Split Company (SSC). Your stock has been climbing for months, sales are fantastic, operations are running smooth, and net profits are improving. The stock has climbed so high that it's almost time for another stock split, which is no surprise since SSC has done a two-for-one stock split 11 out of the last 12 years. Each time the stock climbs above $140 the rumors start, people predict that SSC is going to declare a stock split and the stock shoots up to $160. And now, looking at the current price of $165 even television programs are talking about the predicted SSC stock split.

There is so much excitement; you realize that if SSC does not declare a stock split investors will start to worry that something is wrong. You decide to get the wheels of success moving, you will recommend a two-for-one split to the board of directors. The company will need to follow specific steps to carry out the stock split with precision.

Stock Split Requirements

There are some hoops that all companies must jump through to do a stock split. Here is a list of some of the things a typical company needs to successfully complete a stock split.

1. The stock is in a general uptrend and is expected to continue the trend.
2. The board of directors meet and declare a stock split.
3. The company must have enough unissued authorized shares to split the stock.
4. If authorized shares need to be increased, the company has to seek approval from shareholders.
5. A shareholder meeting is required for a vote to authorize additional shares.
6. The company announces the stock split.
7. The company sets the split date, recording date, shareholder meeting date, et cetera.
8. On the split date, additional shares are issued and price per share is adjusted.

Note: This is a list, not a step-by-step process. These steps may occur in almost any order the company needs.

When a company declares a stock split, there are usually other important announcements made. There might be an increase in the dividend being paid, a stock buyback program, changes to management, expansion announcements, et cetera. A stock split is a symptom of corporate success, not the cause. It is just one of many things that management will be handling.

The Typical Company That Splits Is:

1. Operating successfully with increasing revenues/net earnings.
2. The stock price is near or above the price of the last split (not required, but common), in a general uptrend and expected to continue climbing.
3. Business is good and is forecasted to continue or improve.
4. Legal issues are contained or expected to have minimal impact on the company.
5. Shareholder confidence is high.

Failing To Announce Can Hurt

If a company has a history of splitting and fails to announce as expected, the investment community can sour very quickly. Investors know a stock split indicates business is good, and a failure to split the stock can indicate that business may be getting bad.

The IBM Breakdown

In December of 1998, IBM was expected to announce a stock split. Investors were highly excited and rumors were running wild. Newsletters predicted that IBM would announce a stock split when they released earnings on January 21st. Look at the following chart; there is a big move from $168 to $197 during the month before the earnings date—almost 30 points!

The stock had a very strong run-up because of the upcoming earning announcement and the possibility of a stock split. However, the date came and left and the board of directors said nothing about a stock split. The following day, IBM's share price took an ice bath, opening 13 points lower. The damage continued and IBM lost another five points before the market closed on the 22nd. A few days later IBM's board of directors had their regularly scheduled meeting and voted to approve a two-for-one stock split. That afternoon they announced the split, but it was too little too late.

There was a short-term recovery (very short) but IBM set the split date too far away. Investors decided to drop IBM like a piece of nuclear waste, causing another collapse in stock prices. This downturn started a market-wide depression; tech stocks fell hard, taking the rest of the market with them into a deep canyon. Many people say, "As the techs go, so goes the market." The collapse was so swift and hard that people were caught unaware. Everyone was sure that IBM would announce a stock split when they released earnings. This created such over-confidence people ignored the potential risks!

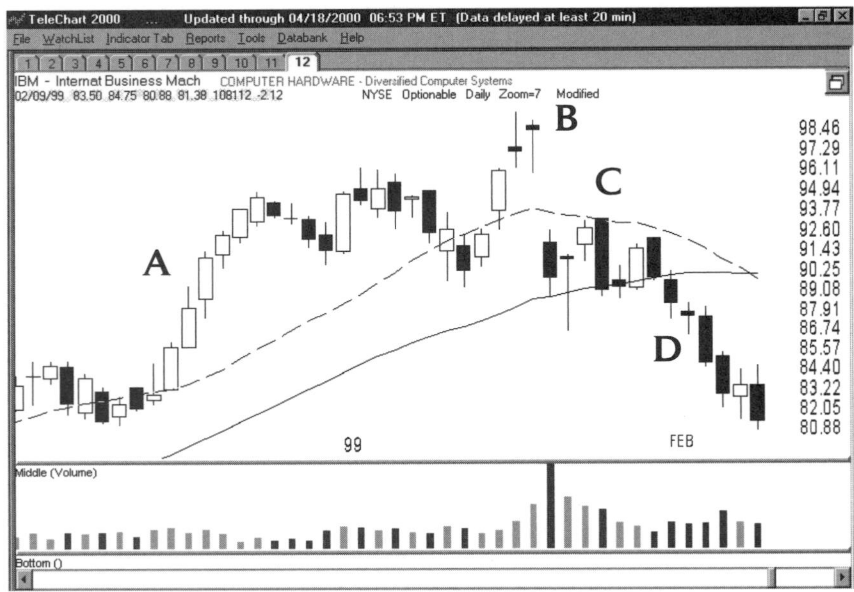

Because IBM failed to announce a split on January 21, the chart shows:

A. Stock run-up prior to split announcements.

B. Earnings released January 21, 1991, but no split announcement as expected.

C. Actual split announcement January 26, 1999.

D. Continued collapse of stock value, after announcement—many said "too little, too late."

This story is a perfect example showing why caution is always needed when heading into earnings. It confirms the rule of thumb—to avoid holding strong positions when a company makes an earnings announcement.

Remember, you want to play the game when you have the best chance of making a profit, and get out of the way when there is a strong chance of loss.

Reasons Not To Split

A company may choose not to split their stock if:

1. There is a chance that revenues will fall far short of expectations.
2. Business has taken a downturn and future earnings are expected to suffer.
3. Company or sector problems could put the stock in a tailspin.
4. Management knows of problems that will cause the stock to collapse when made public.
5. It is planning an acquisition or merger and a split would be detrimental.
6. Other unseen problems exist that make splitting a poor business choice.

The Rules

When a company is publicly traded it must meet requirements of the state in which it is incorporated. Part of that compliance requirement is the creation of the Articles of Incorporation. Included in these articles is the authorization to issue stock. A company might have preferred and common stock, voting and non-voting stock, additional paid-in capital, et cetera.

The most important thing to look at is how many shares are *authorized* and how many have been *issued*. If a company wants to do a stock split, there must be sufficient authorized, unissued shares. If the company wants to issue more shares than have been authorized, they will need shareholder approval.

Having enough authorized shares is just the beginning. There are other rules that we need to know. The rest of this chapter will cover these issues and how the corporation deals with them in order to split its stock.

Authorized Versus Issued Shares

If you look at annual and quarterly statements (i.e., SEC Form 10-K, 10-Q), the company will disclose the number of authorized and issued shares. Before a company can issue shares for a stock split, they must have enough authorized, non-issued shares. If there are *not* enough authorized but unissued shares to complete the stock split, the company will have to get shareholder authorization to issue additional shares.

> ***Authorized Shares Versus Issued Shares***
>
> ***Authorized Shares*** are the number of shares that a company can, but does not have to, issue.
>
> ***Issued Shares*** are the number of shares that the company has issued and placed into service.
>
> ***Shares must be authorized*** before they can be issued.

In order to authorize additional shares the corporation must make an amendment to the articles of incorporation. Making changes to the articles of incorporation requires shareholder approval. Therefore, the company has to hold a shareholder meeting and ask the shareholders to vote, approving an increase in the number of authorized shares. Once authorized, the board of directors can complete the stock split.

Are There Enough Shares Authorized?

Does the company have enough authorized shares to complete a stock split? You can find out by doing the following:

1. Check SEC filings to determine how many shares have already been issued and how many shares are authorized.
2. Estimate how many shares are authorized but unissued.
3. Estimate how many authorized shares the company needs for the split.
4. Compare the two estimates and determine if there are enough unissued shares to do a split.

Shareholders Must Authorize Increase

This section might seem like a review, because I just mentioned it in the last section. I feel it is important to be very clear on this subject, because it is one of the most critical things to consider when looking at potential stock split plays. Plus, I am adding other information, so this section is more than just a review.

If a company does not have enough authorized shares to do a stock split, the board of directors will have to ask the shareholders for permission to increase the number of authorized shares. This permission can only be done as part of a shareholder meeting. *Before a meeting can be held, there must be a public announcement, stating that there will be a shareholder meeting.* Therefore, when you catch wind of a shareholder meeting that includes a vote authorizing additional shares, take that as a strong signal that there is a possible stock split announcement in the future. Run, do not walk—to your research tools and do your homework. If the rest of the market decides a stock split is in the works, there could be a strong run-up.

Shareholders almost always approve the requested increase in authorized shares, because they know that the end result will be money–$$$! In the last 10 years I cannot think of a single shareholder meeting that rejected the request to increase additional authorized shares. As far as you are concerned, the shareholder vote is a formality that you can use as a trading opportunity.

Board Of Directors Declare Split And Issue Shares

Most people think that shareholders must authorize a stock split. This is a common misconception in the investment community. The truth is that the board of directors does *not* have to have permission from shareholders to declare a stock split. That's right. If there are enough authorized shares, the board of directors can declare a stock split without saying anything to the shareholders.

A perfect example of this is a November 1998 stock split announced by Amazon.com (AMZN). In the articles of incorporation, 300 million shares were authorized and only 50 million had been issued. It was a surprise announcement when the board of directors declared the three-for-one stock split. At the time of the stock split announcement the board of directors had not told the stockholders anything. It was a surprise even to AMZN shareholders.

Today, the new game in town is for the board of directors to declare a stock split, pending shareholder approval, to increase additional shares of authorized stock. They don't even have to have enough shares available when they declare a split!

What Meetings To Look For

If you want to predict when a company is going to declare a split, use your understanding of the authorized and issued shares to look for clues. Figure out which meetings are required:

1. Board of Directors Meeting

   If there are enough authorized shares for a split, look for the board of directors meeting. Chances are the board of directors meeting will be the event investors watch.

2. Shareholder Meeting

   If there *are not* enough authorized shares to do a split, look for a shareholder meeting. If there is a shareholder meeting, check the items to be discussed. If there is a request to increase authorized shares—bingo! Chances are other investors will be watching the shareholder meeting, expecting a stock split announcement.

The Split Announcement

This is the moment that the rumors become fact, when supposition becomes reality, and stock split prophets become temporary deities. On the date of the announcement there is no technical change in the nature of the company or its stock. However, the stock price becomes far more volatile and unpredictable.

As a result, market makers get more nervous and increase the cost of transactions. This is reflected in the spread between the buy and the sell price (bid and ask). Before a split announcement a particular stock might be selling for 10 x 10 $^{1}/_{4}$, a $^{1}/_{4}$-point spread (25¢).Then a few minutes after a stock split is announced the market makers usually see a large increase in trading volume. When that happens they widen the spread. Even if the stock has not changed in price, you could see a spread like 10 x 10$^{3}/_{4}$, a $^{3}/_{4}$-point spread (75¢), or even more. Of course, after the announcement the stock price will probably change. I have discussed those changes in prior chapters.

If you look at the options market, similar things happen. Spreads widen and option prices can increase rapidly, even if the underlying stock price stays the same. The market makers tend to boost option values because of the increased volatility.

The Date Is Set

Shortly after a company announces a stock split they will follow up with a more specific news release that provides details of the stock split. This news release may establish:

- The type of stock split (two-for-one, three-for-two, et cetera).
- The recording date.
- The split date.
- The ex-date.

The "recording date," or the "date of record," is the day when the accountant makes a list of the shareholders and counts the total number of shares so that the stock split can be made. It is actually an internal event that has little or no effect on the shareholders. The person who benefits from the stock split is the person who owns the stock (or the option) on the split date.

The "split date" or "pay date" is the actual date of the stock split. People get confused about this and the "ex-date" all the time. You need to own the stock on the split date, the day *before* the ex-date. The split date is the day when the company does the final accounting of who owns what. The market closes and the next business morning the stock split is completed. On the ex-date it is too late to benefit from the split—it's already over.

Note: There is a common mistake made by people wanting to profit from stock splits. They mistake the ex-date for the split date and end up staying in a play longer than their investment formula specifies. If your plan is to exit on or before the split date, be sure you understand that the split date is the day before the stock split adjustment shows up in your account!

The Stock Split Is Completed

After close of market on the split date, the additional shares are issued and credited to your account and the value of each share will be adjusted.

If you are purchasing and selling using an automated system such as the Internet, telephone, or other electronic execution system, be careful. These electronic systems often mess up on the ex-date. You will probably need to talk to a live broker and have them hand-process your transaction. Be sure to tell them that the company has just finished a stock split. If you forget, they might enter your order wrong and you could end up with a real mess.

I had a position in a company that did a two-for-one stock split. The next day I called the broker and told her to close the position by selling my shares. She confirmed the sale and I was a happy puppy. A few hours later I decided to call the broker and confirm that it went as I expected. I was upset to discover that the broker had only sold one-half of my position. She didn't know anything about the two-for-one split and so she only sold half of the shares. (Remember a two-for-one split doubles your number of shares.)

Note to TC-2000™ users: If you are using TC-2000™, the split date that is listed is actually the ex-date. This is especially important if you are using TC-2000™ to track pending stock splits. The program will list future split dates, but these dates are the ex-date, so back up one trading day if you want to know the split date.

Preferred Versus Common Shares

What's the difference between preferred and common shares? When doing stock split plays, the difference is insignificant. In most cases, common shares are what you will be buying and selling. If for some reason you are holding interest in a stock in preferred shares, you will never notice the difference between preferred and common shares. For the sake of simplicity, let's assume that I am talking about common shares any time I discuss authorized and issued shares. What you will find is that almost all companies save the preferred shares for special uses and the general public will have the common shares.

Note: The only time preferred and common shares become important is in the case of bankruptcy. Preferred shareholders get priority over common shareholders. But we are looking at stock split companies not companies that are splitting up.

Par Value Versus Actual Value

When a corporation is created, each share of stock is given what is called a par value. Par value has no bearing on current market value, so as far as I am concerned we can forget about it in a stock split situation. All I care about is the current price of the stock. I'll worry about par value when I'm on the golf course!

Board Of Directors And Shareholders Meetings

A shareholder meeting is a matter of public record. What will be voted on at the meeting, where and when the meeting will be held, and other items must be disclosed to the SEC and shareholders many weeks before the meeting will be held. You can get a sneak preview into shareholder meetings by reading SEC Form 14A, which is discussed later in this chapter.

The board of directors meeting, on the other hand, is not required to be disclosed to the public. If you call the company, about one-half of the time they will tell you when the meeting will be held. Many companies keep the board of directors meetings strictly confidential until they are over, so use history to find clues. After a meeting is held, the board of directors may make press releases and other reports. In some of the SEC filings the board of directors meeting may be discussed.

Many companies are traditionalists at heart and tend to hold their meetings at the same time year after year. Once you know when they have had board of directors meetings in the past, you can predict when they will happen in the future. If a stock is targeted as a split candidate, you may see a price run-up prior to a board of directors meeting, and a drop-off in price afterwards. This can mean extra nuggets of profit for the stock market detectives that are able to figure out when the meetings are held.

Again: Shareholder meetings are public record while board of directors meetings are kept private.

SEC Filing Requirements And Forms

Don't expect this section to provide legal opinions on how to operate a public company, and please be careful of what you learn here. I am providing this information to give you a bird's-eye view of the internal workings of SEC compliance and how you can take advantage of the reports filed by a public company.

All public companies are required to keep the public informed about regular operations and anything substantial that affects the company. The SEC requires several company filings, including annual financial statements, quarterly reports, notices of shareholder meetings, statements regarding pension plans, mergers and takeovers, et cetera. These reports and notices are filed with the SEC, processed, and many are made available to the public through the EDGAR (Electronic Data Gathering, Analysis, and Retrieval) database. Anyone can access these records using a home computer, and they can help you earn truckloads of money when you know where to look.

Using EDGAR – Unfortunately the free EDGAR database system is not ticker symbol friendly. When searching try using the first four characters of the company name. For example: GTW would be found by entering "Gate" because GTW is the ticker symbol for "Gateway." Entering GTW in error could result in "file not found."

I will tell you a little about some forms that must be filed, and investor issues relating to those forms. Most full service brokers can access this information and do the research for you. Give your broker a copy of this book and ask them to read this chapter, so they know what you are looking for. A broker can become a powerful resource if they choose to specialize in stock split plays.

SEC Filing Requirements

The EDGAR system can be accessed via the Internet (World Wide Web) at "www.sec.gov." There is no charge for accessing the system, and all information found is public record, which means that you can print copies without breaking the law. There is only one problem—the free forms are only available on a delayed basis.

This means that you can't access them for at least 24 hours and sometimes for up to a week after filing. Real time access is available for a fee either directly or through a secondary access system.

There is one other limitation. You may find that some companies haven't filed, or that not all the forms are available for your target company. The EDGAR database contains only the forms that were filed electronically. And since some forms are not legally required, they appear only if the company chooses to file. I have found that almost every company meeting my requirements has entries in the EDGAR database. The service may not be perfect, but it's good enough to make me happy.

Public companies have to file tons of different forms. Between the IRS, SEC, states, and other organizations, there are thousands of different papers that can be filled out. I'll only discuss a few.

Of all the forms available, I look at Form 14A first. It is the shareholder proxy form, used to disclose what items shareholders will vote on in the next stockholder meeting. In many cases you can get a sneak peek into future events by reading Form 14A, and usually this shareholder proxy form is filed one to four months before the meeting. If you see a request to authorize more shares, this should perk your ears up for profits!

Filings And Related Form Numbers

Here is a list of the common filings and forms you might see as you scan the EDGAR Database.

Act Filed Under (Filing Type)	Major Forms Used
Act 34 Quarterly Filings - Financial Statements	10-Q, 13F-E
Act 34 Annual Filings - Financial Statements	10-K, 11-K, 20-F
Act 34 Registrations - Pension Plans, etc.	8-A, 8-B, Form 10
Tenders and Acquisitions	SC 13D, SC 13E3, SC 13E4, SC 13G, SC 14D1, SC 14D9
Shareholder Reports	ARS, N-30D, N-30B-2
Proxy Solicitation and Information Statements	PRE14A, DEF14A, DEFA14A, DEF14C, DEFM14A

Annual and Quarterly Statements

Most common reports: 10-K (annual) and 10-Q (quarterly) financial statements.

Form 10-K—Annual

Each year public companies file a financial statement which details how they did over the last 12 months. There is a multi-year comparison showing what increased and what decreased. Included are some of the following:

- Statement of compensation to officers.
- Pension plan.
- Performance history.
- Review of holdings.
- Discussion of mergers in the past and future.
- Expectations of future performance.
- A review of major legal actions that are pending, or recently completed.
- A review of stock splits or other dividends.
- An accounting of the number of authorized shares.
- Statement showing how many shares have been issued.
- Statement of irregularities, risks, and problems.

By reviewing this financial report you can determine how many shares are authorized and how many shares are issued and outstanding. Using that information you can determine if a company has enough shares available to do a stock split. If they do not have sufficient shares to split the stock, you will know to look for a shareholder meeting that will seek authorization to issue more shares. Use the most current 10-K or 10-Q

Form 10-Q—Quarterly

Similar in function to the annual report, this quarterly filing has fewer pages and is lighter on historical information. However, the financial reports are included, and can be used to determine authorized and issued shares. By knowing dates of the quarterly reports you can possibly catch short-term fluctuations in the price of shares. If you know that a company is expected to have a good quarter, the stock price might move up, and if they are expected to have a bad quarter shares will most likely drop.

It is very dangerous to hold a strong investment position on the day a company is reporting earnings. After a stock has declared a split and before the actual split takes place, there might be a financial report filed. If they disappoint the street, their stock will take a hard dip. If they meet the expectations of the street, the stock might still fall. By knowing what to expect, you can determine if you need to adjust your investment plan to increase your income or protect your capital. If the company reports earnings that exceed expectations, the stock might jump in value or it can still take a dive. You need to consider that the stock has probably run up in value in the weeks prior to the report.

The old adage "buy on rumor and sell on fact" holds very true during earnings season. Of course, our rule is to buy on rumor and sell before the news (fact).

Form PRE 14A/DEF 14A—Proxy Statement

The legal definition of form 14A is: "Proxy Statement Pursuant to Section 14(a) of the Securities Exchange Act of 1934." The term to use is: "Proxy Statement." Form 14A is the most enjoyable of all the SEC-required forms, because you get to look into the scheduled events of the next shareholders meeting. If a company needs to increase the number of authorized shares they are required to get the approval of the shareholders. This vote is done as part of the shareholder meeting.

In order to have a shareholder vote, the company must notify all shareholders (as of the Record Date) of the meeting, give them a preview of what will be discussed, and allow time for shareholder responses—before the meeting.

Proxy statements are a fantastic way to predict the future. If a company is increasing the number of authorized shares there is a good chance that a stock split announcement is on the horizon. In a proxy statement filed by Lucent Technologies (LU), I found a proposal to authorize additional shares. Another example of a proxy statement that included a shareholder vote to increase the number of authorized shares was filed by Dell Computer Corporation (DELL).

Excerpt from Lucent Proxy Statement

Lucent proxy statement filed on November 9, 1998

	FOR	AGAINST	ABSTAIN
2. Directors' Proposal — Approve an Amendment to the Certificate of Incorporation to Increase Authorized Common Stock.	[ ]	[ ]	[ ]

Excerpt from Dell Proxy Statement

DELL proxy statement filed May 8, 1998
The Board of Directors is proposing an amendment to the Certificate of Incorporation to increase the number of authorized shares of Common Stock from one billion to three billion. If the stockholders approve this proposal, the first paragraph of Article Fourth of the Company's Certificate of Incorporation will be amended to read in its entirety as follows:

"FOURTH: The total number of shares of capital stock of the Corporation shall be three billion and five million (3,005,000,000), which shall consist of five million (5,000,000) shares of Preferred Stock, of the par value of $0.01 per share, and three billion (3,000,000,000) shares of Common Stock, of the par value of $0.01 per share."

Form 8-K–Change In Material Status

This statement might discuss takeover plans, senior management or board of directors' changes, mergers, and major changes in the company or operations. It can give you a clue to the possible use of shares that are available to be issued. The company might want to offer the shares for sale in order to raise more capital, or take other actions which would prevent them from using the shares to do a stock split.

Form S-8–Registration Of Securities

This is the form used to describe an action like sales of shares, use of shares in pension plans, et cetera. I don't usually look at this form because it doesn't seem to have much to do with stock split plans, at least not directly enough for me to teach the concepts to other people.

However, look at Dell Computer's S-8 filed November 2, 1998 and you can see a perfect example of an Employee Stock Purchase Program. While too many pages to include here, it clearly shows the potential for corporate executives. A company can compensate key individuals using stock options that often have a guaranteed stock purchase price established when the option becomes first available. In many cases, the options have a life of 10 years. Each year many of Dell's board members receive options to purchase 24,000 shares of stock as compensation for their year of service. A few years later, those same options are worth millions.

The fantastic part of this element of the plan is that the company does not have to incur a large cost. The day the options are issued they have a strike price equal to the stock price on the date of issue. For example, if the DELL shares closed at a price of $74.08, the company would issue the stock options with an exercise price of $74.08. Since the options have a strike price equal to the stock price, there is no cost to the company. The key employee can then hold the options for 10 years before exercising them. Can you imagine what those options will be worth in 10 years? Even if the company grows at an average rate, the accumulation would be exciting.

Other choices for the company include providing the options at a cost of 85% of the fair market value and in some cases 50% of the fair market value. These last two options incur a cost to the company of 15% or 50% of the value of the stock, respectively. These costs are a corporate expense that can be deducted according to normal accounting standards using a method that does not make a big difference in corporate earnings. All of these incentives can be contained in a tax-sheltered program like a 401(k), resulting in an unbelievable benefit to the employees.

I did a little figuring last night and it was sobering. So sobering I feel like drafting a resume that can be submitted to every major corporation in the country. Perhaps one of them will want to add my wonderful skills to their board of directors. I'd be happy to serve if I get the same compensation that I'm about to show you.

This is a portion of the incentive package provided by Dell Computer. Options were issued to active members of the board. Many received options for 24,000 shares on July 18, 1997 at a strike price of $74.08, the stock price as of the market close on July 18, 1997. The options will remain available for 10 years from issue. If the board member decides to resign, the options would be fully vested by 2002.

DELL had a few stock splits and the options were adjusted to reflect the split.

Date	Action	Shares	Stock Purchase Price
July 28, 1997	*Option Issued*	*24,000*	*$74.08*
March 9, 1998	*2:1 stock split*	*48,000*	*$37.04*
September 8, 1998	*2:1 stock split*	*96,000*	*$18.52*
March 8, 1999	*2:1 stock split*	*192,000*	*$9.26*

On March 8, 1999 at the close of market, DELL shares were worth $45.375. The holder of the above option could purchase 192,000 shares at a cost of $9.26 per share and turn around and sell the shares for $45.375. This would result in a profit of $36.115 per share. $36.115 x 192,000 = $6,934,080! That's right—almost $7 million dollars! What did this cost the company? Virtually nothing.

How would you like to be on the board of directors at Dell Computer? Do you want to hear the best part of this example? The above 24,000 shares were only for 1997 efforts. Each year the members of the board can receive more options!

Companies use these types of packages to attract and keep quality talent. It also encourages management and officers to do everything they can to assure the company is successful, because the options have no value if the stock stays stagnant.

Is This A Profit Opportunity?

What can you do with this interesting information? You might look at large companies, determine when the options are issued and when their purchase values are set. There might be a very interesting and mysterious drop in value, just before the purchase price of the options is set. And then the stock could slowly drift back up and resume its uptrend.

I'm not saying that corporate executives of large companies would intentionally release rumors or news that could cause the stock to tumble, just so they can purchase the options at a big discount. But, if for some strange reason the stock tumbles, you might just see a buying opportunity.

The following quote is taken directly from the SEC's EDGAR Internet site.

"Companies that have fewer than 500 investors and less than $10 million in net assets are not required to file annual and quarterly reports with the SEC.

The SEC does not require companies that are raising less than $1 million under Rule 504 of Regulation D to be "registered" with the SEC, but these companies are required to file a "Form D" with the SEC. The Form D serves as a brief notice that provides information about the company and the offering. To determine whether a Form D has been filed, or to obtain a copy, call the SEC's Public Reference Branch at (202) 942-8090 or contact them via e-mail at publicinfo@sec.gov.

The presence of co-registrants in a filing can result in duplicate listings.

http://www.sec.gov/edaux/formlynx.htm Last update: 10/23/98"

What this means is that smaller companies may not have to file forms with the SEC.

Running Numbers: Formulas

Here is how you figure out if there are enough authorized shares to complete a stock split.

1. Determine how many shares have already been issued and outstanding. These are the shares that have been sold already. Look at the annual or quarterly statement. There will be a statement on the first page showing the total number of shares issued and outstanding. If the total number of issued shares is not listed on the first few pages, you will have to look deeper for a financial statement that has a section called "Stockholder's equity." This section details the total number of issued shares, and it may state the authorized shares.
2. Determine how many shares are authorized. These are the shares that were available to sell. Look at the annual or quarterly statement, Form 10-K or 10-Q—there will be a financial statement somewhere within it called a "Consolidated Financial Statement." The total number of authorized shares will usually be included in the "Stockholders' Equity" portion of the financial statement—look for "Stockholders' Equity." Or there may be a "note" attached to the financial statement that includes the authorized share information. If the company is new you might look for the authorized shares in the articles of incorporation—of course this is not as reliable because the articles might have been amended.

Save tons of time is using the search feature in your software:

Click on your page and depress the "control" and "F" key or:

Click:	*"Edit" on the command bar*
Select:	*"Search" or "Find Within Page" or "Find (on this page)"*

Then:

Search For:	*"Outstanding"*
Select:	*"Repeat Search" until you find it*

3. **Determine how many authorized shares the company needs for the split. Look at the first page of the annual or quarterly filing for a statement that shows the total number of shares issued. Multiply the number of issued shares by the following factor:**

Split		Factor
3:2	*= issued shares x*	*1.50*
4:3	*= issued shares x*	*1.333*
5:4	*= issued shares x*	*1.25*
2:1	*= issued shares x*	*2.0*
3:1	*= issued shares x*	*3.0*
	Others = you are on your own	

4. **Are there enough authorized shares for the split? Assume there are 400,000 authorized shares and the company has issued 250,000 shares. You think the company will declare a two-for-one split. 250,000 issued shares x 2 = 500,000. There are 400,000 authorized shares and the company needs 500,000 authorized shares—a two-for-one split cannot be completed unless the shareholders approve an increase in the number of authorized shares.**

Using the same facts, you can see that the company has enough authorized shares to do a three-for-two stock split. 250,000 x 1.5 = 375,000. There are 400,000 authorized shares and the company only needs 375,000.

Two Examples

Let's look at two hypothetical examples to see when shareholder approval is needed before a split can be completed.

Example A

A company has issued 2.33 billion of a 2.50 billion authorized shares. Company wants to execute a two-for-one split. Will a shareholder meeting be required?

Shares already issued:	*2.33 billion*
Company to execute a two-for-one split:	*X 2*
Total issued shares after split:	*4.66 billion*

Shares already authorized:	*2.50 billion*
Total shares needed for a two-for-one split:	*4.66 billion*
Is a shareholder meeting required?	*Yes*
Number of shares company will ask shareholders to approve:	*5.00 billion*

Note: Although the company only needs 4.66 billion shares to complete the split, there needs to be a few extra for other things like pension plans, hiring incentives, etc. In addition, companies seem to like round numbers so five billion sounds much better than 4.66 billion.

Example B

A company has issued 1.25 billion of a four billion authorized shares. Company wants to execute a two-for-one split. Will a shareholder meeting be required?

Shares already issued:	*1.25 billion*
Company to execute a two-for-one split:	*X 2*
Total issued shares after split:	*2.50 billion*

Shares already authorized:	*4.00 billion*
Total shares needed for a two-for-one split:	*2.50 billion*
Is a shareholder meeting required?	*No*
Number of shares company will ask shareholders to approve:	*Not required*

Knowing What To Look For

After running the numbers you can decide what steps the company may need to do in order to proceed with a stock split.

- If there are enough shares to complete a stock split, an announcement can be made when the board of directors decides to split the stock.
- If the company needs more authorized shares you know there will be a shareholder meeting.

Wait a minute! So far, I have been talking about predicting if a company is going to announce a stock split. How do you know what kind of a stock split the company will be doing if they have not even made the announcement? Will it be a three-for-two, three-for-one, two-for-one, four-for-five? Start out by using the company stock split history, and find out what type of splits the company has done in the past. If they have always done two-for-one splits, you can be confident that they will do a two-for-one again (which by the way is the most common type of split).

Except

Yes, there are exceptions to every rule. There are times when a company may need to use a different ratio.

Exception #1: Let's say that the usual stock price range is $50 to $100 and the stock is soaring, it is already above $300. The company might end up wanting to do a three-for-one or a four-for-one in order to get the price per share down to the normal range.

Exception #2: The company likes to do two-for-one stock splits, but there are only enough authorized shares to complete a three-for-two split. There might be a three-for-two split declared, so that the company can avoid having to bear the cost of conducting a special shareholder meeting.

The Result

When companies go through the process of declaring a stock split, they have many other events happening at the same time. Although we are sitting on pins and needles waiting for the stock split announcement, the CEO could be meeting with the board of directors with a list of 26 items to be discussed. The stock split could be item number 25.

There are a few other things that can happen just before, at the same time, or shortly following a stock split announcement. The company might:

- Declare a dividend.
- Increase the previously announced dividend.
- Declare a stock buyback program.

- Announce new board members (which means they might have had a board of directors meeting).
- Make changes to pension plans.
- Release major news about new developments, products, or opportunities.
- Announce a special shareholder meeting.
- Increase public confidence to boost share value by:
  - Using national ads
  - Developing public awareness programs
  - Increase future earnings estimates.

Making It Real

One day Miles was looking at Amazon.com's 1998 annual financial statement (Form 10-K). On page three of the report was a consolidated balance sheet. Toward the bottom of the page was a section called "Stockholder's Equity." Lo and behold, there was an accounting of the preferred and common stock. Amazon.com had 300 million authorized shares. According to the June 30, 1998 financial statement, they had only issued 49,669,601 shares. Using a handy dandy calculator he subtracted 49 from 300 and discovered that there were over 250 million authorized shares that could still be issued. Amazon.com had more than enough authorized shares to do a two-for-one or a three-for-one split.

When Miles noticed this, he checked the stock price, which was well within split range. He sent me the following e-mail message predicting that Amazon was going to declare a stock split. It was a great piece of research and the play was solid—a real cash generator.

E-mail message from Miles to Darlene about possible Amazon stock split announcement:

"Dar,
If we look at amazon.com (AMZN), they have 300 million shares authorized and they have only issued 50 million. That means they probably have enough shares to do another two-for-one or three-for-one split. AOL completes their split tomorrow, which frees up attention that AOL has been getting. In addition, Amazon has just announced that they are going to become a seller of tons of stuff, including almost everything in a depart-

ment store. The stock jumped 20 points today. Amazon might keep climbing into the stratosphere.

Should we consider a long-term play to speculate that they will announce a split between now and the next meeting? The uptrend should be real strong. What do you think?

I love you, M"

Do you want to hear the funny part of this story? I didn't respond to him and he was so busy editing the book and some special reports that we both forgot about the e-mail message. Two days later AMZN declared a three-for-one stock split; on the announcement it jumped up 27 points and never looked back! We let the play slip by us like $10,000 blowing in the wind. Oh well—the beauty of knowing these stock market strategies is that there will be another opportunity tomorrow. I pass on great deals every day. With thousands of stocks to choose from, there will always be another great opportunity, always!

8

The Stock Market Is A Cash Cow!

Some people call the stock market the best investment cash cow of all time. There are thousands of companies to choose from and the opportunities are growing each year. I believe, that with the right education, anyone can take advantage of the opportunities presented by the stock market. What people need is basic knowledge, so that they can practice until they develop enough skills to ensure a profitable experience. With the right understanding, you can take an active approach to investing that will allow you to far exceed the buy-and-hold returns experienced by the general population.

It is important to understand the need for practice. Knowledge applied without practice can lead to errors, frustration, and disaster. With knowledge and perfect practice, stock split investment strategies may become a vehicle to fortune, fame, and the achievement of dreams. Let's proceed, and learn how to milk the stock market's cash cow.

How To Milk A Cow

The milk business has many experiences that can be applied to the goal of this book, and relating the two will help you remember the concepts and make learning a unique experience.

The Development Of The Dairy Business

100-Year-Old Methods

For hundreds of years farmers have milked their cows twice a day, usually before dawn and at dusk. Old Bessie was called in, the farmer sat on a three-legged stool, and placed the wooden bucket in position.The milk was extracted and filled the bucket. The more cows the farmer had, the longer the process took. It was a difficult regimen, working twice a day, twelve hours apart, seven days a week, with no vacation or sick leave.

Enterprising farms hired extra hands to help with the milking and maintenance of the farm. If a city was near, the farmer could start a dairy business and deliver bottled milk to the homes and apartments, but this was a time-intensive and difficult process. Then the industrial age arrived for the dairy business.

In Comes Technology

Automatic milking machines were created. Farmers converted their buckets into planter boxes and the three-legged stool was replaced with a stainless steel milking device. Milk was extracted in a quick and efficient process. Farmers were able to handle hundreds more cows with fewer employees. However, because of storage and transportation challenges, the dairy farm was still limited to producing the amount of milk that could be consumed by local customers. Other farms were also challenged, because there were more farmers producing more milk than the market could possibly consume.

With improvements in refrigeration and storage techniques, long distance transportation was finally possible. Trucking and railcar tankers meant milk would survive the trip to mass storage facilities that could package and distribute it to larger metropolitan areas. The shipping developments allowed farmers to widely distribute products, but there was still too much production capacity.

Along Comes Advertising

Enterprising farmers suffering from this over-capacity agreed to create a milk cooperative. One goal of the cooperative was to hire advertising firms to promote the social and health benefits of milk, increasing demand for their products.

When actors and big-name celebrities appeared with the white "moo"-stache, demand for milk and milk products surged. The milk industry had increased profitable productions by developing a larger need for the product. As consumers bought the physical and psychological benefits of milk, farmers smiled all the way to the bank.

Some Refused To Change

Some farmers refused to change. They preferred milking cows by hand and did not take to the idea of attaching some contraption onto old Bessie. As modern dairies increased their ability to produce milk more efficiently, prices fell, demand rose, and the need for increased production grew. The old timers found that milking by hand could not produce enough milk for a competitive cost. Since old-fashioned methods could not earn enough money to stay profitable, their farms had to adapt or go to the auctioneer. Those who resisted developments faded away into the pages of history right next to wagon wheel manufacturers and buggy whip designers.

What Kind Of Farmer Do You Want To Be?

What sort of lifestyle do you want? Do you want to get up before the sun and work 12 to 16 hours a day for the rest of your life? Do you want to milk your cows by hand and have arthritis before you're fifty? Or do you want to go for the gusto, increase demand and production, and keep ahead of the market?

Similar to the dairy business, the stock market has been operating for well over a hundred years and there are established investment techniques that have been around since the beginning. These techniques are very much like that old wooden bucket and three-legged stool, comfortable, well known, and slow.

Recently, breakthroughs in technology have created new opportunities for small investors. Timely news releases, financial reports, and efficient research tools are now available to anyone with a personal computer and a modem. This has caused the development of a grassroots movement that is changing forever the face of stock market investing. For the first time in history, individual investors can trade in the market with the same access formerly reserved for institutions. The opportunities appear unlimited and the potential is absolutely fantastic.

It is up to you. If you are going to go for the big profits, you have to be willing to leave the pack and embrace the most effective methods. I have talked about playing stock splits using options for more leverage. What I'll do now is compare different investment methods and show how they can be used when playing stock splits.

Things are getting fun now. I hope you have your heart medicine, because your blood will be pumping with excitement soon, if it isn't already! When you finish this chapter you'll know the tools that can help you turn stock splits into an efficient, speedy, income-producing cash cow.

How To Milk The Stock Market

Let's start with some techniques that build upon established ways of investing. After laying a strong base of understanding, I'll expand the concepts to investigate more aggressive ways to profit from stock splits. With the correct knowledge and practice, you can milk the stock market with ease and great returns.

Look At Rates Of Return, Not Just Dollar Moves

When looking at trading possibilities, many people miss great opportunities because of ignorance. I learned from one of my mentors, Wade Cook, that you need to look at percentage rates of return, not just dollar returns. If you earn $1,000 profit, but you have to risk $1,000,000 for three months, that's a low return for the money, in my opinion.

Which is a better investment, A or B?

Investment Risk	Capital Invested	Profits on Investment
Investment A	*$1,200 for one year*	*$300*
Investment B	*$10,000 for one year*	*$1,500*

Many people think that Investment B was the better choice, because you end the year with $1,500 income vs. $300. However, if you look at the rate of return you will see a totally different story:

To calculate a rate of return:

Divide the profit by the amount of money at risk (amount invested).

- *Investment A returned $300 and $1,200 was at risk: $300 divided by $1,200 = 25%.*

- *Investment B returned $1,500 and $10,000 was at risk. $1,500 divided by $10,000 = 15%.*

Now—which is a better investment, A or B?

Investment	Risk Capital Invested For One Year	Profits on Investment	Rate of Return
A	*$1,200*	*$300*	*25%*
B	*$10,000*	*$1,500*	*15%*

Rate of Return Computation: Profit ÷ Risk Capital

Both investments took one year to generate the profits, but Investment A provided the greatest rate of return. This concept escapes many people, but it's well known to the bankers and loan officers who play with money all day long. They know that rate of return is the key to increasing income. What counts is not how much money you earn on a trade, but what your rate of return is and in what time frame.

In addition, investing $1,200 is quite different from investing $10,000, $100,000, or $1,000,000. You can divide $10,000 into many different $1,200 investments that return 25%. The same is true in the stock market. Once you have a formula that works, the next step is to put cash into the high-return pipeline and have profits flow out the other end.

There's one more concept I need to introduce to you: the difference between annual and monthly returns. We are a monthly-income society—my bills need to be paid once a month, and I assume so do yours. To be honest with you, when I am working my investments, I would be totally depressed if they only generated 15% to 25% annually. I am much happier with 15% to 25% on a monthly basis.

Compare Rates of Return: Remember, when looking at the potential of a play, you need to consider the rate of return and not just the total dollars returned.

This can mean that you will look at companies or trades that will kick out only one or two dollars. But if you use one dollar and get back three dollars you have made a killing.

Calculating Your Monthly Rate of Return

I compute my rate of return by looking at the monthly interest rate. Since these investment concepts do so well, converting to annual rates is hard to grasp. Sometimes the numbers are so big they don't look realistic, so I use monthly rates to mentally accept them. As you read on you'll see what I mean. Here is the formula I use to determine the monthly rate of return for an investment:

Gather information:

A. *Amount invested:* $________

B. *Amount returned:* $________

C. *Days in trade:* ________
(Calendar days, including week-ends)

Compute the Rate of Return:

D. *Determine the cash profit:* (B – A) ___________
Subtract the amount invested (A) from the total amount returned (B) to get your profit (D).

E. *Determine the rate of return:* (D ÷ A) ___________
Divide your profit (D) by the amount invested (A) to get the rate of return (E).

F. *Convert the return to daily:* (E ÷ C) ___________
Divide the rate of return (D) by the number of days the money was at risk (C) to get the daily rate of return.

G. *Convert daily to monthly:* (F x 30) ___________
Multiply the daily rate of return (F) by 30 to get the monthly return (G).

H. *Convert to percent:* (G x 100) ________ %
Multiply the monthly return (G) by 100.

FYI: Some people like to convert to monthly using a factor of 20 because there are 20 business days each month. However, I look at rates of return like interest, which compounds every day of every month.

Interest Never Sleeps!

Interest operates seven days a week, 52 weeks a year, never takes a vacation, won't call in sick, doesn't have family problems, and never has compassion for anything! For most people, this is a bad thing because they pay interest, but if you can switch sides and put compounding to work for you, imagine where you could be!

Apply the Formula

This is a practice run to see if you understand how to apply the formula. It is vitally important that you get this concept. It needs to be so clear to you that you can do it without thinking. This formula will become a part of your everyday routine as you evaluate investment choices and analyze the results of your activities.

You invest $1,000 in a trade for 1½ months, and when the investment is done you get $1,350 back ($1,000 capital plus $350 profit). Use this information to apply the formula:

A. Invested:	*$1,000*	
B. Amount returned:	*$1,350*	
C. Days in trade:	*42*	
D. Determine cash profit:	*$1,350 – $1,000*	*= $350*
E. Determine rate of return:	*$350 ÷ $1,000*	*= 0.35*
F. Convert to daily:	*0.35 ÷ 42*	*= 0.008333*
G. Convert to monthly:	*0.008333 x 30*	*= 0.25*
H. Convert to percent:	*0.25 x 100*	*= 25%*

If you wanted to convert this monthly return to annual, you would simply multiply by 12. The result is an annualized return of 300%. However, I don't like to do that because I am almost never in a play for an entire year. My typical stock split play lasts less than a month, and I complete some plays in as little as 24 hours. I don't feel that converting returns to annual is realistic.

Stay Liquid. How about keeping your risk capital in cash, sitting in the brokerage account, earning you interest until the right opportunity presents itself. When a fantastic play develops take advantage of the trade for all the profits you can get. Let's face it, even if you were to do only one trade a year, and you earn 35% as the rate of return ($350 on $1,000), that would be a pretty good rate of return – it would beat every CD in the country!

And The Survey Said...

When I decided to write this book I grabbed some stock split calendars and did a little figuring. I looked at a random group of stock splits between the summer of 1997 and the summer of 1998. I made note of the stock price the day after the announcement was made and the price the day before the split ex-date. I threw out companies that averaged share volumes under 100,000 shares per day and stocks that were in a big downtrend prior to the announcement. Of the stocks that fit my criteria more than 90% performed much better than the market. Historically if I kept to the criteria and was selective about investing in stock split companies I could usually have beaten the street. However, I'm not quite satisfied with beating the street. I'd rather buy the street, the block, or even the whole town!

With this non-scientific survey in mind I can establish that investing in stock split companies will provide a predictable opportunity for profit. Let's get more aggressive and look at different ways to profit from stock splits. You might even learn that the most conservative methods can actually be one of the riskiest ways to play the market. Not only do you risk your capital, you risk your true income potential.

Comparing With A Known Quantity

At the beginning of this book I talked about investing in stock split companies using a buy and hold technique. We developed a "stock split portfolio" and compared the long-term success of stock split companies with the market as a whole. The buy and hold technique is the most common trading method taught in investment circles. It is also familiar to the highest number of readers.

Now that we are all comfortable with this vocabulary, it is time you learned how to speak the golden language of profits.

With the solid base that has been built so far, you can begin to compare a buy and hold investment with more progressive investment concepts. What I am talking about doing is an "apples-to-apples comparison," that will allow you to see how the same investment might perform using different investment methods.

It's okay to do nothing! There is no rule that says you have to keep all of your money in play all of the time. Truth is, you will do better holding your money until fantastic plays present themselves

If there are no good plays this week, wait. The law of compound investment says you will not miss a thing by passing bad deals. It's better to pass on a poor play than to end up poor by playing!–Miles Nelson

Playing The Stock Split

What if you were to purchase and hold a stock long enough to take advantage of a particular price-moving event—like a stock split? When that event is over or nearly over, take your money out of that stock and look for another opportunity. This is like a short-term buy and hold technique, where you decide to hold the stock only when it is the most profitable. If we start there, I can show you a small adjustment that could cause your profits to explode.

Let's examine what can happen if you hold a stock long enough to take advantage of a stock split and then move onto another stock.

We'll pretend that you have watched Microsoft (MSFT) for years. (If you had any interest in the market before you picked up this book, this may not be pretending—MSFT is one of the most-watched stocks in history.) You purchased some shares a few years ago and did very well in the last two-for-one stock split. By October 16, 1998, you see that your shares are worth $105 each. You've learned that stock splits can make a big change in the value of a stock, and there is a rumor that America On-Line (AOL) is going to do a two-for-one split in the middle of November. Currently AOL is selling for $102 per share. You decide to be conservative and watch AOL to see what happens.

On October 26th, AOL announces a two-for-one stock split which will be effective November 18th. You can sell the shares of MSFT and purchase AOL shares. You call the broker and confirm the price of each stock. MSFT shares are selling for $107 and you can purchase AOL for $122. That's right—on October 16th, AOL shares were selling for $102, and just ten days later they are at $122. There was a 20% run-up in AOL prior to the split announcement (Phase 1).

Looking at MSFT, you see that it has been stuck in a sideways trading range for a few months and the company has all kinds of legal problems. You think that MSFT is going to be in the trenches for awhile longer. Since you expect MSFT to stay stuck, and AOL has good news, you decide to put the money into AOL so you can take advantage of their two-for-one stock split.

MSFT And AOL Comparison–Buy And Hold

You sell your 200 shares of MSFT for $107. That will result in a credit of $21,400 going into your brokerage account. Since AOL is selling for $122, you can purchase 175 shares at a cost of $21,350. You tell your broker to use a $10 trailing stop-loss and your exit point is November 19th, the day after the split. It would have been better to enter the trade a few weeks earlier when AOL was at the bottom of a dip, but this example will work out anyway.

The next few weeks are uneventful. There are a few ups and downs, which don't matter to you since you own the stock and can hold on forever if you need to. On November 19th you call the broker and get a few quotes. AOL's split is complete and your 175 shares have doubled to 350 shares now selling for $83 (equivalent to a before split price of $166). You place an order to sell your AOL holdings at $83 and close the transaction. Your sell is confirmed for 350 shares of AOL, and your total return of $29,050. You were in the play for 25 days.

Use the formula we learned earlier to determine your monthly rate of return:

A. *Amount invested in AOL:* $21,350

B. *Amount returned:* $29,050

C. *Days in trade:* 25

D. *Determine cash profit:* $29,050 – $21,350 = $7,700

E. Determine rate of return:	*$7,700 ÷ $21,350*	*= 0.3607*
F. Convert to daily:	*0.3607 ÷ 25*	*= 0.01443*
G. Convert to monthly:	*0.01443 x 30*	*= 0.4329*
H. Convert to percent:	*0.4329 x 100*	*= 43.29%*

Note: To convert to annual it would be 43.29% x 12 = 519.48%!

If you wanted to get back into MSFT, which has climbed a little and is now sitting at $111, you could purchase 261 shares. Our apples-to-apples comparison between simply holding MSFT or selling and getting into AOL is that had you done nothing you would have had 200 shares of MSFT worth $111. By taking advantage of the AOL stock split you now have 261 shares of MSFT—still worth $111 each—for a difference in your pocket (or portfolio) of more than $6,771.

Shares	Price Per Share	Total Value
200	*$111*	*$22,200*
261	*$111*	*$28,971*
Difference		*$6,771*

Using Margin To Double Your Profits

Knowing that AOL is a short-term play, you can increase your profits by using the margin portion of your account. Margin is essentially a loan made by the brokerage firm to you, secured by qualifying stock that you own in your account. Typically, margin will lend you up to 50% of the value of your qualifying stock to use for additional stock investments. This is done because the broker has your stocks as collateral so they know they will be paid.

Any time someone is willing to loan you money, there's a cost, risk, or downside. Here's the "downside" of margin:

- If your stocks fall in value, the broker may require you to provide additional money or sell some of your stock to bring the loan ratio back in line. This is known as a margin call. It's a little like being over your limit on your credit line at a bank.

- There is interest charged for money borrowed on margin. These are usually very low rates, but it is an additional expense of investing.
- If the stock moves down in price, you can lose equity quickly.

Since you could be forced to sell assets if there is a downturn in stock prices, be sure to use a stop-loss to limit your downside risk.

Now that we are clear on the risks, here are the benefits—the "upside" of margin:

- You get to use the best investment-leveraging tool available: Other People's Money (OPM).
- You can use margin to increase your stock holdings and your potential profits.
- Using margin can help spread risk by letting you diversify into more stocks.

People tend to blow the risks of margin accounts way out of proportion. Because of fear and insufficient knowledge, the margin risks seem bigger than they need to be, and many investors have either experienced or heard someone else's horror stories about getting a margin call. I have heard many people talk about how much money they lost because they bought stocks on margin, or tell sob stories about getting broker calls at the worst times. These stories made me scared too, until I realized that I was missing some important facts in assessing whether I was likely to have a similar experience.

- What experience or knowledge did that person have before they used margin?
- What were their investment objectives?
- What was their investment plan to achieve those objectives?
- What controls did they use to limit risk of loss?

I think the important things to keep in mind are to use strict entry and exit criteria, use sound investment practices for getting into trades, and quickly cut losses short if a trade starts to go the wrong way! Also keep your investment capital intact so that you can take advantage of the opportunities that present themselves tomorrow—there will always be more opportunities! That is what's so magical about the stock market.

Using margin, you can control as much as twice the stocks with the same amount of investment capital from your portfolio. Since the broker will loan you the money for one-half of the stocks you purchase, you will need to pay margin interest. Don't worry, the margin interest is insignificant—read on.

MSFT And AOL Comparison–Using Margin

Let's back up and start the MSFT and AOL investment comparison over again. This time you use margin to purchase 350 shares of AOL instead of 175. Starting with 350 shares, you use the same trailing stop-loss controls and the same exit point, November 19th. After the two-for-one split you have 700 shares (350 x 2). Doing the math, you end up with 700 x $83 = $58,100 of total profit, without putting any more of your own capital at risk than we did in the first example. You started out with $21,350 and walk away with a cool $58,100! Using a margin account, you have increased your return on investment.

A quick computation will show your monthly rate of return. Let's apply the formula and see how well you did. Invested = $42,700 ($21,350 your money + $21,350 margin loan). Returned = $58,100. Days in play = 25. Since the monthly rate of return was +43% when you did the play without margin, what do you think the rate of return will be with the margin money?

A. Invested:	*$21,350 capital* *($42,700 total invested)*	
B. Amount returned:	*$58,100*	
C. Days in trade:	*25*	
D. Determine cash profit:	*$58,100 – $42,700*	*= $15,400*
E. Determine rate of return:	*$15,400 ÷ $21,350*	*= 0.72131*
F. Convert to daily:	*0.72131 ÷ 25*	*= 0.02885*

G. Convert to monthly:	*0.0285 x 30*	*= 0.86550*
H. Convert to percent:	*0.08655 x 100*	*= 86.55%*

Note: Be careful. You invested $21,350 and borrowed $21,350, so you need to subtract $42,700. However, do not use the margin loan in the "rate of return" computation; only use your out of pocket money invested for that.

Your investment has doubled your original profits and earned you a monthly rate of return of 86.55%! That's fantastic!

Can you see why I am so excited about the power of this book? I get to teach you about stock splits and how they can greatly magnify your income potential. Then I get to take it a step further—I get to show you ways to enhance profits using powerful concepts that cause a tremendous increase in that potential. By using the power of margin buying you have increased your profit by an additional 43%. I intentionally ignored the cost of margin interest here, since it is insignificant.

And now I am going to let you in on a technique that power players use. You will get to see how stock options can push stock split plays light years ahead of where we are now. If you have a problem with options, don't worry. Just read the next section and then I'll discuss the challenges.

Using Options For Leverage

Let's get it out in the open—stock options are risky. Most professionals agree that options should only make up a small portion of any investment portfolio, perhaps 10%. At the same time, I have found that the 10% often creates 90% of my profits. However, preservation of capital is the main and most essential goal. Use no more than a small percentage of your investment capital for stock options. Practice before trading with real cash, and always, *always* use stop-losses and other risk controls.

Another thing to remember is that options provide a tremendous amount of leverage. When there is a small move in the stock, there is a much larger move in the option.

What follows is an options mini-overview. Please do not get stuck on any options terms. A further explanation is provided in Chapter 9, "Options for Stock Splits" on page 143.

Mini-Options Course

Call Option Defined. *A Call Option gives you the right, not the obligation, to purchase the stock for the strike price any time before the expiration date. If the option expires without being exercised, there is no value. Stock options expire on the Saturday following the 3rd Friday in the month of expiration. For our use we will say options expire on the 3rd Friday.*

Purpose Of Options. *Your purpose in purchasing options is to sell them at a profit. Using this investment formula, options are bought and sold. There is no intention or desire to execute the option and purchase the underlying stock.*

Contract Size. *Options typically control 100 shares of stock per contract. In rare circumstances there are odd contract sizes like 50 or 33 shares per contact, but it is extremely unusual.*

Choosing An Expiration Date. *Options expire the third Friday of the month. A full month would be counted from the 3rd Friday of each month. If your exit is in the 4th week of the November, you would need to hold an option that expires in January.*

Purchase options that have expiration dates at least one full month past the planned exit date.

Life changes and the market is full of surprises. The last thing you want is to own an option that expires before your planned exit date.

Options Versus Stock. *"When there is a small movement in the stock, there is a magnified movement in the option." –Wade Cook*

For example: If the stock worth $100 moves $2 that's a 2% movement, while the option worth $5 might move $1 that's a 20% movement!

MSFT And AOL Comparison–Using Options

I'll use the same MSFT and AOL scenario again.

For this example, you will purchase call options. AOL is selling for $122 per share, and you decide to buy January $115 call options.They will not expire until well after the November 18th stock split, so you have plenty of breathing room. The broker says your purchase price for the options will be 16^1/_4$ per share. At that time AOL was selling for $122 per share, so your options let you control a $122 stock for only $16.25.

Each contract will allow you to control 100 shares of stock. The cost is $1,625 per contract of 100 shares (16^1/_4$ x 100 = $1,625). You do not intend to make a stock purchase. Your plan is to hold the options until the exit date and then sell them at a profit.

As in the last two examples, you sell your 200 shares of MSFT stock for $107 per share, which will bring you $21,400. The AOL January $115 calls cost 16^1/_4$ per share, or $1,625 per contract. You can purchase 13 AOL contracts (13 x $1,625 = $21,125).

When you were purchasing the AOL stock you could purchase 175 shares; using margin, you controlled 350 shares. Now with stock options you are controlling 1,300 shares! We do not use margin power here because option purchases are not marginable. You use similar damage control methods, like knowing your exit point and using a trailing stop-loss. On November 19th, your 13 contracts have had babies because of a two-for-one stock split. You now have 26 contracts of AOL. When a stock splits, the options contracts do the same—for each contract you own you get two contracts, which are each worth half as much. After the split, you call your broker. On November 19th each contract was worth 25^1/_4$.

Let's calculate the rate of return and see how this investment method performed. Are you ready? Okay, turn the page.

ALERT! I no longer hold my options through the split date (stocks are okay). What I have found is that after the split, the party is over. The market makers unbeef the option prices sometimes minutes after the market opens on ex-date.

After the split you have control of 2,600 shares of AOL (26 contracts), which are now worth $25\frac{1}{4}$ per share. That's equal to $50\frac{1}{2}$ in pre-split value. You call your broker and sell them in a heartbeat. After selling the options you have received the following: 2,600 x $25.25 = $65,650! Using the formula that I used before, let's figure your monthly rate of return.

A. Amount invested:	*$21,125*	
B. Amount returned:	*$65,650*	
C. Days in trade:	*25*	
D. Determine cash profit:	*$65,650 – $21,125*	*= $44,525*
E. Determine rate of return:	*$44,525 ÷ $21,125*	*= 2.10769*
F. Convert to daily:	*2.1077 ÷25*	*= 0.08431*
G. Convert to monthly:	*0.08431 x 30*	*= 2.52923*
H. Convert to percent:	*2.52923 x 100*	*= 252.92% –Monthly!*

Let's recap. Doing a straight stock purchase your monthly rate of return was $43.29%. Using margin you earned 86.55%, and now using a call option you earned 252.92%. Look at these rates of return again. Look at this power, we are talking about monthly rates of return! The difference is 252%-86.55% = 165.45%. That's right: using the options you have generated an additional MONTHLY rate of return of 165.45%, as compared to buying the stock on margin. This is a huge difference. More than can ever be conceived by most brokers, bankers, and candlestick makers.

How To Beat The Market And The Money Managers

If you look at the actions of money managers and the market's big players, they usually play using long-term investment concepts. The "buy and hold" investment style is probably the most conservative method to invest in the market. I have a problem with "buy and hold" because most individual investors lack the resources and education to identify a stock that will stay a good investment for the next 10 years. Making a decision to own interest in a company for two weeks is much different from owning interest for a decade. Too much can happen in one year; what could happen in ten?

Looking at the challenges and limitations a money manager has, it makes sense that they use the buy and hold technique. I think it would be difficult to move $100 million dollars in and out of a stock when minor changes occur. Selling large chunks of stock can cause massive price swings. Imagine the massive amount of damage a large pension fund manager could cause if they dumped 10% of the shares of a company on the market. To be safe, the transactions have to be slower and more deliberate. In addition, the sale of holdings triggers a taxable event for investors—a big no-no for most funds.

I have a problem with "buy and hold" because most individual investors lack the resources and education to identify a stock which will stay a good investment for the next 10 years. –Miles Nelson

As an individual investor, you can move in and out of investments quickly. Which allows you to take advantage of the predictable price swings made by companies during stock splits.

Explanations And Terminology

Luck Defined. Luck is the place where opportunity and preparedness meet each other. In order to create your own luck, you need to be prepared and then keep looking for opportunity.

9

Options For Stock Splits

We are about to explore the ins and outs of stock options Before I proceed, I'd like to share what my opinion used to be, before I learned the use and power of those misunderstood creatures called "stock options."

About fifteen years ago, Miles and I were driving in the car and heard a radio program about the futures market. Some broker was giving away free tickets to a one-day futures investment seminar. He talked about how his clients had timed the oil market and made half a zillion dollars with only $5,000 in seed capital. This fast talker explained how people were earning fantastic returns with very little up-front money. He made the investments sound easy and safe, a sure thing. Miles almost called and ordered a set of tickets for us, but we were knee deep in tax returns, so we decided to wait until after tax season was over. I often thank goodness for that money-saving decision.

That year was a real bummer for some of our tax clients. They heard the same radio program, attended the seminar, and even wrote checks for $5,000, $50,000 and more. Many of them had decided to go for the whiz-bang profit potential by risking even more in a creative way. That good old whiz-bang opportunity became a wham-blam explosion and everyone lost their money. The more aggressive participants received bills from their brokers; they had lost more than their original investment.

Miles said to me, "These futures options are a crazy way to lose money. I'd rather go to Reno and spend it on room service in the Presidential Suite." That year, none of our clients earned money on those highly promoted deals. Based on our second-hand experience, we made a personal commitment to avoid those types of opportunities no matter how exciting they sounded. I don't care whose belly looks like pork, who eats sugar on their oil tankers, nor do I want to risk $5,000 so that I can corner the market in a winter wheat windfall.

It always astounds me how often people make decisions without enough facts. Let's face it. Those clients were asking for trouble. They called an 800 number, attended a high-pressure seminar then jumped headfirst into the futures market. They did no research, no study and no practice. They spent more time shopping for and learning how to use their last VCR! Give me a break. If getting rich was that easy, everyone would be wealthy.

Back then I had no idea that stock options and commodity options lived on separate planets. Commodities have a limited number of options available; stocks have thousands. I prefer the consistency, stability and expandability of the stock market.

Feelings Change With More Knowledge

My feelings about the stock market have changed; I now have a healthy respect for stock options. I see options as a tool that, when used correctly, can make a business more profitable. Before my stock market education, I only had bad experiences to use as a point of reference and so I thought that options were a foolish idea. However, with proper education and some successful experiences, I now see that options can mean the difference between success and failure for many business enterprises.

The Use Of Options Is Common

It is common for large companies to use options of many types to control assets, real estate and business opportunities. They might want to make a purchase later, or just control an asset while they do research and development. Options are a common tool in real estate, manufacturing, retailing and the stock market. Have you ever gone to a car rental desk and had them show you the different rental "options" they had available? How about your local telephone company? You pay a monthly fee so that you can exercise the "option" of making long distance calls. You can even log onto the Internet and choose a menu "option."

I feel like I've beat this concept to death, but it is so important to eliminate the preconceived notion that options are new, unusual or untested. Options can of course become dangerous when they are used incorrectly or without understanding. What makes the difference between a crazy option trade and a profitable one is knowledge and experience.

I will suggest, right now, that you need to consider using only a small portion of your investment capital for option plays. Leave the largest part of your capital in safe, secure, simple vehicles such as stocks, bonds, mutual funds, money market accounts, REITs, etc. Personally, I love hard assets like silver, gold and especially diamonds—just ask Miles.

What Is An Option, Really?

An option is an opportunity, not an obligation. It can also be the gateway to life, liberty and overwhelming financial happiness. I once heard someone say that money is not the doorway to happiness, but with enough cash you can have a key made. I say that as a kind of tongue-in-cheek joke, but at the same time, I know we've all felt that having more income would make a huge difference in the quality of our lives.

The word option means the opportunity for you to act—if you choose. According to Webster's™, the word option means:

"option åp/sh(n), n.

1. *The act of choosing;*
2. *the right of choosing;*
3. *the right to buy or sell something at a certain price within a certain period of time."*

The Options Clearing Corporation (OCC) defines the term option this way:

"An option is the right either to buy or to sell a specified amount or value of a particular underlying interest at a fixed exercise price by exercising the option before its specified expiration date. An option which gives a

right to buy is a call option, and an option which gives a right to sell is a put option. Calls and puts are distinct types of options, and the buying or selling of one type does not involve the other." (Characteristics And Risks of Standardized Options, p.1, February, 1994)

Those are the textbook definitions of options. Now let's create a human definition of an option. In business, the term option usually means that the holder of the option has the ability to ask or require the seller to do something.

Real Estate Options

In real estate, people use options to control property for a period of time. If you choose to exercise the options and purchase the property, the terms are described in the option agreement. A few years ago Miles and I wanted to purchase a home in a new area. We found a wonderful home and wanted to have twelve months before we completed the purchase. We worked out a deal with the seller to allow us to have a one-year lease-option on the house. We paid a non-refundable option fee and we had an entire year to exercise the option. In addition, we lived in the house during the 12-month option period and paid a fair market rental rate. Here were the option terms:

Option Premium	*$3,000*	*Non-refundable, transferable*
Exercise Price	*$125,000*	*Purchase price of the home*
Expiration Date	*12 months*	*An actual date was set*

One of the benefits of the option was we had control over a $125,000 asset with only $3,000 at risk. The worst thing that could happen is we would lose $3,000, but our upside potential was unlimited.

We had a 12-month option on a beautiful six-bedroom home. We lived in it, enjoyed it and had an entire year to get financing arranged and make a final decision on the purchase. What happened next taught me the power of options.

We lived in the home, fell in love with the area and wanted to live there forever. At the same time, the job market collapsed. People were moving out of the city in caravans. The city's real estate values dropped almost 25%. When the time came for us to exercise our option, the home was worth about $110,000. If we wanted to exercise the option we would have paid $125,000, which meant that we were out of the money by $15,000 in value. Who in their right mind would exercise a $125,000 option for a $110,000 home?

In addition to the valuation problem, there were structural challenges and other troubles. This situation was actually very fortunate, because we ended up moving out of the area. If we had purchased the home, we would have had to sell it at a big loss.

We decided to count ourselves lucky! That's right, we were happy to have lost the $3,000. Why? Think about it—what if we had purchased the house in the beginning? We would have paid $125,000, and when our circumstances changed we would have had to sell the home for $110,000 (or less)—a $15,000 loss.

We paid $3,000 for the option that allowed us to avoid a $15,000 loss. That option saved us a potential $12,000 in capital loss, plus commissions, taxes and closing costs. Looking at the option this way, we got a great deal.

What if the house had skyrocketed in value? The market was searing hot when we moved in and we expected to see the house move up in value. If the house had increased in value we could have exercised the option and purchased the house for $125,000, even if the value had moved up to $200,000.

Or, since we held a transferable option, we could have sold the option. If the house was worth $200,000, we could have sold that option for $75,000 cash! That means the option would have been in the money by $75,000. In the stock market, the $75,000 cash value is called "Intrinsic Value."

To recap, the option on this house allowed us to control our risk to a maximum of $3,000, but our potential for gain had no limit other than the expiration date. We had the opportunity to take advantage of any increase in value of the home for 12 months. That means we risked $3,000 for the opportunity to control $125,000 in assets for an entire year. What a wonderful concept; our downside risk was contained and our upside potential was wide open.

I hope that this example has illustrated the power of options. They are respected and valued in business, real estate and the stock market. Now, let's move on to terms and rules for stock options.

Stock Options

Can you see that real estate options allow you to control a large amount of money (in the form of real estate) with a small outlay of cash? The same is true for the stock options market (equity securities). By paying a small fee, called a premium, you can control a larger cash value of stocks. While you own the option, you get to benefit from any increase or decrease in the stock value. At the same time, you do not have to suffer substantially if the stock moves in the wrong direction. It's like having your cake and eating it too.

Of course, there are different kinds of options and some have more restrictions and requirements than others. I'll describe many of them in this chapter. I'll also show you how to use the stock options market to increase the profitability of your investments.

For the sake of simplicity, from this point on I will use the word "option" to mean "stock option."

Call Option

When you purchase a call option, you are locking in the right to purchase stock at an agreed price within an agreed time frame. A call option is very similar to the real estate option that I discussed earlier.

Purchase a call option when you expect the price of the stock to increase, making the option more valuable.

Sell a call option when you expect the price of the stock to decrease. As the stock price falls, the call option loses value and you can buy it back to close your position or allow it to expire.

Note: Selling uncovered call options (meaning you don't own the underlying stock) represents a high-risk trade that is beyond the ability of many investors.

Put Option

People usually steer away from put options because they do not understand them. Essentially a put option is the opposite of a call option. A put option gives you the right to force someone else to buy your stock. Buying puts is a common strategy to minimize the risk of loss.

Purchase a put option when you expect the price of the stock to decrease. Puts increase in value as the price of the stock falls.

Sell a put option when you expect the price of the stock to increase. As the stock price climbs, the put option loses value and you can buy it back to close your position.

That's about all I'm going to say about put options in this book. For more information about using put options, check the appendix for a list of books and tapes that will detail how to profit greatly using puts.

Note: From this point forward, you need to assume that I am discussing "call options" unless I specifically mention something else.

Stock Option Terms

This section is kind of like the chicken before the egg dilemma. I need to present option terms, but I need to define the terms in order to present them—it's difficult to know which to present first. My solution is to discuss the major elements of an option and then provide definitions.The most important elements of a stock options contract include:

Strike Price—The strike or exercise price is the guaranteed price at which you can buy the stock.

Option Premium—The price you pay for your option. In simple terms this includes the value of time (time cost), a charge for volatility (historical and implied), plus any cash value (intrinsic value).

Expiration Date—Stock options expire on the third Friday of the expiration month.

Contract Size—A contract is usually 100 shares of stock.

Strike Price

The strike price is also called the "exercise price." The exercise price is the guaranteed price for which the underlying stock can be purchased.

Option Premium

A portion of the option premium includes: time value, volatility and intrinsic value. Also included in the option premium are factors for interest, dividends and other items.

1. Time Value (extrinsic value) is the price you pay for the right to control the stock until the expiration date. As the option gets closer to expiration, the cost of time value decreases.
2. Volatility is based on historical and expected movements of a stock. Which means volatility is broken down into these two distinct types of risk:
    a. "Historic Volatility" takes into consideration the potential movement of a stock based on prior experience.
    b. "Implied Volatility" is an estimated figure based on current and future events, which may cause exaggerated stock price movements, such as a stock split, news events, change in market, et cetera.
3. Cash Value (Intrinsic value) is the liquidation value of the option. When an option is "in the money," it has intrinsic value. There is no intrinsic value for options that are at the money or out of the money. When purchasing an option it can be in, at, or out of the money:
    a. Out of the money: If the call option strike price is higher than the stock price, then the option is considered out of the money.
    b. At the money: If you purchase a call option contract that is at the money, the strike price is equal to the stock price.
    c. In the money: If you purchase a call option that is in the money, the option strike price is lower than the stock price. This is also called the cash value or "intrinsic value."

When considering call options

Is the Strike Price in the money?

(Assume that the stock price is $45 for each of the examples)

Option	Stock Price	Option Strike Price	Comment
Out	*$45*	*$50 (or higher)*	*Strike price is above stock price $5, it is out of the money $5*
At	*$45*	*$45*	*Strike price is the same as the stock price, it is at the money*
In	*$45*	*$40 (or lower)*	*Strike price is below stock price $5, it is in the money $5*

Expiration Date

Stock options have a stated expiration date based on a monthly cycle. Stock options expire at 11:59PM on the Saturday following the third Friday of the month, in the month of expiration. Since the general public cannot execute trades after the market closes on Friday (or the last business day of the week), we use the rule of thumb that says options expire on the third Friday of the month.

It is very important to understand expiration, because it can be a big source of problems for new investors. Expiration can hurt your profits in a few ways: you could miss an important event, lose value or even lose your market. When you buy options you need to consider these things:

1. I prefer to have an expiration date that is at least one full month beyond my planned sell date.
2. As the expiration date nears, option premiums (what you get when you sell) shrink.
3. The closer you are to expiration, the fewer buyers there are for your option.

Contract Size

A stock option contract controls 100 shares of stock. When you look at premiums for the option, they are stated in terms of cost per individual shares. Thus, an option premium of $4.50 would need to be multiplied by 100 to arrive at the total cost of one contract, e.g., $4.50 x 100 = $450 per contract.

In most cases, a stock option contract controls 100 shares of stock. There are rare instances when a contract will be a nonstandard size of 50 shares, 33 shares, et cetera, which may happen because of an unusual distribution, merger or split. If the option contract will be other than 100 shares, your broker will let you know. However, in all of the trades I have handled, I have never dealt with anything other than 100-share option contracts.

Example Option

Let's say today is January 1, and I purchase a January $45 call option for $9 per share. If the stock is at $50, the $45 option is "in the money" by $5 so the option price of $9 includes $5 of cash value and $4 of time value. If the stock stays at $50 until a few moments before it expires, I could still sell the option for $5 (the cash value), or exercise the option, buy the stock for $45, then sell it for $50.

Stock Option Considerations

Expiration Date One Full Month Beyond Sell Date

Imagine purchasing an option that expires this coming Friday only to realize that the big stock split event is not until next Wednesday. Your option will expire before you have any chance to benefit from the expected final run-up in the stock price. Make sure that you give target dates a wide berth. Purchase options with an expiration date at least one full month past the planned exit date.

As the expiration date nears, option premiums shrink because there is less time for the option to change in value. During the last two weeks of the option's life, the cost for time value can lose 5% to 10% per day in value.

As Expiration Nears, Buyers Run

When the option expiration date gets closer, option volume will fall off. Since there is less time for a price jump, fewer people will be interested in buying your option, thus lowering demand and driving prices even lower—perhaps to the point where you can't even give your option away! Then you are faced with that worst of feelings, an option that expires worthless.

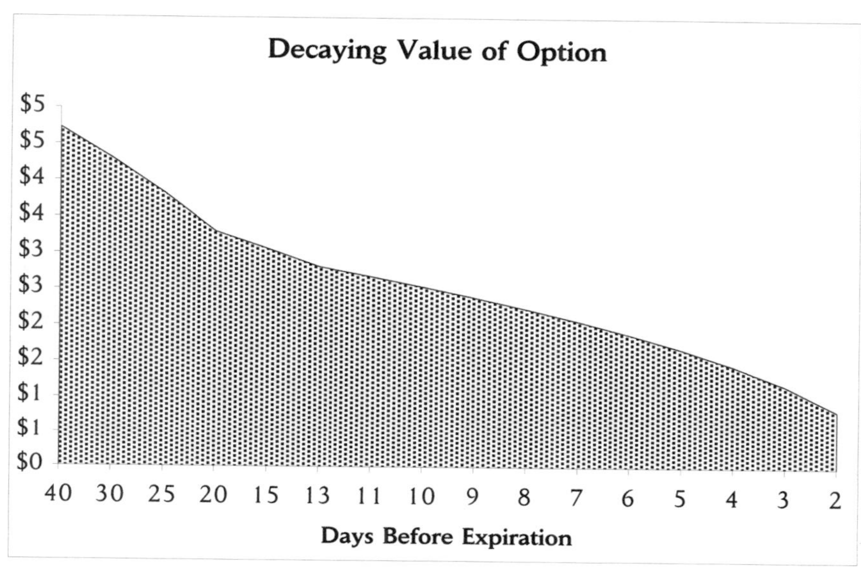

Time Value

Time value, also known as extrinsic value, is the price you pay to control the fate of the underlying stock for the period of the option. The more time you control the stock, the larger the time value of the premium.

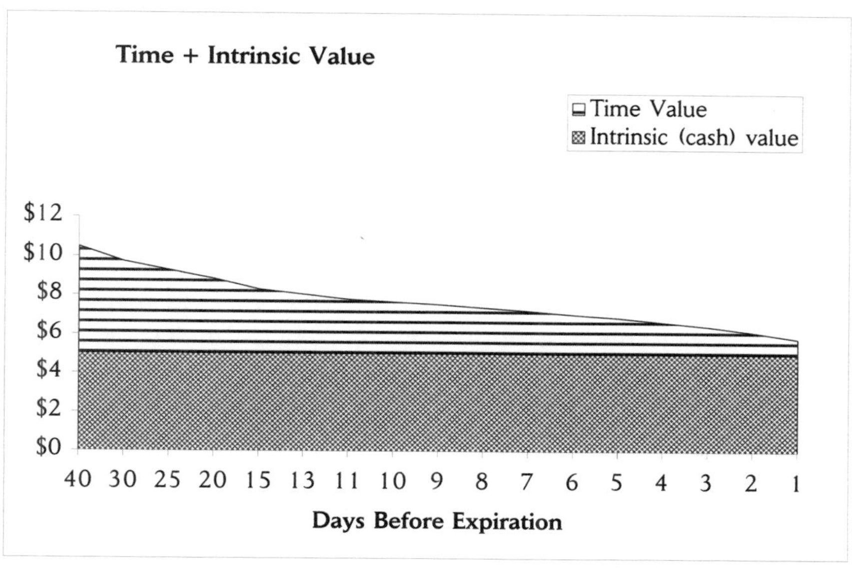

Open Interest–Exception To The Rule

Don't forget to look for a minimum of 100 contracts of open interest when considering purchasing an option. There is an exception to this rule: when new options become available they will have zero open interest, because they are brand new. Even if the stock is great, there will be zero open interest for a short time. Here is a real life example of new options being created:

There is no open interest for these options, because they were created at market open. Dell Computer had split its stock the night before. Although there is zero open interest, you can see that there is volume for the current day. Since DELL is a big company, there will be plenty of open interest within a few days.

Dell Computer Corporation (DELL) $44^7/_{16}$ $+1^7/_{16}$ Calls

Last	Sale	Net	Bid	Ask	Volume	**Open Int**
APR 32.5	*12 3/8*	*0*	*12*	*12 3/4*	*10*	***0***
APR 35	*10 1/4*	*+7/8*	*9 7/8*	*10 3/8*	*41*	***0***
APR 37.5	*7 5/8*	*0*	*7 3/4*	*8 1/8*	*52*	***0***
APR 40	*6*	*+1/4*	*6*	*6 1/8*	*471*	***0***
APR 42.5	*4 1/4*	*+1/4*	*4 1/4*	*4 1/2*	*674*	***0***

 Dell Computer, March 08, 1999, 11:16 A.M. P.S.T.

Option Price Volatility

One thing that you need to be very aware of is how the market makers play with the value of options. Even when the stock price is staying the same, they change the price of the option based on the amount of interest investors are giving the stock and options. This is called "implied volatility." For example, if IBM were to announce a stock split in the middle of the trading day, excited investors jump on the news and the market makers would see a spike in the number of option orders. When this happens, they immediately raise the price of the most popular contracts. You might see the price of an option jump as much as $1 to $5 in a matter of minutes—in some of the more volatile tech and Internet stocks, prices can run even faster, both up and down. Later that day or the following morning, purchase activity slows and the market makers drop the price of the option. It's all a matter of supply and demand; the market makers charge what investors are willing to pay.

Just for fun sometime, you should see the amazing changes that happen to an option when a split announcement is made. Call your full-service broker and ask for a printout of the bid and ask prices for a particular option from five minutes before the announcement until 30 minutes after it. Your broker can print out a tick by tick report showing the changes to the option prices. It's fantastic.

Delta △

Delta is a figure that refers to the relationship between the price movement of an option and the price movement of the underlying stock. When looking at call options, a delta of one would mean a $1 for $1 relationship—for every dollar the stock price moves up or down, the option premium moves a dollar in the same direction. A 0.50 delta means that for every $1 in stock movement the option will move 50¢. The higher the delta number, the more your option premium changes as the stock price moves.

Delta △ indicates how far an option will move for the next $1 of stock movement.

Stock	Option	Delta △
↑ *$1*	↑ *$1.00*	*1.00*
↑ *$1*	↑ *$0.50*	*.50*
↑ *$1*	↑ *$0.25*	*.25*

Be aware that delta is always changing, and just because it is high now does not mean it will stay there. I use delta as a reference tool while comparing different potential options. If I want to use delta tomorrow, I will need to get a new quote because it will have changed, a little. For short term trades, I prefer using deltas of .70 or higher. What this means is that I can get in and get out of the trade faster.

Note: If you want to use delta numbers for put options, you will need to do some research because everything is reversed in puts, including delta numbers. When comparing put options, keep in mind that delta numbers are expressed in negative numbers, a put delta of –0.79 means that for every $1 in stock movement the put changes $0.79 in value.

Option Holder

The holder of the option is the person that purchased and controls the option.

Option Writer

The writer of the option is the person that sold and must comply with the option. When you buy an option you will never know who wrote it, because they all go into a big pot at the OCC's electronic "warehouse" (a computer system) and executions are assigned randomly.

Note: The OCC (Options Clearing Corporation™) regulates and administers the stock options market. When option contracts are executed, the OCC distributes the purchase or sale orders in a random order, like a lottery.

Exercise

To exercise an option is to use your right to purchase the underlying stock at the strike price. I hope you are beginning to understand that option traders almost never buy calls with the idea of buying the stock. Instead, we want the value of our options to increase, so we can sell them for more than we paid and pocket the difference as our profit!

Day Order

A day order is sometimes called "good for the day only." Meaning that the order is good for the current day until the order is filled or the market closes. If the order is not filled by the end of the day, it is no longer valid.

GTC

GTC stands for "good till canceled." This type of order stays in force until it is filled, or 30 to 90 days have passed, depending on the broker. If you use GTCs, track them closely or you will end up getting surprised down the line when you find you've purchased a stock or option after you have forgotten all about the play. Or even worse, you could be filled when the stock is on its way down!

Pros Expect Options To Expire Worthless, Sometimes

Here is where the prophets of doomsday and the professional traders part ways. The doomsday people warn repeatedly, "options are risky, 80% expire worthless, so most people are losing money on options." This statement is true only if you assume that options are purchased with the intent to exercise them.

Yes, options do expire worthless. But most professionals purchase options for reasons other than exercising them to buy stock. Professionals buy options in order to sell them when the options increase in value. This is a critical concept to grasp. Very rarely have I purchased an option and then held onto it until it expired. I usually purchase the option to have it go up in value (or down if the trade goes against me) and sell it. There are times when I have purchased an option, intending that it will expire worthless, because I bought it to cover another option, which I sold for a higher premium. When this happens and the options expire, I pocket the difference between the premium I sold and the premium I paid. This scenario shows up in many advanced strategies, such as spreads, butterfly spreads, straddles, selling puts and more. Many investment techniques use options as a tool, so having them expire is to be expected and can even lead to profits.

Long Positions Versus Short Positions

There are two types of positions in the market: long and short. Being long in a stock or option means you own it in your account and you are expecting it to increase in value, so you can sell it for a profit. Being short means you have sold something you don't own, expecting to buy it back at a lower price when the stock or option has lost value. It is still the same old "buy low, sell high," but in reverse—"sell high, then buy low."

Selling stock short is a very risky, aggressive strategy that requires a great deal of knowledge. In the options market, being short in a position is called "uncovered" or "naked," meaning that you do not have protection from massive loss. Avoid being short or naked until you have extensive experience and successful practice.

LEAPS®

LEAPS stands for Long-term Equity AnticiPation Securities. LEAPS are very long-term call or put options with a January expiration up to three years in the future. They always expire on the third Friday of January of the coming year, the year after, or the January after that.

LEAPS are a wonderful way to do extended plays that last many months, such as the one to two-year plays I used for the example portfolio in the chapter titled "The Power of Stock Splits." By purchasing LEAPS, you reduce the need for intense daily monitoring. As long as the stock is in a general up-trend, you only need to become concerned if the trend changes. I wrote a special report about LEAPS called "Poolside Investing with LEAPS"—look for information in the Appendix.

Risks of Options Made Simple

When Miles was eight, he spent the night at his best buddy Greg's house. The next morning Miles discovered a baggy full of cash in the freezer. Greg said his dad kept it there because he wanted to have plenty of cold cash around. It's a great story, and it demonstrates something about life. You can keep your money in "buy and hold" investments like the deep freeze, but they will be slow to grow. In fact, some will not keep up with the rising costs of life. You can lose money without even getting out of bed in the morning. Nevertheless, you can't earn money until you do!

Are options risky? Yes, options are risky. So is driving a car during rush hour. The difference between earning money and losing it is knowledge and experience. My daughter Hollie is 16 and she wants to start driving. Talk about scary! But we all have to start somewhere. When she passes the learners' permit test, she'll start learning how to drive. Now, would anyone in their right mind take a 16 year old just learning to drive to downtown Seattle and say, "Watch out for traffic?" No! That would be a guaranteed accident. You start the kid in a parking lot with plenty of room for error. Then, after patience, practice and time, she can venture out onto deserted streets and gradually increase her confidence and skill.

The wonderful and risky thing about the stock market is that you can leave the parking lot and take to the freeway as soon as you want. But for heaven's sake, and your financial health, get a learners' permit and practice on paper first. Then, when the paper trades prove the concepts valid and your skill sufficient, venture out into real trading with money and confidence.

10

Technical Concepts

There are three distinct forms of research used when making investment decisions.

1. Fundamental Analysis looks at financial information and company operations.
2. Technical Analysis looks at the historical changes in the price of the stock.
3. Reality Analysis looks at the news.

The truth is that most professionals talk about the "big two" forms of research—technical and fundamental analysis. The reason I separated news into a third section is that news is the master controller of stock prices for short and mid-term investments. You have to consider the news, always.

Most of this book has discussed the use of fundamental analysis techniques. In this chapter I'll make a mini-venture into technical analysis, especially the use of support and resistance. Then I'll share a few other technical concepts.

Support And Resistance

Of all the sections in this book, this piece on support and resistance is one of the most critical. Support and resistance are the ultimate indicators, and all other investment rules come in second. Can a stock break support or resistance? Of course, and those breakouts themselves become strong indicators. As you read along you will see what I am talking about. Keep in mind that the information presented here is overly simplified.

It's How We Started

I can remember when Miles and I first started investing in the market. A few times a week Miles would get an updated list of stock split announcements, sort through the companies, and pull up charts. He looked at the news, recent events, and market conditions, making sure that there were no major problems. He confirmed that the stocks were optionable and selected some of the better companies. He then printed out a chart of the last three to six months of stock price movement. With a ruler and red pen, Miles marked lines indicating the bottom prices (Support) and the top prices (Resistance). Then he put a big red S and R, with numbers next to both letters, and identified the companies that had share prices close to their support level. When he was done, we talked and chose companies we would consider investment candidates.

In the morning, we watched CNBC before the opening bell, listening for news that might affect the companies we had selected. After the market opened, we checked prices. If one of our target companies had bounced off the support line, we looked to see if it was making a climb back up. About 30 minutes after the market was open, we called our broker and got in. When the stock price climbed up to the resistance point, we watched it—the moment it started to move down, we called our broker and got out. That was our "great" investment strategy. The funny thing is, the system worked most of the time, and we earned money. As we developed our understanding and improved our skills, it worked even better.

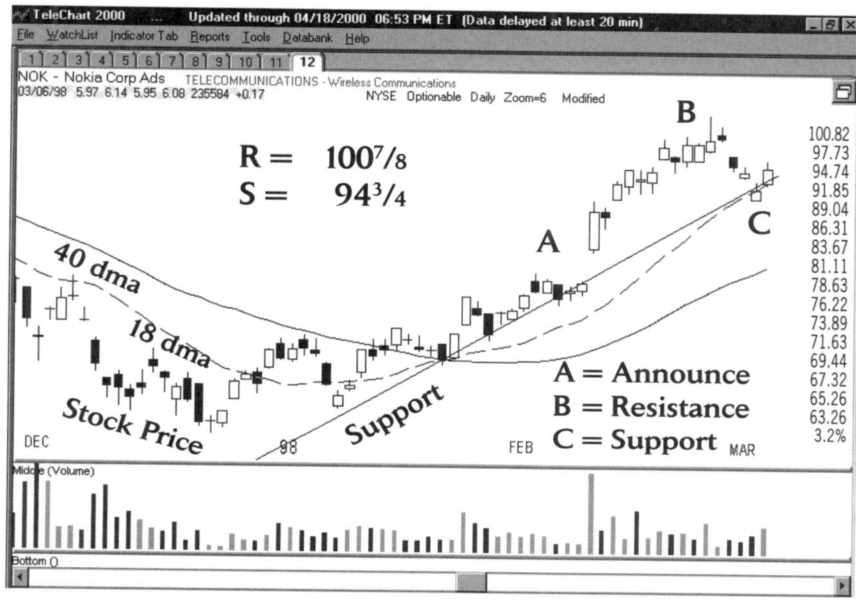

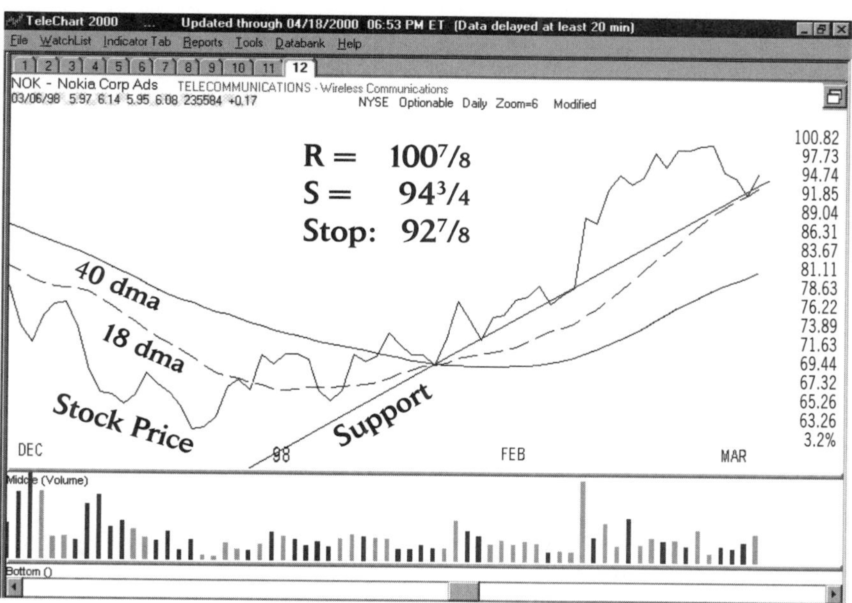

This "candlestick" chart and the "line" chart for Nokia are identical. I prefer candlestick charts, but when looking for support and resistance, line charts make the job simpler.

The next chart shows a flat trading range. In an uptrending stock, there are times when the stock needs a rest. It will get stuck in a trading range, until something causes it to push out. In most cases, when a stock breaks out of a flat period, it will usually continue the direction the stock was moving. Which means you could have expected Nokia to break to the upside, at some point, which this chart confirms.

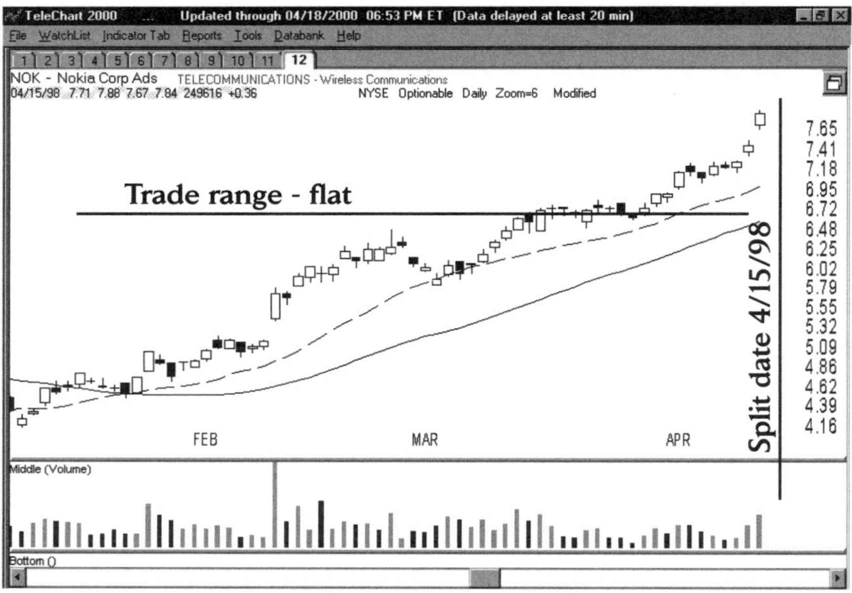

Support And Resistance Defined

Stock prices are defined by supply and demand. When a stock is dropping in price, it indicates that buyers are not willing to pay as much as it is selling for—prices drop when demand is low. Support is the bottom of this supply/demand range, where the stock is perceived to be a good value and demand increases. If there is enough demand, the stock price stops falling and begins turning upward. Support can be viewed as the wholesale price of a stock.

Resistance is the top (ceiling) of a stock's trading range, when the rising demand dries up and most people think the stock could be overpriced. Resistance is viewed by many as the price where people can sell "retail"—for a profit.

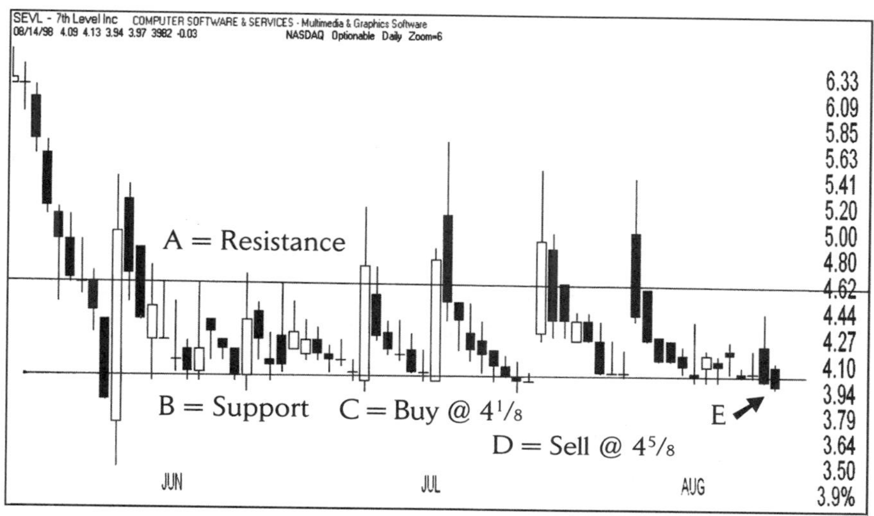

Professionals use support and resistance as a guideline for making entrance and exit decisions. There is a daily battle fought between the bulls and the bears. Each morning the bulls bellow loudly that the stock market is going to reach new heights. The bears growl in return that nothing goes up forever, the end of prosperity is near, and the stock market will head into the toilet. At the end of the day the observers tally up how many prices rose for the day versus how many fell on the day, and declare either the bulls or the bears victorious—for the moment.

Right in the middle of this battlefield are individual investors trying to read the tide of emotion to predict and profit from the future direction of their choice stocks. When individual investors are caught holding stocks at a loss, they look for the price to climb up far enough so they can get out without a loss, or with less of a loss. When the stock climbs up to that point, swarms of people call in their sell orders. This drives supply to outpace demand (more sellers than buyers for the stock), causing a resistance point to be created. At the same time, individual investors look at charts and place buy orders with prices close to a support level. There is always a point when the majority of investors say, "This is a good time to buy the stock," and there is always a point when those same investors think, "I'd better get out now."

This morning I was thinking about the workings of large investment funds. I read an article about a particular fund that was receiving new deposits at a rate of $300 million dollars each month! That's a lot of money that has to be invested before the cash burns a hole in the profit ratio of the fund. If the fund has a history of earning 25% per year, too much cash in a money market account can be a problem.

To maximize profit potential, fund managers often choose to keep as much money in the market as possible. These managers choose which stocks to buy, hold and sell. When they have too much cash in their holding account, the funds will be used to buy stocks as quickly as is practical. If cash funds are depleted, managers need to liquidate holdings as soon as possible.

Fund managers know what is happening in the market and they set the purchase and sale prices to take maximum advantage of high and low price points. Each trading day, managers contact brokers with instructions to place orders in a "basket." The broker's firm then seeks to fill the basket with stocks or cash, providing the purchase or sale conditions can be met.

The purchase and sell decisions made by fund managers and individuals create the waves of movement in the stock market, simply because of the huge amounts of money involved. These choices determine support and resistance for each stock. It is critical to stay aware of and use this knowledge when making your purchase and sell decisions. Watch the trend and work with it. Don't try to play against the money managers, or you will get hurt as surely as if you lay down in front of a Mack truck.

Breaking Through: A Strong Indicator

As outlined above, support and resistance tend to be predictable. Usually a stock approaching either support or resistance will bounce off that psychological barrier and stay within the trading range. That range between support and resistance could be trending up, trending down, or moving sideways, but the price will tend to stay within the range.

If a stock breaks through support or resistance it may continue in that direction for a while and establish a new trading range with new support and resistance, or it could reverse direction and return to the former trading range after a short run. As long as the stock is within the longer-term support and resistance, it is considered a strong indicator that can be traded for profits.

- A stock can be viewed as establishing a lower range if it breaks through support and stays below the support line for more than one trading day.
- A stock can be viewed as establishing a higher range if it breaks through resistance and stays above that resistance line for more than one trading day.

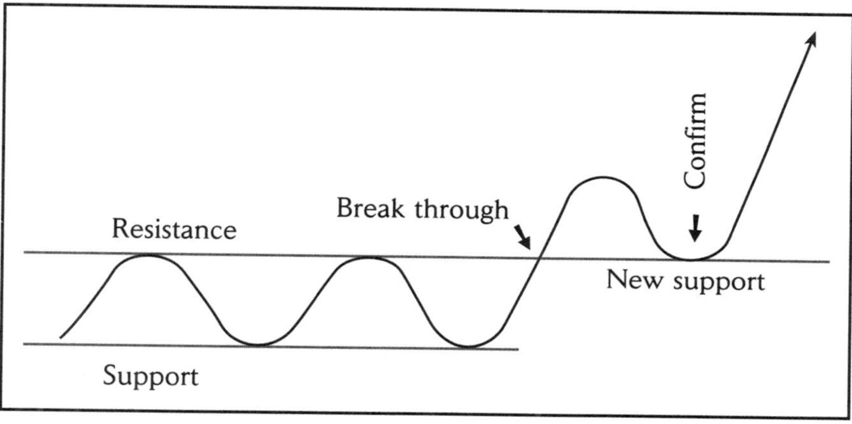

Resistance Can Become Support And Vice Versa

Support and resistance lines become very strong points of reference. They can change often, so consider them guides and not guaranteed entry or exit points.

When a stock makes a move up through the resistance line and stays above that the old resistance line, it could become a new support line for the future. This new support level is confirmed when the stock falls to this breakthrough point and bounces off.

When a stock makes a move down through the support line and stays below that point, the old support line could become the new resistance line. Confirmation of this new resistance works the same way, occurring when the stock price approaches the resistance breaking point and backs away.

When making investment decisions, many investors forget how valuable support and resistance lines are for setting their entrance and exit points.

Note: If a stock breaks through resistance or support on lighter than normal volume, the breakthrough could be a false indicator. Be very careful as the stock could turn quickly and move back through the break point with tremendous energy.

Moving Averages

Moving averages are another technical indicator that let you estimate how far a stock is likely to fall before it reaches support. The interesting thing is that moving averages, like support and resistance and other technical indicators, tend to become self-fulfilling prophecies. The more investors know about these tools and use them to predict and place their entry and exit points, the more accurate psychological predictors they become and the more they are relied upon. Sometimes it seems that these indicators can almost be causing investor behavior more than tracking it!

I usually have 18 and 40-day moving averages showing on my charts. If a stock is being slammed, I'll add a 50-day moving average to get a sense of the longer-term trend. Recently the tech stocks took a turn for the worse, as all sectors do eventually. At first, the stocks appeared to be in free fall, then they stopped abruptly. Without technical indicators, it looked like they stopped for no visible reason and were hanging in mid-air. When the moving averages are added to a chart, it provides contrast, and at times the reason for the new support line becomes very clear.

Understanding moving averages is especially important when you are in long-term plays. A stock that breaks below the 40- or 50-day moving average lines could be on the way to establishing a new trend in the opposite direction. As a final confirmation, look at the 200-day moving average; it is considered a significant support. If the stock violates the 200-day moving average, a recovery may be in a galaxy far, far away.

Technical analysis is fascinating and powerful. I love exploring it and introducing the principles to individual investors. I wish I could write 100 more pages on this topic, but I'll forgo that pleasure and stick to stock split concepts—that's where I'm an expert, and there are others who are better than I am at explaining technical analysis and charting.

On the next page you can see how charts can look very different, when moving averages are added. DELL experienced a short term set back. The stock fell though major support lines and seemed to be hanging in mid air. By adding a 200-day moving average line, it becomes clear why DELL stopped falling

DELL Chart—Without Moving Averages—see how DELL was hanging in mid air?

DELL Chart—With Moving Averages—see how DELL stopped falling because of the 200-day moving average?

What you can learn from this example is far more than the use of moving averages. It also illustrates the need to look at charts from different angles, with moving averages, without averages, with support lines, weekly views, daily, monthly, et cetera.

Watch For Round Numbers

It may seem strange, but support and resistance are often established on round numbers, like: 10, 20, 25, 50, 75, 90, 100, 120, 150, and 200. This interesting occurrence is the reason that some investors use a rule of thumb to avoid setting purchase and sell orders on round numbers. In many cases they may set a stop-loss at $\$49^{7}/_{8}$ instead of \$50, because a stock may fall to \$50 then bounce back up. They also may set a purchase order at $50^{1}/_{4}$ instead of 50, because the stock may not go down far enough to get a \$50 fill. Don't forget that there are two prices, bid and ask. For a \$50 order to get filled, the ask must be at \$50, but the stock may not move down that far.

You do need to be careful because big money professionals know that people set stop-losses at $\$49^{7}/_{8}$ instead of \$50. I see stocks fall to $\$49^{7}/_{8}$ all the time. The stop-losses are triggered, tons of automatic orders flood the market, and when the stop-losses are all hit, the stock makes a move back up. To avoid becoming a victim of temporary dips, set your stop-loss order low enough to get triggered only if the stock really falls past the support level. Keep this in mind and watch out for round numbers—use them to your benefit.

Another "round number" observation is when a stock climbs up to the low $90s, chances are it will continue climbing until it reaches $100 within a few days. Once the stock reaches $100, it will then make a strong short-term decision to break through or fall back.

The previous diagram shows EFII. It has attempted to break through $50 two times, but has not had enough strength.

The next chart is of CSCO. What a powerful run this company has been on. They are right in the middle of the technology explosion, growth is geometric and success seems never ending. However, CSCO has been stuck in a trading range, with $95 as support and $120 as resistance, for six months! What will it take to break through $120? That is a question that people ask about many companies—$120 is a very solid barrier. Perhaps great earnings with a surprise report, and better than expected projections for future quarters could break the $120 barrier. There is so much energy stored in that six-month barrier that breaking $120 could be followed with a long hard run into outer space.

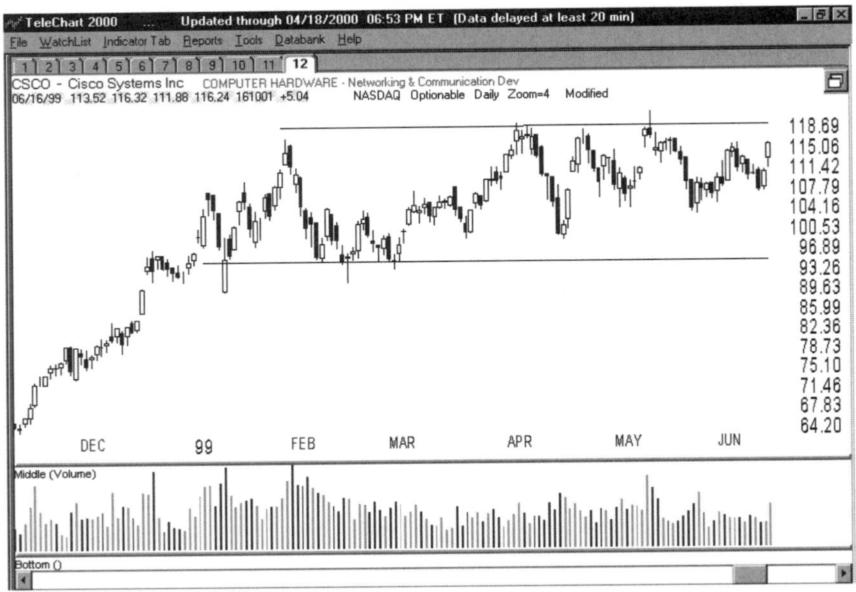

The chart shows stock prices through June 16th. There is a stock split pending for the 22nd. This is a perfect example of stock split Play #4 in the making. The stock has reached support and made a move up. The split is only a few days away and it is a perfect time to open a position. Make a purchase, set your stop-loss for protection and get ready for fun. With a stock split on the horizon, and three months of sideways movement, there is plenty of pressure. This play could turn out to be a short run that stops when the stock hits $120, or it could break through and run strong and hard.

If you had been watching CSCO, you would have entered the play in the morning on June 16th. By the end of the day, it would have moved up from $114 to $116¼. A stop-loss would be set, just in case the stock goes below $110. The following chart shows the results of the play.

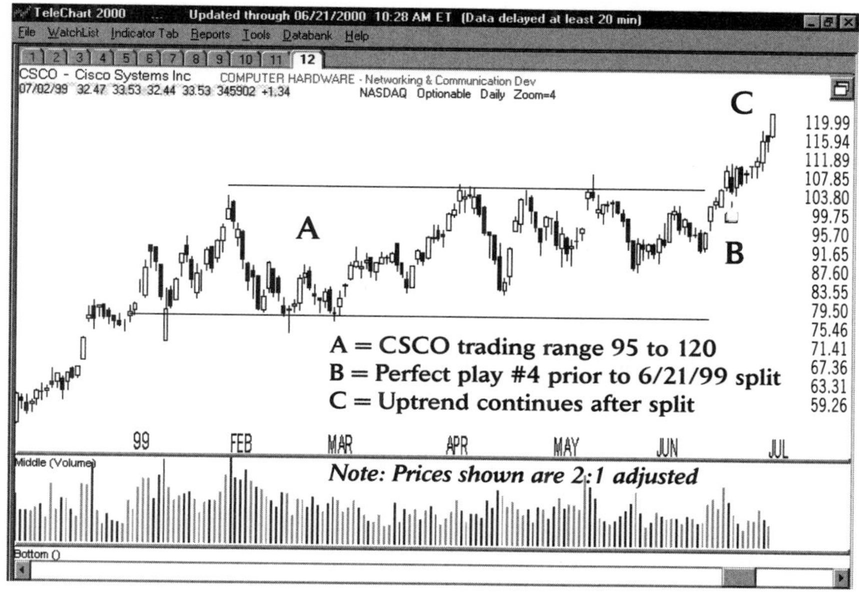

Buy Low And Sell High

When people discover my tax and accounting experience, the most common question they ask me is, "How can I save on my taxes?"

I quickly respond "buy high, sell low."

People get a blank look on their face and eventually say, "Don't you mean buy low, sell high?"

I reply, "Not if you want to get a tax deduction!" When I invest in the stock market, tax deductions are the furthest thing from my mind. I want to buy low and sell high, higher, highest!

This concept is extremely critical and more important than almost anything else. Look for opportunities to purchase at a discount, buy low—near support—and then give the stock an opportunity to move up, selling high—near resistance.

I am not suggesting that you purchase stock or options simply because the price is at an all-time low. I am proposing that you use the techniques presented in this book and make your entry points when it makes sense. It is unwise to buy high, hoping to sell higher. If a stock is at an all-time high and you open a position, you could end up being the last person to get in before the stock pulls back.

Think about it. When you look at any chart there will be a high point on the chart—someone made a purchase at that high price, and tonight they will go to bed depressed. No one wants to admit they are the sucker who established the all-time high price of a stock—especially if that price has been unchallenged for the last 10 months!

When possible, look for opportunities to purchase stocks and options as close to support as possible. Support is the wholesale price. Then sell at retail—when the stock is near resistance. This is especially important when you are new at investing. Get in a little late and sell a little early. There is no reason to stretch the risk. By getting out early you lock in your gains. As you develop more experience and expand your knowledge base you can use technical indicators to look for bigger trading ranges.

Know When to Get In

As I travel around the country, I hear a common problem from many students. They bought near resistance and the stock collapsed the next day. They got in because some hot news came out and they just knew it would send the stock shooting up. If the hot news happens near resistance, I pass on the deal. There are too many great deals waiting out there for me to risk buying high, hoping for it to go even higher. Hope rhymes with dope.

There are techniques and formulas for entering deals when the stock hits a high, breaks through resistance, gaps up, announces news, et cetera. I am not going to cover them in this book. When playing stock splits look for opportunities to open positions close to support. This gives you the best potential for success.

Know When to Get Out

To become an old soldier, you have to survive. To become an experienced trader, your capital has to survive. The way to do this is to use stop-losses and other damage controls. If you get into trades that go wrong, you can decide to ride out the storms, but in so doing you may end up losing tons of money, or having your cash tied up for months waiting for a recovery. One benefit of using the buy and hold technique is the fan mail you get from the loser stock companies in your portfolio, while news reports remind you daily of the consequences of your long—L O N G—L O N G—term purchase decision.

I'm just not very patient. If I have a hard time waiting for hot water in the shower, how can I wait three years (much less ten to fifteen!) for an investment decision to turn profitable? I prefer the McDonalds' method—get it done quickly or move to another job! Investment capital can only provide monthly returns if it is allowed to be in profitable plays every month. If a particular investment appears to be locked in a long-term holding pattern, it's time to make an adjustment and seek a pathway for escape.

This is where stop-loss controls come in. There are other damage recovery techniques, so many in fact that I cannot possibly discuss them all in this book. I am specifically writing to teach you how to profit from stock split events. I expect that you will also learn stock market investment techniques from other sources. Please take the time to look in the Appendix at the end of this book. It will provide you with a list of resources for advancing your investment education.

It's better to pass on a poor play than to end up poor by playing! –Miles Nelson

Stop-Losses

I have a friend that sold his family residence, netting about $80,000 cash. He saw that I was having fun with the market and he decided to open a brokerage account. He went to a top-rated firm and picked one of the better-looking brokers in the office. She helped him make his purchase decisions, and 12 months later he had lost more than $30,000 in cash, because of broker margin calls (the stocks that she had recommended had fallen that far in price).

One particular stock he purchased for $27 is now worth less than $3. I realize that unlike options which quickly become worthless, he owns the stock and therefore has a boat to ride out the storm, but who wants to wait half a lifetime for a stock to scratch and climb its way back from $3 to $27? In the same amount of time he would have been better off buying a car, driving it off a cliff, and watching it burn—at least that might have been fun.

If my friend had used a stop-loss, he would still have lost money, but far less than $30,000. He would have avoided the stress of looking at a $3 stock that cost him $27!

All investments in the stock market carry risk. Your job as an investor is to be aware of that risk, manage it and keep it in control. The way to do that is to use specific trading formulas to minimize the twin disaster agents of fear and greed, and never stray from the path. Success is a matter of following a pattern that you know works.

Setting Stop-loss Limits

A stop-loss is a way of setting your downside exit. You are telling the broker the lowest price at which you are willing to hang onto the stock. If the stock or option price reaches that limit, it is automatically liquidated. Experience has shown me that when a properly set stop-loss is reached, the stock price usually continues to fall and I am glad to be out of it even with the loss. The stop-loss gets you out of a deal before it falls off the cliff. Then you can watch the stock and decide when and if you want to get back into the deal.

The concept of a stop-loss is simple. Before you enter a trade, decide how much money you are willing to lose should the stock or option move against you. It is important to make that choice *before* you start the transaction! Once you get confirmation from your broker that the buy order was filled, set your stop-loss order right away. If the stock moves too far in the wrong direction, the broker will automatically close the transaction. You are "stopped out" and your loss is contained.

Please, please face reality right now. Everyone will have some plays that go wrong. The problem is that inexperienced investors are often afraid to admit error, so they stay in the deal watching their capital evaporate as their investment slowly bleeds to death. They become "hope dopes," thinking, "Tomorrow will be better, it has to be. I know it looks bad now, but I couldn't have been that wrong. Things will turn around any day now." All the while this dialogue is going on in their head, the capital they wanted to have working for them drops from $2,000 to $1,500, then $1,000, then $750, then $500, and finally to zero. The truth is that if it is bad now, it will probably get worse later. Denial can wipe out your portfolio.

What If The Stock Recovers?

What happens if the stop-loss price is hit causing the sell order to trigger, and the stock changes direction to resume its upward climb? Well, you can always get back into the play if it makes sense. I know that the stop-loss may have cost you a broker's commission and possibly some money because of price movements, and that can be irritating. If this happens repeatedly, you are probably setting your stop-losses too tightly and you should review the formulas on the following pages to discover where your plan is going wrong. As I gain more and more experience, I find getting back in is rare. When I get stopped out, it's usually because the stock is going down for the count and I'm happy to have most of my money back.

Most Common Stop-loss Formulas

As I share the following rules, I intend them to be only a starting point for your own research and practice. In practicing these techniques on paper, you will find adjustments that better fit your preferred companies or your own risk tolerances.

DANGER! When does a hiker get lost? When they leave the established path. When you are investing in the stock market and leave the established path, you don't get lost, you get killed! If you want to change the rules or make adjustments, save your money by scouting the territory first–do several trades on paper to test your new strategy before you risk your cash.

Tight Stop-losses

Determine the current value of your option and set a stop-loss $1 to $2 below the current option price. If the option goes below that limit, a sell order is automatically entered and the option is sold. This is a very tight limit and you need to be careful that you don't set your stop too tight, otherwise a minor downtick in stock prices can activate the stop-loss. The time to use a tight stop-loss is when you are planning an extremely short-term trade. If the particular option you are working with has daily price swings of about $3, setting a $1 stop-loss will almost guarantee you will be stopped out. With this in mind, take into consideration the daily price swings of a stock before setting the stop-loss.

Loose Stop-loss

A loose stop-loss is set at 50% of the purchase price of the option. You don't want to see your option double and then still end up losing if it drops quickly to your original stop-loss. As the option increases in value, you can switch to a trailing stop-loss to lock in your profits. A loose stop-loss might be used when beginning a long-term trade that you expect to last more than a few days.

Trailing Stop-loss

Trailing stop-losses are usually set at 1.5 to 2.0 times the average daily movement of the option. A broker can tell you how far the particular option has moved in an average day (based on the last 7 to 14 days). Multiply that average daily movement by 1.5 or 2.0, subtract that amount from your purchase price, and set the stop-loss using that figure. Each day as the option price increases you will raise the stop by an equal amount. Adjust the stop order in the morning before the market opens.

Here's how it works: The option was at $3 and your stop-loss was $2. After the market closed you check the current prices. The option moved up to $5, that's an increase of $2. You would then add $2 to your stop-loss. Before the market opens, call your broker and set a new stop-loss at $4. Each night, check the option values and continue increasing the stop-loss if the option increased.

When the stock stops increasing in value, so will the option, but don't adjust your stop-loss downward. As the option price backs off, the stop-loss is hit and the option is sold, locking in maximum profits. The trailing stop-loss is a good tool to use when you do not know how high an option will climb and you want to ride it as long as the trend continues. It is also very common in long-term trades. The following chart illustrates the action of a stop-loss.

Stop-loss Action

Note: Read from the bottom up – start at "Day 1"

	Option Price	Stop-Loss	Action
Day 5	*$7*	*$7*	*The option falls to $7, the stop-loss activates, the option is sold.*
Day 4	*$8*	*$7*	*The option falls back to $8, do not reduce stop-loss—leave it at $7.*
Day 3	*$9*	*$7*	*The option jumps to $9, change stop-loss to $7.*
Day 2	*$5*	*$3*	*The option increased in value to $5, raise stop-loss to $3.*
→ *Day 1*	*$3*	*$1*	*You buy a call option worth $3, set a $1 stop-loss.*

In this example, you have purchased a call option at a value of $3, a stop-loss is set at $1. When the option increases in value, the stop-loss is also increased. Eventually, when the option value starts to fall back, the stop-loss is not changed! Once the option value drops equal to the stop-loss, the option will be sold.

This concept is actually a challenge for many people. They get confused about how the trailing stop-loss is applied in real life. The following chart puts the trailing stop-loss concept in a graph format, which might help you more fully comprehend this technique.

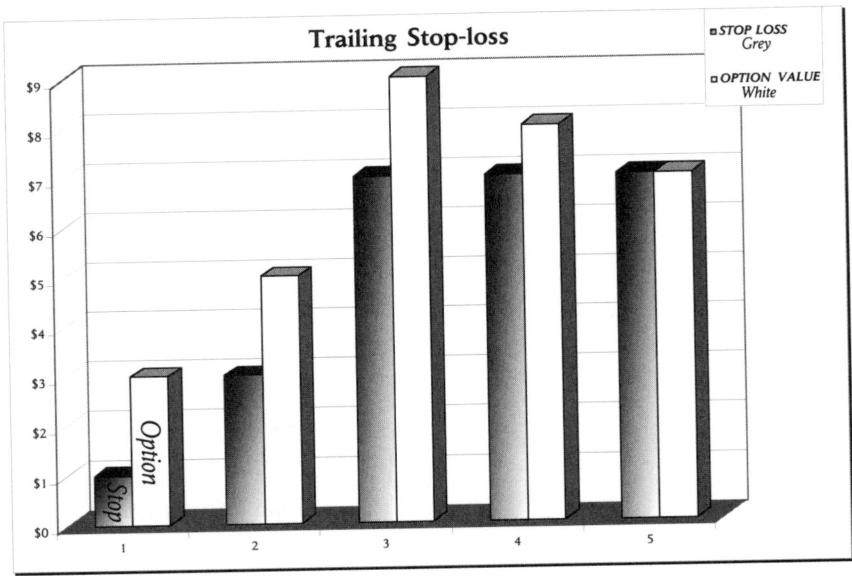

Use Support And Resistance

Earlier I talked about how I started investing using support and resistance. I had a few strict rules for damage control—if the stock went below the support line, I got out. If the option lost 50% of its value, I made a decision and moved on. By looking at support and resistance it becomes clear when a stock might be in trouble. If you find you purchased near the resistance level, when the stock was close to its high, you might end up getting hurt, so use tighter stop-loss limits to minimize your risk. If you have purchased just above the support line, you might set a stop-loss that would activate if the stock dropped below support.

Use Your Eyes

Stop-losses work as an automatic protection valve to prevent disaster, but nothing can replace your own observation skills and decision making. If you can see that a stock is going to nose dive, why wait for the stop-loss to kick in? Call the broker and sell the puppy. Just remember to cancel your stop-loss order at the same time, or you will be surprised to find you have sold something you don't own, and you might be faced with a margin call to cover your short position! Stop-losses are used to protect your investment capital, but they do have their limitations!

The Problem With Stop-losses

When a stop-loss is activated, it immediately becomes a market order. Let me say that again: When your stop-loss is activated, it automatically and immediately becomes a market order. (I'll review market orders shortly.) If the stock or market is in a free fall, the stop-loss you expected to save your bacon could end up getting filled at a price much lower than you were prepared for. Personally, I have had many stop-losses activated with no surprises, but if you use a stop-loss on a highly volatile stock, you could run into this problem. If this is a concern you could use a "Stop-loss Limit" which means the stop-loss activates, but the sell order will only happen if your price limit is met—or better.

A second challenge is that some brokers will only allow one order at a time. This means you can have a stop-loss order to limit your downside or a GTC sell order for your upside target, but not both. A solution is to have your broker set an alarm to alert you for the second order.

A third challenge is that some brokers have limited stop-loss abilities. Some of them have to do everything manually. In this case, if the broker happens to be away from the desk when the stock falls out of bed, the stop-loss may be filled late and at a lower price.

The fourth and final challenge is that some brokers will not work with stop-losses. They may require you to do the monitoring and decision making. If this happens, ask them if they are willing to set alarms and contact you when they are reached. If the broker refuses, it's time to get a new broker.

Review of Basic Trading Terms

This section is exactly what the heading says—a review. The following concepts have already been covered in various areas of the book. It is important to repeat them in this condensed format so that you have a single reference point to review the trading terms used through the rest of the book. I have condensed these topics and enhanced them a little. Enjoy.

"Run-up" and "Profit Taking" Defined

"Run-up" means the stock price has increased. This is an event or emotion-caused surge in volume with an accompanying jump in stock price, creating a momentum which becomes self-feeding (causing even higher stock prices and volumes).

"Profit Taking" is a natural result of an increase in stock prices. After the run-up there is almost always a period of "profit taking," when people sell to lock in their profits. Some traders sell their entire position, others lighten their holdings and take their capital to use in another trade.

Uptrends And Downtrends

A stock is in an uptrend if it is generally increasing in value over time. If the stock is reaching continually lower levels over time, it is in a downtrend.

Uptrends

A stock is in an "uptrend" if the price climbs for a few days, then falls back, hits support, climbs a little higher, falls back, climbs a little higher, falls back, et cetera, but over all continues to head higher. As a general rule, nothing shorter than a two-week period can be called a trend, and the longer the time period, the stronger the trend indicated. A true uptrend develops when the 18-day moving average climbs above the 40-day average and continues to stay above it.

Downtrends

A stock is in a downtrend when the lows are a little lower each time and the highs are also a little lower with each swing. Again, nothing shorter than a two-week period can be called a trend, and the longer the time period, the stronger the trend indicated. A true downtrend develops when the 18-day moving average falls below the 40-day average and continues in that direction.

Up-Market/Down-Market Rules

When anticipating market reaction to an event, you need to look at the market as a whole. Market trends are short-term events. Look at the last seven to 14 days. What has happened with the large indexes: OEX, S&P 500, Dow Jones 30, NASDAQ, et cetera? If these indices indicate a general market uptrend, then the majority of investors are excited and money is flowing into the market. If the trend is down, investors as a group are nervous and taking their money out of the market. Remember that you want market psychology in your favor. Modify your entrances or exits based on how the market is behaving. You can fine tune this by looking at the market your stock is in.

In an upmarket plan longer-term trades. If the market as a whole is headed up, you can enter the play earlier and stay in longer. Sell indicators are often clear and you can usually take profits as expected.

Plan shorter-term trades in a downmarket. In a downtrending market you have to get in the deal later than you might like and you need to get out earlier, with a smaller amount of profit. Stop-losses must be tight and so should your personal scrutiny. This is when you need to watch your trades more closely. Rules for the play are based on the expectation of sudden, large, unexplained downturns in share values.

Limit Orders Versus Market Orders

By using a limit order, you set in advance the maximum price you are willing to pay or accept for your stock or option. If the price is not met, you don't do a deal. If you place a market order, you are letting the market makers tell you what you will pay, and it most likely will not be in your favor. When purchasing stocks or options, I use a limit order. In my opinion, market orders are usually stupid, naïve and very dangerous. I do sometimes use a market order to sell, but rarely to purchase.

Note: I do make an exception, which is the use of stop-losses. I only use stop-loss limit orders in unusual situations.

Roll Up/Roll Out

Rolling up is a technique that allows you to take profits and stay in the deal. If you have an option that is deep in the money, you can roll up a few strike prices by selling the current option and purchasing one that is not as deep in the money. The new option will be cheaper, which means you could sell an option for $20 per share and purchase a new one for $5 per share. Now your $15 is secure and you can still ride the wave a little longer.

Rolling out is a technique where you want more time. You sell your current option and purchase the same strike price option that has a few more months of time (a longer expiration date). In this situation, you are selling a lower cost option and paying a higher price because of the additional time.

Rolling up and rolling out can be fantastic techniques, but there is danger. If you are near resistance, you might be approaching the end of the upward movement. At times it's better to take your money and run. Check your technical chart and make sure you are making a good decision. I find that I am tempted to roll up or roll out when I should really be getting out of the deal. My emotions get in the way and I want to hang on for a few more pennies. Why play for pennies and risk your dollars?

Short-term Plays

A short-term play is one you expect to be complete within a few minutes to a few days. If you expect a play to last longer than a few days, you will need to use the rules for mid-term or long-term plays instead. To do short-term plays:

1. Purchase in-the-money options.
2. Use expiration dates of one to three full months. (Current month options are very dangerous.)
3. Enter the deal expecting to capture $1 to $2 in profits, or less.
4. Use tight stop-losses, a few dollars below the option price. (You don't want to lose more money than you can earn.)

Note: The use of current month options provides the biggest delta bang for the buck, but it also carries the biggest risk of loss. Time is not on your side, premiums evaporate right before your eyes, and bad news is a death sentence. My suggestion is to save this type of trade until you have tons of successful trades under your belt.

Be careful not to set your stop-loss too close to the current price or the market will swoop down and stop you out. You also need to allow for the typical daily ups and downs of the stock. You might use a mental stop-loss, but only if you can watch the market.

Mid-term Plays

A mid-term play uses a mixture of short-term and long-term concepts. It is perfect for plays that you expect to last longer than a few days, but expect them to end within a few weeks. Often this is because you have a specific sell date such as a fixed event like earnings, stock splits, et cetera. To do mid-term plays:

1. Purchase at-the-money options.
2. Use options one to three full months or longer.
3. Use trailing stop-losses that follow the stock up as it increases in value.
4. Determine your exit point, such as:
   a. the stop-loss,
   b. the target event or date is reached,
   c. when volume slows or technical indicators tell you to get out, or
   d. when you are happy with the profits.

Note: Be sure the option does not expire before the split! To be safe–set the expiration date for one or more months following the split date.

Long-term Plays

A long-term play is defined as a play that you expect to last more than a few days, especially if you think it may take weeks to hit your target. If you expect a play to last less than a few days, you need to consider using the rules for short-term plays. To do a long-term play:

1. Purchase out-of-the-money options.
2. Use options that have an expiration of four full months or longer.

3. Enter the deal expecting to keep the position open until the stock changes directions.
4. Use trailing stop-losses that follow the stock up as it increases in value.
5. Your exit point is determined by:
    a. the stop-loss,
    b. the target event or date is reached,
    c. volume slows or technical indicators tell you to get out, or
    d. when you are happy with the profits.

Note: Out-of-the-money options have a lower delta than in-the-money options. This means the stock will have to make larger moves than when in-the-money options are used. Using out-of-the-money options is acceptable because time is on your side.

11

The Five Power Profit Plays

In previous chapters I have given you numerous aspects of stock splits in general, and an overview or mini-play book of each phase. In this chapter I'll give you a more detailed picture of the five phases of a stock split, including the specific elements of how to do each play. I'll show you again how to take advantage of each phase, and what kinds of things can be done to increase your profits. And best of all, I'll show you the most profitable way to play each of the five phases, and I'll include trade confirmation and run the numbers on actual plays.

As I have said again and again, there are five different phases that a stock split frequently passes through. You need to think of each one of these phases as an opportunity to earn money, five different times to profit. Each phase has a specific behavior. Each presents a buying and selling opportunity. All it takes to turn a typical investment portfolio into a money making machine is to master any one of the five phases. That's right—you only need to master one of these techniques to create fantastic returns. Again, please do practice trading before you start applying the concepts.

Phase 1

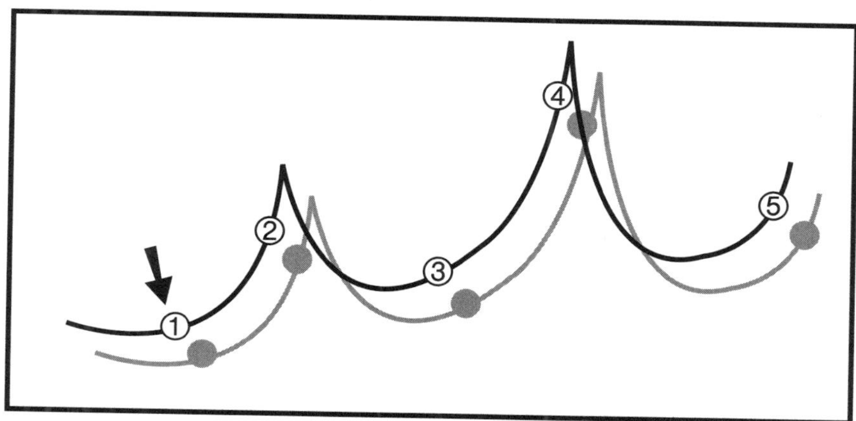

Before the Announcement

This play is based on a short-term increase in stock price before the expected or rumored announcement of a stock split.

Term:	Long-term play.
Option:	Four months or longer. Out of the money.
Enter:	Seven to 14 days before anticipated announcement.
Exit:	Day of the announcement if an up-market; one to two days before the announcement if a down-market.
Protection:	Trailing stop-losses, 1.5 to 2.0 times the average daily movement. If it's a down-market, tighten stops as you near the expected announcement.
Adjustment:	If profits have accumulated, consider doing a rollup, pocketing your profits, and leaving only a small amount in the deal. If the current option is in the money two or more strike prices, switch to an at-the-money option or one strike price in the money.

This is a long-term play in the period just before a company makes a stock split announcement. Usually there are a few weeks where rumor is running wild and excitement is in the air. The bigger the company, the more rumors will spread. It is this rumor and excitement that causes the stock price to climb at a faster than normal rate. This is probably my favorite stock split play because the market makers have not inflated the option premiums yet. I can purchase options when they are cheap and sell them after the premiums are pumped up because of rumor and excitement.

Since the company has not officially declared a stock split, there is no guarantee that the announcement will be forthcoming, which is the reason for making this a long-term play. However, you do not need an announcement to earn money. All you need is to be positioned in the stock and for rumor to move the stock prices higher.

Handled correctly, Play #1 is very profitable. It can also be a challenge because of the research involved. Making an announcement prediction is a matter of research and experience. We'll discuss indicators of a potential announcement in a moment.

Profit from the rumor. Played right, most of your money will be earned during the runup caused by stock split rumors. The stock split announcement will be a bonus!

Once you decide that the company is a stock split contender, look for evidence that indicates the possible announcement date. Don't forget to check for any indications that the company might not declare a stock split.

The most profitable time to play is usually seven to 14 days before the target date. It is not uncommon for a stock to run up 5% to 25% in the weeks prior to an announcement. Protect your investment by setting exit points in case the stock doesn't perform as you expect.

Remember: You are taking advantage of an "expected announcement." You are looking to profit from stock movement, regardless of what actually happens with the stock or company. It does not really matter if the company announces a stock split–all that matters is that you profit from the increase in stock prices before the expected event.

Danger: First, if the company does not announce a stock split when the investment community anticipates, there will usually be a severe "beating," which could erase all profits in a matter of moments. When possible, take profits before the event, and if you want to stay in the deal, leave only a small amount of risk capital in the play.

Second, if the announcement is expected to occur at the same time that financials are being released, it's even more important to take profits early. After an earnings announcement, stocks usually fall in price, even if there is a good report and a stock split announcement.

Selecting Stock Split Candidates

There are over 10,000 viable companies to choose from. The following list will help you determine which companies have the potential of declaring a stock split:

- Has the stock split before?
- What was the stock price in prior announcements? (Typical price range)
- Does the company split at regular intervals? (Annually, every two years, et cetera.)
- Have other companies in the sector declared a split recently? (Within the last six months.)
- Is the company included on a list of potential stock splits?
- Are there rumors of a stock split?

Once you determine the stock split candidates, you need to eliminate companies that are high risk. You then investigate the remaining companies looking for the best investment targets. The following list will help you sort and choose candidates that are worth your effort and attention.

Which Companies Merit Investigation?

Choosing which companies are worth investigating will help you narrow down the 10,000 plus choices. Here are a few minimum criteria I suggest:

- Share volume: A minimum of one million shares transacted each day (average daily volume).
- Option volume: Look for a minimum of 100 contracts of open interest before participating.
- Play well-known companies.
- Look for split ratios of two-for-one or better; three-for-two on big companies is acceptable.
- Look at the history. Did they do well the last time they split?
- Is the company profitable?
- Are there good newsy things happening?
- Has the stock been in a general uptrend for the last year?

Average Shares Per Day		Comment
Over	*1,000,000*	*Great pick; lots of shareholders.*
Over	*500,000*	*Need to monitor and be cautious.*
Over	*250,000*	*Be very careful; usually highly volatile.*
Over	*100,000*	*Dangerous; often a small base of shareholders, usually a closely held company.*
Under	*100,000*	*Suicide play! Walk away.*

It is very important to watch daily share volume. The smaller the number of shares transacted, the harder it gets to sell in an emergency (like bad news).

Now you get to determine which companies may be getting ready to declare a stock split. Members of the board seem to live by pre-determined schedules, adhering to a set pattern for making stock split announcements. Nevertheless, the magic of this business is that there are always surprises; a stock split announcement can occur at any time.

The most common times a split announcement is made include:

- During the board of director's meeting.
- When the company conducts the annual meeting of shareholders.
- At the same time as an earnings release.
- A few hours or days after an earnings release.
- At the same time dividends are announced.
- During special conferences held for the industry, sector, or major investors.

Look at the history and see if there is a set pattern for the company split announcements: when, where, why, et cetera. When attempting to determine a possible announcement date, some important things to know include the following:

- What is the most common split ratio used by the company (two-for-one, three-for-one, three-for-two)?
- Are there enough shares authorized to do a split?
- If there are enough authorized shares to complete a stock split, is there a board of directors meeting scheduled?
- If there are not enough authorized shares, is there a shareholder meeting scheduled that includes a vote to approve additional shares?
- Have they filed a 14A report with the SEC seeking approval for an increase in the number of authorized shares? (Look for SEC form—PRE 14A, DEF 14A.)

A company may end up foregoing a split announcement. Determine:

- Has there been any bad news recently?

- Are they having big legal or financial problems?
- Has the stock price been falling for a while, creating a downtrend for the stock?

A company may have behind the scenes problems preventing them from announcing:

- Management believes that revenues will fall short of expectations.
- Business has taken a downturn and future earnings are expected to suffer.
- There may be company or sector problems that could put the stock in a tailspin.
- Management knows of problems that, when made public, will cause the stock to collapse.
- It is planning an acquisition or merger and a split would be detrimental.
- Other unseen problems exist that make splitting a poor business choice.

It is not unusual for me to identify a stock split candidate weeks before I open a position. Time is on your side—you choose the entry and exit point. It's a relaxing, enjoyable, profitable experience. With a little practice, this process can become a consistent resource for amazing amounts of cash flow. It is imperative that you remain alert and be ready to get out if circumstances change.

Protect your investment—just before opening a position, take one last look at the news. Are there any new situations developing that could create difficulties? While you have an open position, keep your eyes on the news, it can change at any time.

Keep a journal of your research by company for future reference.

The next few pages are a few of our Play #1 trades for fun.

Split Play #1

Company:	Oracle Corp.	
Target Announcement Date:	12/20/99	
Open:	$11,930.00	12/15/99
Close:	$13,944.53	12/15/99
Profit:	$2,014.53	
Monthly %:	506%	

CONFIRMATION
OF TRANSACTION

Nondeposit investment products are not insured by the FDIC, are not deposits or other obligations of or guaranteed by Association or its affiliates, and involve investment risks, including possible loss of the principal amount invested. Bank Certificates of Deposit are FDIC insured up to $100,000 per institution.

MILES NELSON
DARLENE NELSON

INVESTMENT EXECUTIVE NAME & TELEPHONE NUMBER

BRANCH OFFICE SERVICING YOUR ACCOUNT

YOU	INVESTMENT DESCRIPTION
BOUGHT 10	CALL ORQ ORACLE CORP STK PX 80 EXP 01/22/00 S/D 12/16/99 OPEN UNSOLICITED
PRICE: 11 7/8	MKT: 04 SYMBOL: ORQ AP

PRINCIPAL AMOUNT	COMMISSION/ SERVICE CHARGE	ACCRUED INTEREST	TRANSACTION FEE	CERTIFICATE FEE	S.E.C. FEE	OTHER
11,875.00	50.00		5.00			

ACCOUNT NUMBER BR | ACCOUNT | T* IE

CUSIP NUMBER

NET AMOUNT 11,930.00
TRADE DATE 12/15/99
SETTLEMENT DATE 12/16/99

YOU	INVESTMENT DESCRIPTION
SOLD 10	CALL ORQ ORACLE CORP STK PX 80 EXP 01/22/00 S/D 12/16/99 CLOSE UNSOLICITED
PRICE: 14.000	MKT: 04 SYMBOL: ORQ AP

PRINCIPAL AMOUNT	COMMISSION/ SERVICE CHARGE	ACCRUED INTEREST	TRANSACTION FEE	CERTIFICATE FEE	S.E.C. FEE	OTHER
14,000.00	50.00		5.00		.47	

ACCOUNT NUMBER BR | ACCOUNT | T* IE

CUSIP NUMBER

NET AMOUNT 13,944.53
TRADE DATE 12/15/99
SETTLEMENT DATE 12/16/99

Split Play #1

Company:	Oracle Corp.	
Target Announcement Date:	12/20/99	
Open:	$4,930.00	12/15/99
Close:	$5,944.80	12/17/99
Profit:	$1,014.80	
Monthly %:	205%	

CONFIRMATION
OF TRANSACTION

Nondeposit investment products are not insured by the FDIC, are not deposits or other obligations of or guaranteed by Association or its affiliates, and involve investment risks, including possible loss of the principal amount invested. Bank Certificates of Deposit are FDIC insured up to $100,000 per institution.

MILES NELSON
DARLENE NELSON

INVESTMENT EXECUTIVE NAME & TELEPHONE NUMBER

BRANCH OFFICE SERVICING YOUR ACCOUNT

YOU	INVESTMENT DESCRIPTION	MKT	SYMBOL
BOUGHT 10	CALL ORQ ORACLE CORP STK PX 100 EXP 01/22/00 S/D 12/16/99 OPEN UNSOLICITED	04	ORQ AT
PRICE: 4 7/8			

PRINCIPAL AMOUNT	COMMISSION/ SERVICE CHARGE	ACCRUED INTEREST	TRANSACTION FEE	CERTIFICATE FEE	S.E.C. FEE	OTHER
4,875.00	50.00		5.00			

ACCOUNT NUMBER BR | ACCOUNT | T* — IE

CUSIP NUMBER

NET AMOUNT	TRADE DATE	SETTLEMENT DATE
4,930.00	12/15/99	12/16/99

YOU	INVESTMENT DESCRIPTION	MKT	SYMBOL
SOLD 10	CALL ORQ ORACLE CORP STK PX 100 EXP 01/22/00 S/D 12/20/99 CLOSE UNSOLICITED	04	ORQ AT
PRICE: 6.000			

PRINCIPAL AMOUNT	COMMISSION/ SERVICE CHARGE	ACCRUED INTEREST	TRANSACTION FEE	CERTIFICATE FEE	S.E.C. FEE	OTHER
6,000.00	50.00		5.00		.20	

ACCOUNT NUMBER BR | ACCOUNT | T* — IE

CUSIP NUMBER

NET AMOUNT	TRADE DATE	SETTLEMENT DATE
5,944.80	12/17/99	12/20/99

Split Play #1

Company:	General Electric	
Target Announcement Date:	12/17/99	
Open:	$9,430.00	12/13/99
Close:	$9,944.66	12/14/99
Profit:	$514.66	
Monthly %:	81%	

CONFIRMATION OF TRANSACTION

Nondeposit investment products are not insured by the FDIC, are not deposits or other obligations of or guaranteed by Association or its affiliates, and involve investment risks, including possible loss of the principal amount invested. Bank Certificates of Deposit are FDIC insured up to $100,000 per institution.

INVESTMENT EXECUTIVE NAME & TELEPHONE NUMBER

BRANCH OFFICE SERVICING YOUR ACCOUNT

MILES NELSON
DARLENE NELSON

YOU	INVESTMENT DESCRIPTION
BOUGHT 10	CALL GE GEN ELECTRIC STK PX 145 EXP 01/22/00 S/D 12/14/99 OPEN UNSOLICITED

PRICE	MKT	SYMBOL
9 3/8	04	GE AI

PRINCIPAL AMOUNT	COMMISSION/ SERVICE CHARGE	ACCRUED INTEREST	TRANSACTION FEE	CERTIFICATE FEE	S.E.C. FEE	OTHER
9,375.00	50.00		5.00			

ACCOUNT NUMBER BR | ACCOUNT | T* IE

CUSIP NUMBER

NET AMOUNT	TRADE DATE	SETTLEMENT DATE
9,430.00	12/13/99	12/14/99

YOU	INVESTMENT DESCRIPTION
SOLD 10	CALL ORQ ORACLE CORP STK PX 80 EXP 01/22/00 S/D 12/16/99 CLOSE UNSOLICITED

PRICE	MKT	SYMBOL
10.000	04	ORQ AP

PRINCIPAL AMOUNT	COMMISSION/ SERVICE CHARGE	ACCRUED INTEREST	TRANSACTION FEE	CERTIFICATE FEE	S.E.C. FEE	OTHER
10,000.00	50.00		5.00		.34	

ACCOUNT NUMBER BR | ACCOUNT | T* IE

CUSIP NUMBER

NET AMOUNT	TRADE DATE	SETTLEMENT DATE
9,944.66	12/14/99	12/15/99

Phase 2

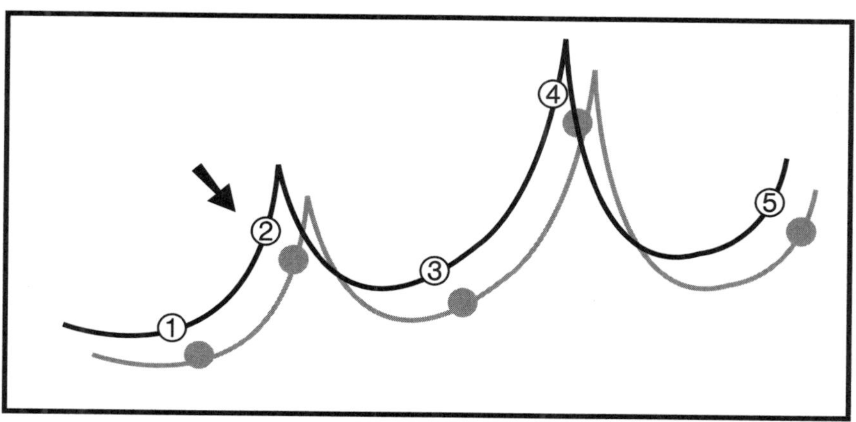

The Announcement

Within seconds of the announcement, the stock price makes a temporary jump up.

Term:	Short-term play—very short.
Options:	One to three full months. In the money. Delta of .70 or higher.
Enter:	Within seconds of the announcement.
Exit:	Set a sell order to capture \$1 to \$2 of profit (GTC). In an up-market expect up to \$2. In a down-market, watch out—passing is advisable.
Protection:	Small stop loss (\$1 to \$4).
Adjustment:	If the stock is not moving up in value within 10 minutes of the announcement, it might be time to jump out before everyone else does.
Pass:	If the announcement is made before the market opens, the stock is halted when the announcement is made, or if you cannot act quickly, walk away.

I've shown you how to play split announcements, but I warn you—it's hard to make this play work! Read "The Fast Pitch" for more information.

Phase 2 is kind of like a baseball game. There are winners and losers. If you know the rules, practice enough, and know when to bunt, you can win the game and take home the pennant.

For years, the most common way to play stock split announcements has been to jump in as fast as possible and take advantage of the short-term jump in prices. The only problem with this technique is that technology has changed the ball field and made it nearly impossible to win at the split announcement game. However, there is more than one way to play the announcement game.

This section will cover the following techniques:

- Stealing Home—Sell when others are buying (my favorite).
- The Fast Pitch—The old-fashioned announcement game.
- The Double Play—A second chance to profit.
- The Triple Play—A combination of techniques.

Stealing Home

A fantastic way to play the stock split announcement is to use it as a selling opportunity. If you did Play #1 and got into the stock before the announcement, you can sell when everything is inflated in value. While the rest of the market is trying to get into the stock, you can be selling! What a wonderful way to profit from the excitement created when a company declares a stock split announcement.

The rules for stealing home are simple:

1. Watch for the announcement.
2. Wait for the stock or option prices to become inflated.
3. Sell!

If you did not get into the stock before the announcement, you have nothing to sell. However, there are other ways to take advantage of the split announcement, read on.

The Fast Pitch

Trying to jump on the announcement is a difficult experience. The biggest problem is the market makers have the upper hand and you have two strikes against you before you even start. The market makers throw you a fast pitch, you swing, miss, strike three—you're out! Please be careful.

This play is all about getting into a deal the moment an announcement is made so that you can take advantage of the short-term increase in prices caused by too many investors heading for the same stock at the same time. This is only possible if you have an accurate, fast, reliable paging or notification service. Old news can cost you the deal. It is a good idea to have a broker who uses the same pager/notification service. My personal favorite is an information pager which provides news and market updates. We don't have to rely on our broker to call us when a split announcement breaks; we have our pager beeping happily when the news is released.

This is a short-term opportunity. When a stock split announcement is made, jump on the news and make an immediate decision to play or pass. Then, within as little as five minutes of getting in, you close the play and take your profits. All you are looking for is a $1 to $2 profit!

Phase 2 can be very exciting, but it can also be very disappointing. You will need a real-time news reporting service that alerts you to new stock split announcements within seconds. Make an immediate call to your broker and execute a pre-planned trade. If much thought or research has to be involved, the play will be over before you get started.

Timing the purchase and sale based on the announcement of a stock split takes experience, accuracy and skill. Frankly, most people do not have the necessary resources to successfully play stock split announcements. Seconds can make the difference between a wonderful play and a terrible loss. The only way to make this event profitable is to have accurate, up-to-the-second information and a broker that is quick on the draw. If they have to run an order down the hall, it's too late!

Arrange for your broker to have the same reporting service that you do, and give clear training on what types of plays you want to do. When your pager fires off a message, call your broker and in the background hear his pager beeping the same message! When the call is made, the conversation is very brief. "Broker Joe, this is me. AT&T just announced a two-for-one."

The broker responds, "I'm on it already, do you want X-options, or Y-options?" That way no time is wasted and the play can be executed profitably.

Implied Volatility

When option volume increases, market makers need to boost option premiums because of a greater risk caused by "implied volatility" causing a jump of $1 to $10 per share.

When volume slows down, implied volatility will also fall resulting in a lowering of option premiums (even if the stock price is unchanged).

The Problem—Hitting The Fast Ball!

Here is the big problem—the pros already know the rules and they have the fastest "pitchers" in the world. When a stock split announcement is made, they throw you a fast ball—before you have a chance to buy anything.

Here's how the market makers throw you a fast pitch: when news is released about a stock split, those in control know about it at the same time or even faster than the general public. While you are getting paged, calling your broker, checking prices, and making a decision—the market makers have already changed prices, thus throwing a fast pitch. After the market makers raise stock and option prices, they allow trading to resume. That's right, the market makers halt or delay trading when important announcements are made. They will not allow any trades to execute until they have assessed the situation and change their prices. In the mean time, you are swinging at air.

Tons of excited investors all rush to the phone trying to get in first. The only way you can earn money is if you happen to get in the front of the line, make a purchase, get a broker fill confirmation and issue a sell order while other excited people are still trying to get positioned. Before you know it, "wham" the stock prices fade and split announcement profits are gone.

There's absolutely no way to get the upper hand on the market makers, which is why I don't even try! I prefer to do a double play or even steal home.

There...I said it...I've shown you how to play Phase 2 the old-fashioned way. You can now decide for yourself what to do with the information. Just keep in mind that you are batting against the fastest pitchers in the world. Here is what Miles says: "I don't really like playing the announcement, because of my lifestyle I can't seem to act that fast. I know that I'm not Marshall Dillon. I'll stick to what I know and do best."

The Double Play

After the initial "announcement surge," the stock price will fall back down and the option prices will be adjusted to moderate levels. On a big company, news reports will mention the stock split announcement frequently during the day. That night, the evening news will be full of talk about this big company announcing a stock split. News anchors will talk about the growth of the company, its officers, and other information. Newspapers may have the split announcement on the front of their business page and the Internet will be awash in split discussions.

The next morning thousands of individual investors will call their broker with market orders to buy stock in this fantastic company. For two or three days the excitement may continue. You can take advantage of this "mom and pop" buying frenzy by doing the double play.

After the initial announcement and the excitement is over, the stock will settle down to a mid-day trading range. (Or the stock might be making a gradual increase as the afternoon progresses.) The best time to enter the play is usually one to three hours after the announcement. Play this as a mid-term play and only if the market is in an uptrend. If the market is having a down day, wait until the following morning. Get in only if you see upward movement in stock prices.

This play tends to be more effective if the split announcement was a surprise, because there was no pre-announcement runup in price! It is rare that a large company sneaks by without notice, so this type of event will be rare, but sweet. What you want is a stock that is near the bottom of its trading range, or at least has room to run before it hits resistance.

This play can be profitable, but it has its own risks. It is an advanced play that requires you to be highly sensitive to market conditions and trends. My suggestion is to paper trade this strategy and see what success rate you have. Once you have done enough successful practice trades, you will be able to decide how to proceed.

I've mentioned this play because it is exciting and can be profitable, however, as you do the practice trades you will notice that it is very wild.

- When it works, it works big. There can be a 1% to 10% jump in stock prices over a few days.
- When it fails, it fails in a big way. There can be a 1% to 20% collapse in stock prices, overnight!

One big disadvantage of playing the announcement is the morning after the announcement. A stock can take a hard dive, gapping down because of overnight profit taking. Be careful. This is a play worth looking into, but practice it first, please!

Check The Chart

Support and resistance are important. If the stock is already at the top of its range, near resistance, there will be little room left for upward movement. If the stock is at the bottom of its trading range, there is plenty of room for upward movement. If the stock is near support, this play has a good chance of success.

The Triple Play

This play is simply a matter of combining the double play and stealing home. If you are in the stock before the announcement, wait for the announcement, then sell when prices are inflated—according to the rules of stealing home.You then wait a few hours. When things calm down you can get back into the stock and ride it again—according to the rules of the double play.

Check The Chart

The triple play is most effective in stocks that are highly volatile. If there is a wide range of intra-day movement, this volatility makes playing in both directions possible. Especially since stock split announcements exaggerate all movements, because of investor excitement.

The next few pages are some of our Phase 2 trades.

Split Play #2 (Stealing Home)

Company:	General Electric	
Open:	$8,180.00	12/16/99
Close:	$13,569.54	12/17/99
Profit:	$5,389.54	
Monthly %:	988%	

Goal: *Sell on announcement date.*

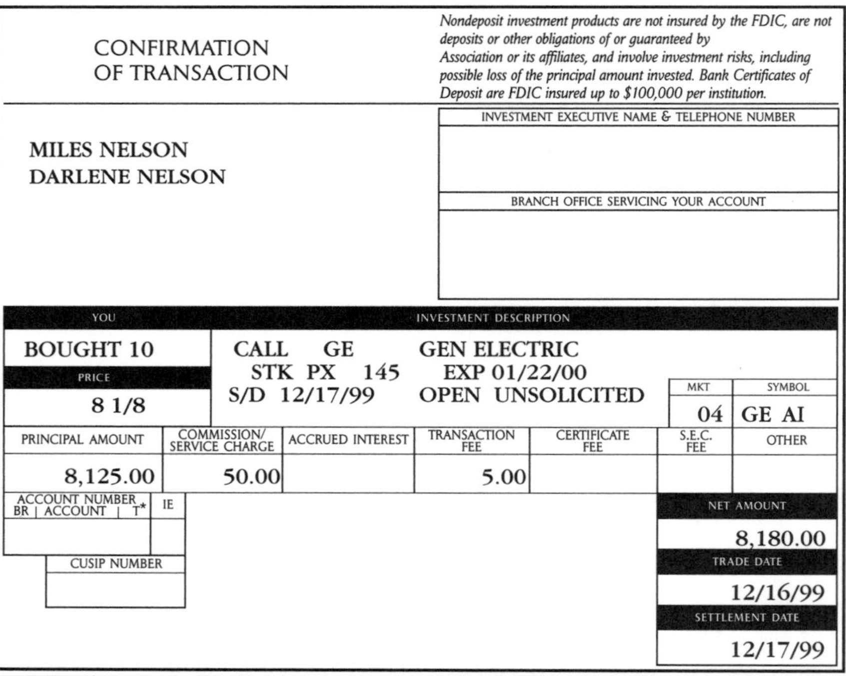

CONFIRMATION OF TRANSACTION

Nondeposit investment products are not insured by the FDIC, are not deposits or other obligations of or guaranteed by Association or its affiliates, and involve investment risks, including possible loss of the principal amount invested. Bank Certificates of Deposit are FDIC insured up to $100,000 per institution.

MILES NELSON
DARLENE NELSON

INVESTMENT EXECUTIVE NAME & TELEPHONE NUMBER

BRANCH OFFICE SERVICING YOUR ACCOUNT

YOU	INVESTMENT DESCRIPTION
BOUGHT 10	CALL GE GEN ELECTRIC STK PX 145 EXP 01/22/00 S/D 12/17/99 OPEN UNSOLICITED
PRICE: 8 1/8	MKT: 04 SYMBOL: GE AI

PRINCIPAL AMOUNT	COMMISSION/ SERVICE CHARGE	ACCRUED INTEREST	TRANSACTION FEE	CERTIFICATE FEE	S.E.C. FEE	OTHER
8,125.00	50.00		5.00			

ACCOUNT NUMBER BR | ACCOUNT | T* IE

CUSIP NUMBER

NET AMOUNT 8,180.00
TRADE DATE 12/16/99
SETTLEMENT DATE 12/17/99

YOU	INVESTMENT DESCRIPTION
SOLD 10	CALL GE GEN ELECTRIC STK PX 145 EXP 01/22/00 S/D 12/20/99 CLOSE UNSOLICITED
PRICE: 13 5/8	MKT: 04 SYMBOL: ORQ AP

PRINCIPAL AMOUNT	COMMISSION/ SERVICE CHARGE	ACCRUED INTEREST	TRANSACTION FEE	CERTIFICATE FEE	S.E.C. FEE	OTHER
13,625.00	50.00		5.00		.46	

ACCOUNT NUMBER BR | ACCOUNT | T* IE

CUSIP NUMBER

NET AMOUNT 13,569.54
TRADE DATE 12/17/99
SETTLEMENT DATE 12/20/99

Split Play #2 (Double Play)

Company:	Microsoft Corp.	
Announcement date:	1/25/99	
Open:	$2,198.00	1/25/99
Close:	$2,769.89	2/02/99
Profit:	$571.89	
Monthly %:	86%	

Goal: *Enter after initial "announcement" surge.*

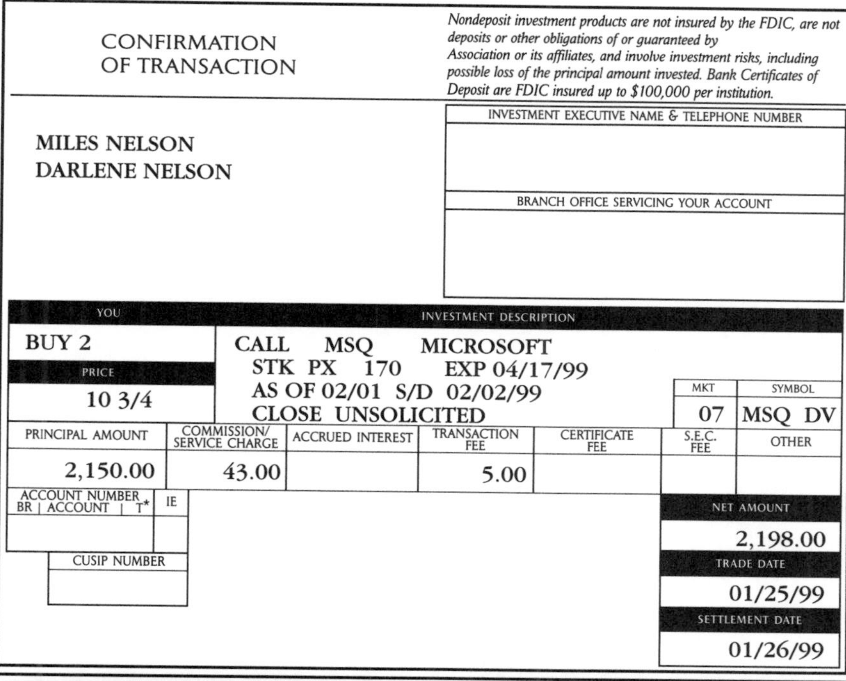

CONFIRMATION OF TRANSACTION

Nondeposit investment products are not insured by the FDIC, are not deposits or other obligations of or guaranteed by Association or its affiliates, and involve investment risks, including possible loss of the principal amount invested. Bank Certificates of Deposit are FDIC insured up to $100,000 per institution.

MILES NELSON
DARLENE NELSON

INVESTMENT EXECUTIVE NAME & TELEPHONE NUMBER

BRANCH OFFICE SERVICING YOUR ACCOUNT

YOU	INVESTMENT DESCRIPTION
BUY 2	CALL MSQ MICROSOFT STK PX 170 EXP 04/17/99 AS OF 02/01 S/D 02/02/99 CLOSE UNSOLICITED
PRICE: 10 3/4	MKT: 07 — SYMBOL: MSQ DV

PRINCIPAL AMOUNT	COMMISSION/ SERVICE CHARGE	ACCRUED INTEREST	TRANSACTION FEE	CERTIFICATE FEE	S.E.C. FEE	OTHER
2,150.00	43.00		5.00			

ACCOUNT NUMBER BR \| ACCOUNT \| T* — IE

CUSIP NUMBER

NET AMOUNT: 2,198.00
TRADE DATE: 01/25/99
SETTLEMENT DATE: 01/26/99

YOU	INVESTMENT DESCRIPTION
SOLD 2	CALL MSQ MICROSOFT STK PX 170 EXP 04/17/99 AS OF 02/01 S/D 02/02/99 CLOSE UNSOLICITED
PRICE: 14 1/8	MKT: 04 — SYMBOL: MSQ DV

PRINCIPAL AMOUNT	COMMISSION/ SERVICE CHARGE	ACCRUED INTEREST	TRANSACTION FEE	CERTIFICATE FEE	S.E.C. FEE	OTHER
2,825.00	50.01		5.00		.10	

ACCOUNT NUMBER BR \| ACCOUNT \| T* — IE

CUSIP NUMBER

NET AMOUNT: 2,769.89
TRADE DATE: 02/02/99
SETTLEMENT DATE: 02/02/99

Phase 3

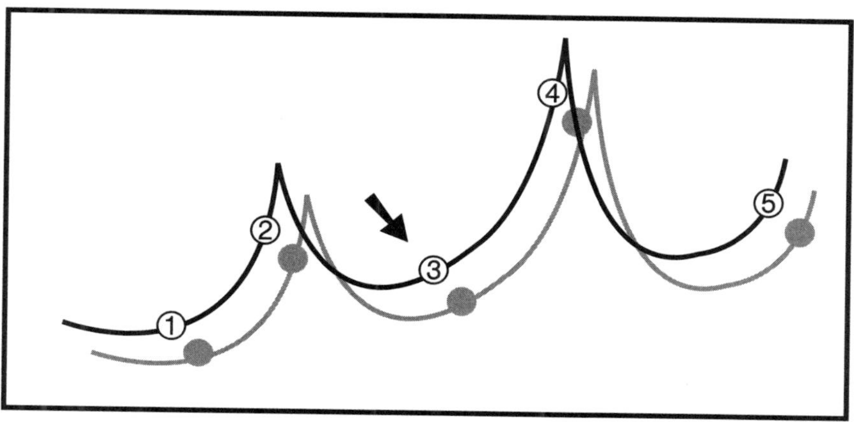

Pre-Split Dip Event

After the announcement, profit taking causes the stock to fall. It collects strength and makes another attempt to climb up.

Term:	Mid-term play.
Options:	One to four full months or more. At the money, or in the money.
Enter:	When the stock makes an upward move from support.
Confirm:	Make sure the stock dropped because of profit taking, not bad news.
Exit:	Use a trailing stop-loss to ride the upward movement. In an up-market the stock can break above the resistance.
Protection:	Watch out for the actual split event. The stock may give in to profit taking three to 10 days before the split.
Adjustment:	If the market is in a downtrend, the stock will make sharp downward movements early. If the market is in a strong uptrend, you may ride through to actual split date.
Pass:	If the stock falls below the support line, check for bad news. If there is none, wait. Look for it to stabilize and make a strong move back up before considering a play. Moving too early is like catching a cement basketball.

This is a mid-term play. After the initial excitement over the announcement ends there will usually be a period of profit taking. As investors close their positions, the stock price will fall until it reaches a support level, where it will usually take a breather and then resume its climb. When the stock reaches resistance it will generally fall victim to profit taking. The price may fall back to the support level once again, gather energy and start climbing up. This up and down movement can happen one or more times before the stock splits.

When the stock price drops down, a dip play is possible. Look for the stock to back off in value—when it hits support the price should stabilize. When it begins to move back up, jump in and ride as it climbs up. As the stock nears resistance, watch it closer because it will probably bounce off the resistance line and stop climbing. This is your exit. At that point the stock may move back down to its support line.

In some cases you can play two or three cycles of excitement and profit taking before the stock splits. This is the workhorse for many stock split investors, because they can watch the stock and make their decisions at night when the house is quiet.

Check the Chart

In order to handle this play effectively you need to understand how to identify the support and resistance lines for a stock. A top quality charting service can be a very valuable tool to assist you in tracking stocks, locating support and resistance lines, and analyzing trends. As I mentioned earlier, a picture is worth a thousand words.

Remember: Since this is a mid-term play, you have some room for comfort. Having longer-term options gives you the opportunity to ride out short-term disappointments, providing news or other events have not changed the overall stock trend.

Other Events to Play

In some cases a stock split announcement is made, but the company does not have enough authorized shares to perform the stock split. When this occurs, the company will have to hold a shareholder meeting and request permission to issue additional shares. This shareholder meeting provides you with a fantastic opportunity to capture profits. The shareholders almost always approve the request (in my memory it has always happened). It's a rare and easy event to play. Of course, caution is always required because the stock market loves to throw us a curve when we are expecting a fastball.

How To Play The Shareholder Event

Enter the play three to five days before the shareholder meeting. This is a short-term play, using in-the-money options that have an expiration date of one to three full months, and a delta of .70 or higher. Exit the play after capturing $1 to $2 in profits using tight stop-losses. If market conditions permit, use trailing stop-losses to let the profits ride until the day of the shareholder meeting. This is an emotion-driven event.

IBM Revisited

Recently I told you about the IBM breakdown (page 99) where they announced a stock split too late and the entire technology sector headed into a tailspin.

IBM led the way into a large pullback. The entire technology sector seemed locked into a never-ending spiral of deeper and deeper price losses. The captains of depression announced their belief that IBM's disaster was proof the world was going to run out of money and everyone was headed to soup lines at the local mission. Many investors believed these horrid predictions and sold their stock holdings at terrible losses.

Don't be fooled. Stocks move up and down for a reason, real or imagined. It is critical that you learn to identify opportunities when others only see disaster—it will allow you to turn frustration into freedom.

As IBM fell, it caused many people to lose faith. Eventually the stock found a support level and it stabilized. For the next few months, it was a great Play #3.

IBM headed sideways for months, waiting for something to change its trend. A great news report turned the tides on IBM's pattern. The following morning the stock gapped up and IBM never looked back. By the time the split ran its course, IBM reached all-time highs and the January disaster was a faint memory.

The next few pages are some of our Phase 3 trades.

Split Play #3

Company:	Qualcomm Inc.	**Open:**	$15,795.00	11/12/99
Announcement:	11/02/99	**Close:**	$24,969.16	11/12/99
Split Date:	12/30/99	**Profit:**	$9,174.16	
X-Date:	12/31/99	**Monthly %:**	1,742%	

Goal: *Take a few dollars profit. Sell order was triggered, got filled higher than order price.*

CONFIRMATION OF TRANSACTION

Nondeposit investment products are not insured by the FDIC, are not deposits or other obligations of or guaranteed by Association or its affiliates, and involve investment risks, including possible loss of the principal amount invested. Bank Certificates of Deposit are FDIC insured up to $100,000 per institution.

MILES NELSON
DARLENE NELSON

INVESTMENT EXECUTIVE NAME & TELEPHONE NUMBER

BRANCH OFFICE SERVICING YOUR ACCOUNT

YOU	INVESTMENT DESCRIPTION
BOUGHT 5	CALL AAF QUALCOMM INC STK PX 370 EXP 12/18/99 S/D 11/15/99 OPEN UNSOLICITED
PRICE: 3 1/2	MKT: 04 — SYMBOL: AAF LN

PRINCIPAL AMOUNT	COMMISSION/ SERVICE CHARGE	ACCRUED INTEREST	TRANSACTION FEE	CERTIFICATE FEE	S.E.C. FEE	OTHER
15,750.00	40.00		5.00			

ACCOUNT NUMBER BR | ACCOUNT | T* — IE

CUSIP NUMBER

NET AMOUNT: 15,795.00
TRADE DATE: 11/12/99
SETTLEMENT DATE: 11/15/99

YOU	INVESTMENT DESCRIPTION
SOLD 5	CALL AAF QUALCOMM INC STK PX 370 EXP 12/18/99 S/D 11/15/99 CLOSE UNSOLICITED
PRICE: 50.000	MKT: 04 — SYMBOL: AAF LN

PRINCIPAL AMOUNT	COMMISSION/ SERVICE CHARGE	ACCRUED INTEREST	TRANSACTION FEE	CERTIFICATE FEE	S.E.C. FEE	OTHER
25,000.00	25.00		5.00		.84	

ACCOUNT NUMBER BR | ACCOUNT | T* — IE

CUSIP NUMBER

NET AMOUNT: 24,969.16
TRADE DATE: 11/12/99
SETTLEMENT DATE: 11/15/99

Split Play #3

Company: Sun Microsystems		**Open:**	$7,430.00	09/29/99
Announcement:	09/17/99	**Close:**	$8,194.72	10/05/99
Split Date:	12/07/99	**Profit:**	$764.72	
X-Date:	12/08/99	**Monthly %:**	44%	

Goal: *Take 3/4 profit.*

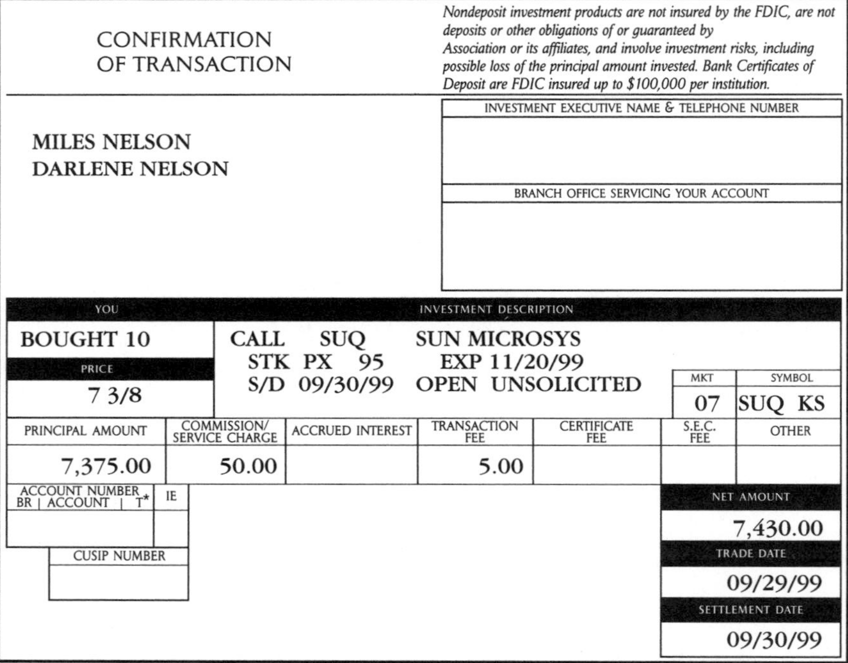

CONFIRMATION
OF TRANSACTION

Nondeposit investment products are not insured by the FDIC, are not deposits or other obligations of or guaranteed by Association or its affiliates, and involve investment risks, including possible loss of the principal amount invested. Bank Certificates of Deposit are FDIC insured up to $100,000 per institution.

MILES NELSON
DARLENE NELSON

INVESTMENT EXECUTIVE NAME & TELEPHONE NUMBER

BRANCH OFFICE SERVICING YOUR ACCOUNT

YOU	INVESTMENT DESCRIPTION	MKT	SYMBOL
BOUGHT 10	CALL SUQ SUN MICROSYS STK PX 95 EXP 11/20/99 S/D 09/30/99 OPEN UNSOLICITED	07	SUQ KS
PRICE: 7 3/8			

PRINCIPAL AMOUNT	COMMISSION/ SERVICE CHARGE	ACCRUED INTEREST	TRANSACTION FEE	CERTIFICATE FEE	S.E.C. FEE	OTHER
7,375.00	50.00		5.00			

ACCOUNT NUMBER BR | ACCOUNT | T* | IE

CUSIP NUMBER

NET AMOUNT	TRADE DATE	SETTLEMENT DATE
7,430.00	09/29/99	09/30/99

YOU	INVESTMENT DESCRIPTION	MKT	SYMBOL
SOLD 10	CALL SUQ SUN MICROSYS STK PX 95 EXP 11/20/99 S/D 10/06/99 CLOSE UNSOLICITED	07	SUQ KS
PRICE: 8 1/4			

PRINCIPAL AMOUNT	COMMISSION/ SERVICE CHARGE	ACCRUED INTEREST	TRANSACTION FEE	CERTIFICATE FEE	S.E.C. FEE	OTHER
8,250.00	50.00		5.00		.28	

ACCOUNT NUMBER BR | ACCOUNT | T* | IE

CUSIP NUMBER

NET AMOUNT	TRADE DATE	SETTLEMENT DATE
8,194.72	10/05/99	10/06/99

Split Play #3

Company:	Sun Microsystems	**Open:**	$11,805.00	11/03/99
Announcement:	09/17/99	**Close:**	$19,569.34	11/08/99
Split Date:	12/07/99	**Profit:**	$7,764.4	
X-Date:	12/08/99	**Monthly %:**	328%	

Goal: *Ride until stop loss is triggered.*

CONFIRMATION
OF TRANSACTION

Nondeposit investment products are not insured by the FDIC, are not deposits or other obligations of or guaranteed by Association or its affiliates, and involve investment risks, including possible loss of the principal amount invested. Bank Certificates of Deposit are FDIC insured up to $100,000 per institution.

MILES NELSON
DARLENE NELSON

INVESTMENT EXECUTIVE NAME & TELEPHONE NUMBER

BRANCH OFFICE SERVICING YOUR ACCOUNT

YOU	INVESTMENT DESCRIPTION
BOUGHT 10	CALL SUQ SUN MICROSYSTEM STK PX 100 EXP 12/18/99 S/D 11/04/99 OPEN UNSOLICITED
PRICE: 11 3/4	MKT: 07 SYMBOL: SUQ LD

PRINCIPAL AMOUNT	COMMISSION/ SERVICE CHARGE	ACCRUED INTEREST	TRANSACTION FEE	CERTIFICATE FEE	S.E.C. FEE	OTHER
11,750.00	50.00		5.00			

ACCOUNT NUMBER BR \| ACCOUNT \| T* — IE

CUSIP NUMBER

NET AMOUNT	TRADE DATE	SETTLEMENT DATE
11,805.00	11/03/99	11/04/99

YOU	INVESTMENT DESCRIPTION
SOLD 10	CALL SUQ SUN MICROSYSTEM STK PX 100 EXP 12/18/99 S/D 11/09/99 CLOSE UNSOLICITED
PRICE: 19 5/8	MKT: 07 SYMBOL: SUQ LD

PRINCIPAL AMOUNT	COMMISSION/ SERVICE CHARGE	ACCRUED INTEREST	TRANSACTION FEE	CERTIFICATE FEE	S.E.C. FEE	OTHER
19,625.00	50.00		5.00		.66	

ACCOUNT NUMBER BR \| ACCOUNT \| T* — IE

CUSIP NUMBER

NET AMOUNT	TRADE DATE	SETTLEMENT DATE
19,569.34	11/08/99	11/09/99

Split Play #3

Company: Sun Microsystems		**Open:**	$5,680.00	10/27/99
Announcement:	09/17/99	**Close:**	$13,694.54	10/29/99
Split Date:	12/07/99	**Profit:**	$8,014.54	
X-Date:	12/08/99	**Monthly %:**	2,116%	

Goal: *Ride until tight stop loss is triggered.*

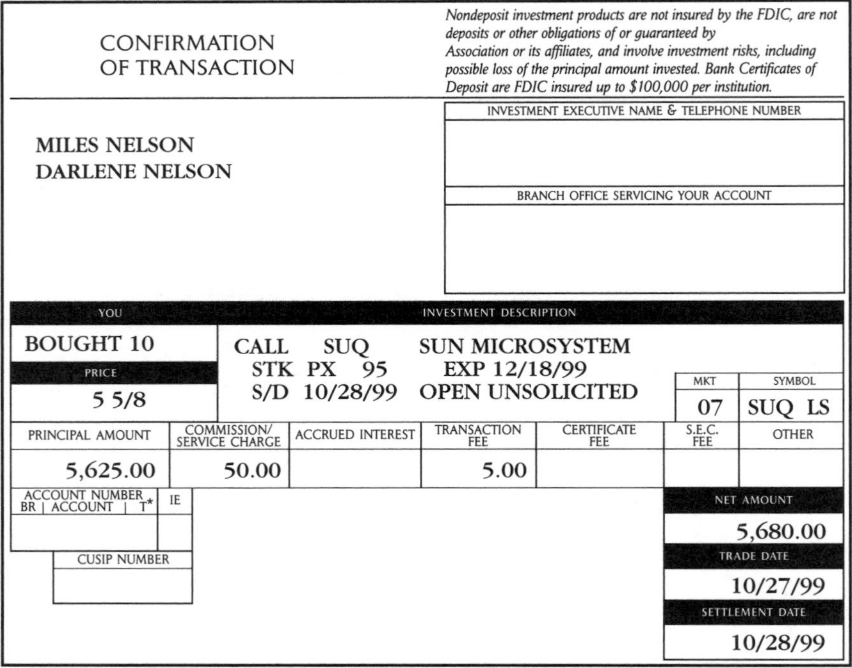

CONFIRMATION OF TRANSACTION

Nondeposit investment products are not insured by the FDIC, are not deposits or other obligations of or guaranteed by Association or its affiliates, and involve investment risks, including possible loss of the principal amount invested. Bank Certificates of Deposit are FDIC insured up to $100,000 per institution.

MILES NELSON
DARLENE NELSON

INVESTMENT EXECUTIVE NAME & TELEPHONE NUMBER

BRANCH OFFICE SERVICING YOUR ACCOUNT

YOU	INVESTMENT DESCRIPTION
BOUGHT 10	CALL SUQ SUN MICROSYSTEM STK PX 95 EXP 12/18/99 S/D 10/28/99 OPEN UNSOLICITED
PRICE: 5 5/8	MKT: 07 — SYMBOL: SUQ LS

PRINCIPAL AMOUNT	COMMISSION/ SERVICE CHARGE	ACCRUED INTEREST	TRANSACTION FEE	CERTIFICATE FEE	S.E.C. FEE	OTHER
5,625.00	50.00		5.00			

ACCOUNT NUMBER BR | ACCOUNT | T* — IE

CUSIP NUMBER

NET AMOUNT	TRADE DATE	SETTLEMENT DATE
5,680.00	10/27/99	10/28/99

YOU	INVESTMENT DESCRIPTION
SOLD 10	CALL SUQ SUN MICROSYSTEM STK PX 95 EXP 12/18/99 S/D 11/01/99 CLOSE UNSOLICITED
PRICE: 13 3/4	MKT: 07 — SYMBOL: SUQ LS

PRINCIPAL AMOUNT	COMMISSION/ SERVICE CHARGE	ACCRUED INTEREST	TRANSACTION FEE	CERTIFICATE FEE	S.E.C. FEE	OTHER
13,750.00	50.00		5.00		.46	

ACCOUNT NUMBER BR | ACCOUNT | T* — IE

CUSIP NUMBER

NET AMOUNT	TRADE DATE	SETTLEMENT DATE
13,694.54	10/29/99	11/01/99

Phase 4

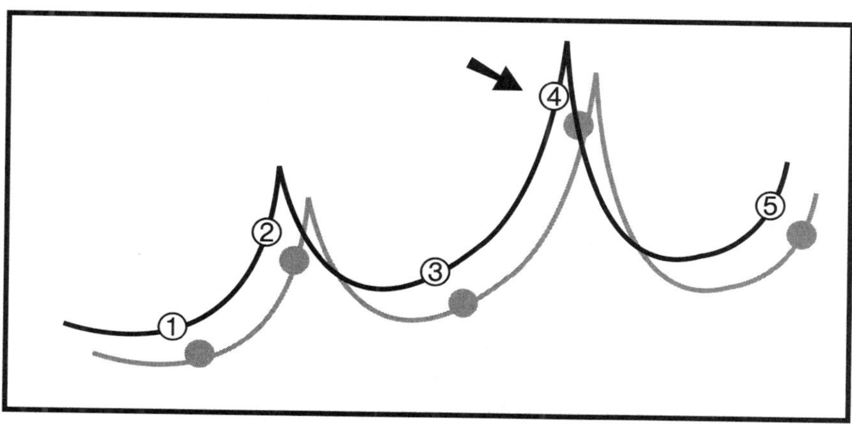

Split Play Event

One to three days before the split, the price runs up. The greatest price increase tends to be the day before and the day of the split event.

Term:	In uptrend markets—short-term play. In downtrend markets—very short-term play.
Options:	One to three full months. In the money. Delta of .70 or higher.
Enter:	One to seven days before the split. The stock should have taken a small dip. When the stock starts to move up (this might be an inner day observation), get in.
Exit:	By the split date.
Protection:	In uptrend markets, tight trailing stop-loss; in downtrend markets, tight stop-loss.
Adjustment:	It's important for the stock to be moving up in value. In some cases you have to wait until the eve of the split to enter the play.
Pass:	If the stock is not moving up or it is falling, pass, unless it shows signs of strength. If you get to the eve of the split and the stock has shown zero life, it's a dead play—pass.

This is a short-term play lasting from a few hours to as much as a few days. Look for an entry point before the stock split. This might be done one to seven days before the split (usually one to five days), or even a few hours before the close of market on the eve of the split. In some cases you can enter the trade a few days before the split and take your profits just before the actual split event. If the stock price is falling prior to the split, wait for it to stabilize and start climbing before you open a position. If it does not start to recover, forget it—there is something wrong. Pass on the play and look for another stock to profit from.

The exit point on the play can actually happen on the eve of the split. If there has been enough run up and you are happy with the profit—get out! In addition, if the stock starts to show some weakness, it's time to walk away. The rule of thumb is to take $1 to $2 profit and sell! The only time to stick in any longer is if you can watch the "moment-by-moment" movements of the stock and get out very quickly.

Be careful, some stocks do a big profit taking pullback a few days before the split. Use this to your advantage.

Phase 4 is a quick in and out. It is very important to use a tight stop-loss to limit your downside. Since you are only looking for a few dollars profit, you do not want to risk more than you plan to earn.

In large companies, there might not be any more than an intra-day dip prior to the split, especially when the market is in an uptrend and the stock is popular with day traders.

FYI: Intra-day = same day. In this case, the stock moves down, bounces off support, and heads back up with strong volume–all in the same day.

Remember: Emotion and rumor are the driving forces behind Play #4. People are coming out of the wood-work talking about the company doing a stock split. Many investors may think that the split is new news and they have an upper hand over the market. If the market is in an uptrend, emotion can become so powerful that option values can double, triple, quadruple, or more. If I am letting the option ride, I use tight stops to protect my interest. I can also "roll up" a few strike prices, taking profits but keeping an in-the-money position that captures additional cash flow. See "Rollout/Rollup–For Profits" on page 257. See my QCOM trade at the end of this section.

Split Date Versus Ex-Date

The split-date is the day the stock split becomes effective—after the market closes! Meaning that on the day of the split the company makes a final tally of issued stocks.When the market closes, the stocks and options will split and the following morning (the ex-date), the additional stocks and options will have been issued, and share prices are adjusted.

When I talk about the "split date," I am referring to the day before the ex-date. If you need to learn the definitions see "The Date is Set" on page 105.

Exit Phase 4 by the split date if you are in options. Market makers often reduce the price of the option drastically the morning after the split, because the party is over, and you could end up losing when you thought you were winning. This happened to me on JDSU. My options were worth $32 on split date.The two-for-one split adjustment the next morning made my shares worth $16, but 10 minutes into market they were unbeefed to $9, then $7! The lucky news for me was JDSU announced another split a few days later, and I ended up making $6,000 versus losing money!

The next few pages contains some very exciting Phase 4 trades we did.

Split Play #4

Company:	Microsoft Corp.	**Open:**	$3,150.37	03/23/99
Announcement:	01/25/99	**Close:**	$4,288.08	03/26/99
Split Date:	03/26/99	**Profit:**	$1,137.71	
X-Date:	03/29/99	**Monthly %:**	270%	

Goal: *Sell on split date.*

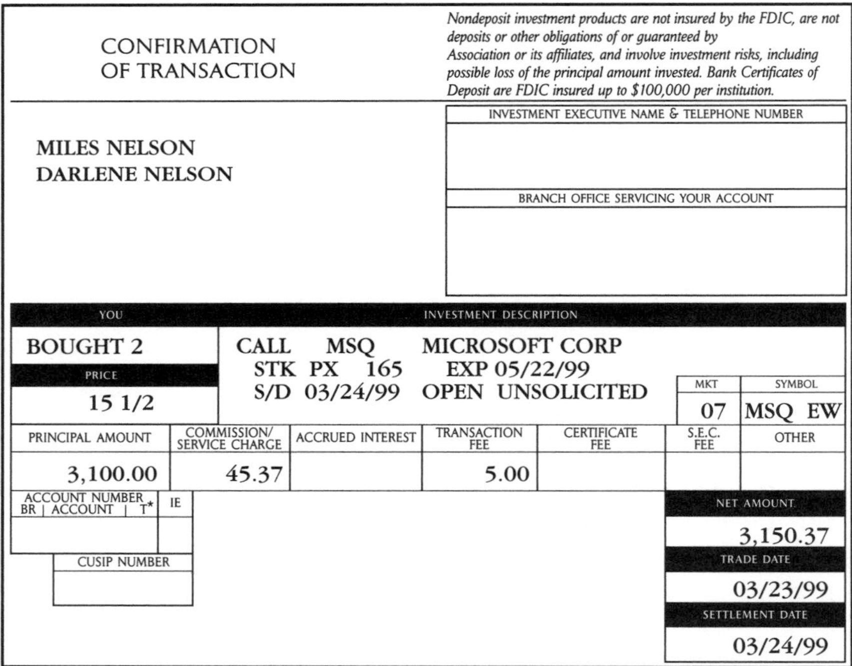

CONFIRMATION OF TRANSACTION

Nondeposit investment products are not insured by the FDIC, are not deposits or other obligations of or guaranteed by Association or its affiliates, and involve investment risks, including possible loss of the principal amount invested. Bank Certificates of Deposit are FDIC insured up to $100,000 per institution.

MILES NELSON
DARLENE NELSON

INVESTMENT EXECUTIVE NAME & TELEPHONE NUMBER

BRANCH OFFICE SERVICING YOUR ACCOUNT

YOU	INVESTMENT DESCRIPTION
BOUGHT 2	CALL MSQ MICROSOFT CORP STK PX 165 EXP 05/22/99 S/D 03/24/99 OPEN UNSOLICITED
PRICE: 15 1/2	MKT: 07 — SYMBOL: MSQ EW

PRINCIPAL AMOUNT	COMMISSION/ SERVICE CHARGE	ACCRUED INTEREST	TRANSACTION FEE	CERTIFICATE FEE	S.E.C. FEE	OTHER
3,100.00	45.37		5.00			

ACCOUNT NUMBER BR | ACCOUNT | T* — IE

CUSIP NUMBER

NET AMOUNT	3,150.37
TRADE DATE	03/23/99
SETTLEMENT DATE	03/24/99

YOU	INVESTMENT DESCRIPTION
SOLD 2	CALL MSQ MICROSOFT CORP STK PX 165 EXP 05/22/99 S/D 03/29/99 OPEN UNSOLICITED
PRICE: 21 3/4	MKT: 07 — SYMBOL: MSQ EW

PRINCIPAL AMOUNT	COMMISSION/ SERVICE CHARGE	ACCRUED INTEREST	TRANSACTION FEE	CERTIFICATE FEE	S.E.C. FEE	OTHER
4,350.00	56.77		5.00		.15	

ACCOUNT NUMBER BR | ACCOUNT | T* — IE

CUSIP NUMBER

NET AMOUNT	4,288.08
TRADE DATE	03/26/99
SETTLEMENT DATE	03/29/99

Split Play #4

Company:	JDS Uniphase	**Open:**	$19,492.50	12/27/99
Announcement:	09/28/99	**Close:**	$22,881.73	12/27/99
Split Date:	12/29/99	**Profit:**	$3,389.23	
X-Date:	12/30/99	**Monthly %:**	521%	

Goal: *Sell on split date, use tight stop-loss. Order was filled mid-day when the stock backed off its high.*

CONFIRMATION OF TRANSACTION

Nondeposit investment products are not insured by the FDIC, are not deposits or other obligations of or guaranteed by Association or its affiliates, and involve investment risks, including possible loss of the principal amount invested. Bank Certificates of Deposit are FDIC insured up to $100,000 per institution.

MILES NELSON
DARLENE NELSON

INVESTMENT EXECUTIVE NAME & TELEPHONE NUMBER

BRANCH OFFICE SERVICING YOUR ACCOUNT

YOU	INVESTMENT DESCRIPTION
BOUGHT 5	CALL XXZ JDS UNIPHASE STK PX 290 EXP 01/22/00 S/D 12/28/99 OPEN UNSOLICITED
PRICE: 38 7/8	MKT: 07 SYMBOL: XXZ AR

PRINCIPAL AMOUNT	COMMISSION/ SERVICE CHARGE	ACCRUED INTEREST	TRANSACTION FEE	CERTIFICATE FEE	S.E.C. FEE	OTHER
19,437.50	50.00		5.00			

ACCOUNT NUMBER BR | ACCOUNT | T* — IE

CUSIP NUMBER

NET AMOUNT: 19,492.50
TRADE DATE: 12/27/99
SETTLEMENT DATE: 12/28/99

YOU	INVESTMENT DESCRIPTION
SOLD 5	CALL XXZ JDS UNIPHASE STK PX 290 EXP 01/22/00 S/D 12/28/99 CLOSE UNSOLICITED
PRICE: 45 7/8	MKT: 07 SYMBOL: ZZX AR

PRINCIPAL AMOUNT	COMMISSION/ SERVICE CHARGE	ACCRUED INTEREST	TRANSACTION FEE	CERTIFICATE FEE	S.E.C. FEE	OTHER
22,937.50	50.00		5.00		.77	

ACCOUNT NUMBER BR | ACCOUNT | T* — IE

CUSIP NUMBER

NET AMOUNT: 22,881.73
TRADE DATE: 12/27/99
SETTLEMENT DATE: 12/28/99

Split Play #4

Company: Qualcomm Inc.		**Open:**	$29,867.50	12/29/99
Announcement:	11/02/99	**Close:**	$37,943.73	12/29/99
Split Date:	12/30/99	**Profit:**	$8,076.23	
X-Date:	12/31/99	**Monthly %:**	811%	

Goal: *Sell on split date.*

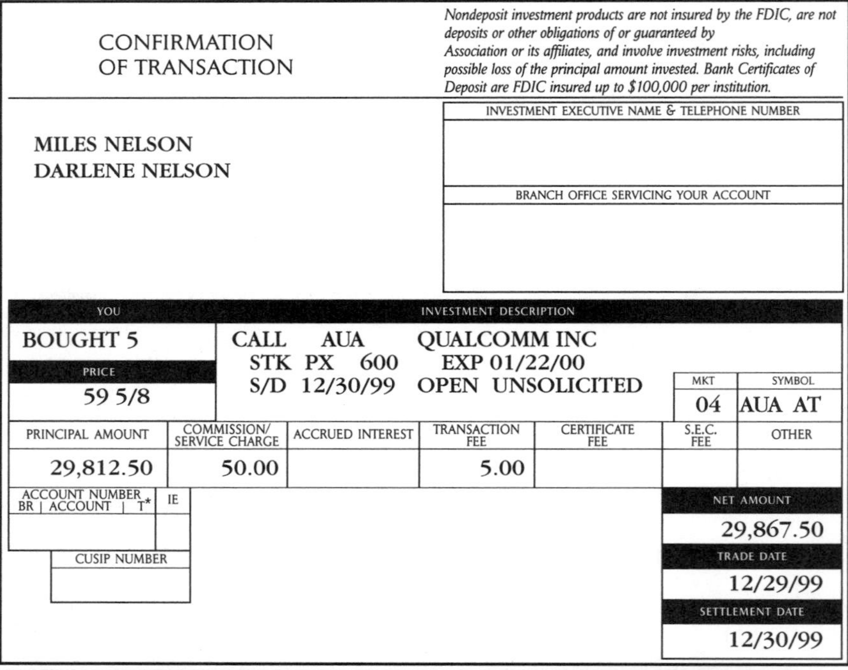

CONFIRMATION OF TRANSACTION

Nondeposit investment products are not insured by the FDIC, are not deposits or other obligations of or guaranteed by Association or its affiliates, and involve investment risks, including possible loss of the principal amount invested. Bank Certificates of Deposit are FDIC insured up to $100,000 per institution.

MILES NELSON
DARLENE NELSON

INVESTMENT EXECUTIVE NAME & TELEPHONE NUMBER

BRANCH OFFICE SERVICING YOUR ACCOUNT

YOU	INVESTMENT DESCRIPTION
BOUGHT 5	CALL AUA QUALCOMM INC STK PX 600 EXP 01/22/00 S/D 12/30/99 OPEN UNSOLICITED
PRICE: 59 5/8	MKT: 04 SYMBOL: AUA AT

PRINCIPAL AMOUNT	COMMISSION/ SERVICE CHARGE	ACCRUED INTEREST	TRANSACTION FEE	CERTIFICATE FEE	S.E.C. FEE	OTHER
29,812.50	50.00		5.00			

ACCOUNT NUMBER BR | ACCOUNT | T* | IE

CUSIP NUMBER

NET AMOUNT	TRADE DATE	SETTLEMENT DATE
29,867.50	12/29/99	12/30/99

YOU	INVESTMENT DESCRIPTION
SOLD 5	CALL AUA QUALCOMM INC STK PX 600 EXP 01/22/00 S/D 12/30/99 CLOSE UNSOLICITED
PRICE: 76.000	MKT: 04 SYMBOL: AUA AT

PRINCIPAL AMOUNT	COMMISSION/ SERVICE CHARGE	ACCRUED INTEREST	TRANSACTION FEE	CERTIFICATE FEE	S.E.C. FEE	OTHER
38,000.00	50.00		5.00		1.27	

ACCOUNT NUMBER BR | ACCOUNT | T* | IE

CUSIP NUMBER

NET AMOUNT	TRADE DATE	SETTLEMENT DATE
37,943.73	12/29/99	12/30/99

Split Play #4

Company:	Qualcomm Inc.	**Open:**	$29,055.00	12/29/99
Announcement:	11/02/99	**Close:**	$42,881.06	12/30/99
Split Date:	12/30/99	**Profit:**	$13,826.06	
X-Date:	12/31/99	**Monthly %:**	713%	

Goal: *Sell on split date; the stock gapped up and started backing off. We took our profits and ran!*

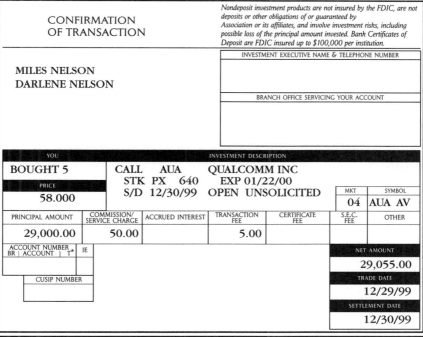

CONFIRMATION OF TRANSACTION

Nondeposit investment products are not insured by the FDIC, are not deposits or other obligations of or guaranteed by Association or its affiliates, and involve investment risks, including possible loss of the principal amount invested. Bank Certificates of Deposit are FDIC insured up to $100,000 per institution.

INVESTMENT EXECUTIVE NAME & TELEPHONE NUMBER

MILES NELSON
DARLENE NELSON

BRANCH OFFICE SERVICING YOUR ACCOUNT

YOU	INVESTMENT DESCRIPTION	MKT	SYMBOL
BOUGHT 5	CALL AUA QUALCOMM INC STK PX 640 EXP 01/22/00 S/D 12/30/99 OPEN UNSOLICITED	04	AUA AV
PRICE: 58.000			

PRINCIPAL AMOUNT	COMMISSION/ SERVICE CHARGE	ACCRUED INTEREST	TRANSACTION FEE	CERTIFICATE FEE	S.E.C. FEE	OTHER
29,000.00	50.00		5.00			

ACCOUNT NUMBER BR | ACCOUNT | T* — IE

CUSIP NUMBER

NET AMOUNT	TRADE DATE	SETTLEMENT DATE
29,055.00	12/29/99	12/30/99

YOU	INVESTMENT DESCRIPTION	MKT	SYMBOL
SOLD 5	CALL AUA QUALCOMM INC STK PX 640 EXP 01/22/00 S/D 12/31/99 CLOSE UNSOLICITED	04	AUA AV
PRICE: 85 7/8			

PRINCIPAL AMOUNT	COMMISSION/ SERVICE CHARGE	ACCRUED INTEREST	TRANSACTION FEE	CERTIFICATE FEE	S.E.C. FEE	OTHER
42,937.50	50.00		5.00		1.44	

ACCOUNT NUMBER BR | ACCOUNT | T* — IE

CUSIP NUMBER

NET AMOUNT	TRADE DATE	SETTLEMENT DATE
42,881.06	12/30/99	12/31/99

Split Play #4

Company:	Qualcomm Inc.	**Open:**	$47,480.00	12/28/99
Announcement:	11/02/99	**Close:**	$92,691.90	12/29/99
Split Date:	12/30/99	**Profit:**	$45,211.90	
X-Date:	12/31/99	**Monthly %:**	1,428%	

Goal: *Sell on split date, use tight stop-loss. The stock moved up, sold options, locking in profits. Note: Purchased 5 contracts, then 5 more.*

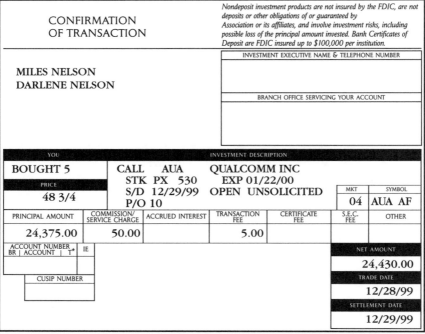

CONFIRMATION
OF TRANSACTION

Nondeposit investment products are not insured by the FDIC, are not deposits or other obligations of or guaranteed by Association or its affiliates, and involve investment risks, including possible loss of the principal amount invested. Bank Certificates of Deposit are FDIC insured up to $100,000 per institution.

MILES NELSON
DARLENE NELSON

INVESTMENT EXECUTIVE NAME & TELEPHONE NUMBER

BRANCH OFFICE SERVICING YOUR ACCOUNT

YOU	INVESTMENT DESCRIPTION
BOUGHT 5	CALL AUA QUALCOMM INC STK PX 530 EXP 01/22/00 S/D 12/29/99 OPEN UNSOLICITED P/O 10
PRICE: 48 3/4	MKT: 04 SYMBOL: AUA AF

PRINCIPAL AMOUNT	COMMISSION/ SERVICE CHARGE	ACCRUED INTEREST	TRANSACTION FEE	CERTIFICATE FEE	S.E.C. FEE	OTHER
24,375.00	50.00		5.00			

ACCOUNT NUMBER BR | ACCOUNT | T* | IE

CUSIP NUMBER

NET AMOUNT	TRADE DATE	SETTLEMENT DATE
24,430.00	12/28/99	12/29/99

YOU	INVESTMENT DESCRIPTION
BOUGHT 5	CALL AUA QUALCOMM INC STK PX 530 EXP 01/22/00 S/D 12/29/99 OPEN UNSOLICITED
PRICE: 46.000	MKT: 04 SYMBOL: AUA AF

PRINCIPAL AMOUNT	COMMISSION/ SERVICE CHARGE	ACCRUED INTEREST	TRANSACTION FEE	CERTIFICATE FEE	S.E.C. FEE	OTHER
23,000.00	50.00					

ACCOUNT NUMBER BR | ACCOUNT | T* | IE

CUSIP NUMBER

NET AMOUNT	TRADE DATE	SETTLEMENT DATE
23,050.00	12/28/99	12/29/99

Split Play #4 (continued)

NOTE: This is a continuation of the play on the previous page.

CONFIRMATION
OF TRANSACTION

Nondeposit investment products are not insured by the FDIC, are not deposits or other obligations of or guaranteed by Association or its affiliates, and involve investment risks, including possible loss of the principal amount invested. Bank Certificates of Deposit are FDIC insured up to $100,000 per institution.

MILES NELSON
DARLENE NELSON

INVESTMENT EXECUTIVE NAME & TELEPHONE NUMBER

BRANCH OFFICE SERVICING YOUR ACCOUNT

YOU	INVESTMENT DESCRIPTION
SOLD 10	CALL AUA QUALCOMM INC STK PX 530 EXP 01/22/00 S/D 12/30/99 CLOSE UNSOLICITED
PRICE: 92 3/4	MKT: 04 — SYMBOL: AUA AF

PRINCIPAL AMOUNT	COMMISSION/ SERVICE CHARGE	ACCRUED INTEREST	TRANSACTION FEE	CERTIFICATE FEE	S.E.C. FEE	OTHER
92,750.00	50.00		5.00		3.10	

ACCOUNT NUMBER BR | ACCOUNT | T*	IE

CUSIP NUMBER

NET AMOUNT: 92,691.90

TRADE DATE: 12/29/99

SETTLEMENT DATE: 12/30/99

Split Play #4

Company:	Ariba, Inc.	**Open:**	$2,555.00	12/16/99
Announcement:	11/16/99	**Close:**	$5,194.82	12/17/99
Split Date:	12/17/99	**Profit:**	$2,639.82	
X-Date:	12/20/99	**Monthly %:**	1549%	

Goal: *This was actually a bull put spread. Opened this play on Thursday and the December options were expiring the next day (Friday). Thought this was a great way to take advantage of Play #4 and a bull put spread. Note: This advanced technique is not covered in the book, but I decided to include it anyway.*

CONFIRMATION OF TRANSACTION

Nondeposit investment products are not insured by the FDIC, are not deposits or other obligations of or guaranteed by Association or its affiliates, and involve investment risks, including possible loss of the principal amount invested. Bank Certificates of Deposit are FDIC insured up to $100,000 per institution.

MILES NELSON
DARLENE NELSON

INVESTMENT EXECUTIVE NAME & TELEPHONE NUMBER

BRANCH OFFICE SERVICING YOUR ACCOUNT

YOU	INVESTMENT DESCRIPTION	MKT	SYMBOL
BOUGHT 10	PUT IRU ARIBA INC STK PX 220 EXP 12/18/99 S/D 12/17/99 OPEN UNSOLICITED	07	IRU XD
PRICE: 2 1/2			

PRINCIPAL AMOUNT	COMMISSION/ SERVICE CHARGE	ACCRUED INTEREST	TRANSACTION FEE	CERTIFICATE FEE	S.E.C. FEE	OTHER
2,500.00	50.00		5.00			

ACCOUNT NUMBER BR | ACCOUNT | T* | IE

CUSIP NUMBER

NET AMOUNT	TRADE DATE	SETTLEMENT DATE
2,555.00	12/16/99	12/17/99

YOU	INVESTMENT DESCRIPTION	MKT	SYMBOL
SOLD 10	CALL IRU ARIBA INC STK PX 230 EXP 12/18/99 S/D 12/17/99 OPEN UNSOLICITED	07	IRU XF
PRICE: 5 1/4			

PRINCIPAL AMOUNT	COMMISSION/ SERVICE CHARGE	ACCRUED INTEREST	TRANSACTION FEE	CERTIFICATE FEE	S.E.C. FEE	OTHER
5,250.00	50.00		5.00		.18	

ACCOUNT NUMBER BR | ACCOUNT | T* | IE

CUSIP NUMBER

NET AMOUNT	TRADE DATE	SETTLEMENT DATE
5,194.82	12/16/99	12/17/99

Phase 5

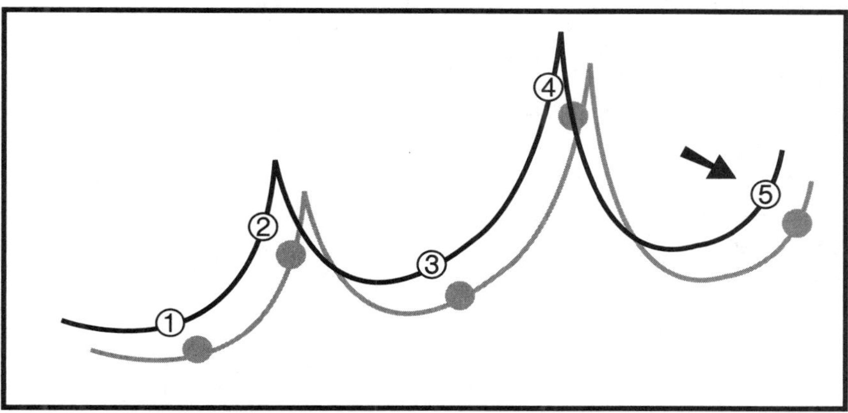

Post-Split Dip

Within hours or days of the split, the stock dips down because of profit taking, it levels out, collects energy and starts climbing again. Remember, the stock can move sideways for 30 to 45 days or more before it starts moving up.

Term:	Long-term play.
Options:	Four or more full months. Out of the money.
Enter:	After the split, wait for the stock to back off in price. When it starts to move back up, get in.
Exit:	When the stop-loss order is activated, or when the stock is moving too slow for your investment objectives.
Protection:	Trailing stop-losses, based on 1.5 to 2.0 times the average daily movement or based on the support lines established <u>after</u> the split (if you want a longer-term investment).
Adjustment:	If profits have accumulated, rollout and/or rollup, keeping gains and leaving a small amount in the deal. Rolling out or rolling up might be done by choosing a slightly out-of-the-money option if there is still plenty of time for upward movement.

This is a long-term play. After the stock splits, there is usually a short runup in the stock price. Then, within a few hours or days of the split, people finally take their profits. The stock will usually take a break, dipping in value, and then collect strength near the support line. There may be an extended period of consolidation anywhere from a few hours to 45 or more days before the stock resumes an upward climb. Jump into the play when the stock starts to show life again and begins to move up in price. The exit point might be when it reaches resistance, when a better deal comes along, or when other sell indicators occur.

Remember: Don't forget that many stocks climb back up to their pre-split price within three years of splitting. In some cases stocks recover their pre-split price within much shorter times.

This is essentially a "Range Rider Up" using a rolling option play. To be effective, you need to watch news, volume, and the normal indicators that are used for rolling options and Range Riders. Watch out for earnings reports, trouble-making news, sector problems, et cetera. Since this is a very long-term play, purchasing LEAPS might be indicated, because they have a life of up to three years. With time on your side you can wait out the mini-dips and ride the stock as it climbs up to its pre-split level.

Caution: If you plan to acquire LEAPS®, don't do it before the split! Wait until the split is completed and option prices pull back–<u>they always do</u>. This is important because the market makers have beefed up the option prices. Once the split is over, volatility slows and the options become cheaper. If you want more info on using LEAPS® see the Appendix for "Poolside Investing with LEAPS®."

Dell and Sun Microsystems have been great Phase 5 trades for us...see the next few pages.

Split Play #5

Company:	America Online	
Last Split Date:	11/22/99	
Open:	$9,680.00	12/10/99
Close:	$13,949.53	12/10/99
Profit:	$4,269.53	
Monthly %:	1,323%	

Action: *Stock hit a high and backed off; took profits the same day!*

CONFIRMATION
OF TRANSACTION

Nondeposit investment products are not insured by the FDIC, are not deposits or other obligations of or guaranteed by Association or its affiliates, and involve investment risks, including possible loss of the principal amount invested. Bank Certificates of Deposit are FDIC insured up to $100,000 per institution.

MILES NELSON
DARLENE NELSON

INVESTMENT EXECUTIVE NAME & TELEPHONE NUMBER

BRANCH OFFICE SERVICING YOUR ACCOUNT

YOU	INVESTMENT DESCRIPTION
BOUGHT 10	CALL AOO AMERICA ONLINE STK PX 85 EXP 01/22/00 S/D 12/13/99 OPEN UNSOLICITED P/O 20
PRICE: 9 5/8	MKT: 04 — SYMBOL: AOO AQ

PRINCIPAL AMOUNT	COMMISSION/ SERVICE CHARGE	ACCRUED INTEREST	TRANSACTION FEE	CERTIFICATE FEE	S.E.C. FEE	OTHER
9,625.00	50.00		5.00			

ACCOUNT NUMBER BR | ACCOUNT | T* — IE

CUSIP NUMBER

NET AMOUNT	TRADE DATE	SETTLEMENT DATE
9,680.00	12/10/99	12/13/99

YOU	INVESTMENT DESCRIPTION
SOLD 10	CALL AOO AMERICA ONLINE STK PX 85 EXP 01/22/00 S/D 12/13/99 CLOSE P/O 20 UNSOLICITED
PRICE: 14.000	MKT: 04 — SYMBOL: AOO AQ

PRINCIPAL AMOUNT	COMMISSION/ SERVICE CHARGE	ACCRUED INTEREST	TRANSACTION FEE	CERTIFICATE FEE	S.E.C. FEE	OTHER
14,000.00	50.00		5.00		.47	

ACCOUNT NUMBER BR | ACCOUNT | T* — IE

CUSIP NUMBER

NET AMOUNT	TRADE DATE	SETTLEMENT DATE
13,949.53	12/10/99	12/13/99

Split Play #5

Company:	Dell Computer	
Last Split Date:	03/08/99	
Open:	$8,305.00	03/16/00
Close:	$9,144.69	03/16/00
Profit:	$839.69	
Monthly %:	303%	

Action: *Set a GTC for 3/4 point; I got a better fill than expected.*

CONFIRMATION
OF TRANSACTION

Nondeposit investment products are not insured by the FDIC, are not deposits or other obligations of or guaranteed by Association or its affiliates, and involve investment risks, including possible loss of the principal amount invested. Bank Certificates of Deposit are FDIC insured up to $100,000 per institution.

MILES NELSON
DARLENE NELSON

INVESTMENT EXECUTIVE NAME & TELEPHONE NUMBER

BRANCH OFFICE SERVICING YOUR ACCOUNT

YOU	INVESTMENT DESCRIPTION		
BOUGHT 10	CALL DLQ DELL COMPUTER STK PX 45 EXP 04/22/00 S/D 03/17/00 OPEN UNSOLICITED	MKT	SYMBOL
PRICE: 8 1/4		04	DLQ DI

PRINCIPAL AMOUNT	COMMISSION/ SERVICE CHARGE	ACCRUED INTEREST	TRANSACTION FEE	CERTIFICATE FEE	S.E.C. FEE	OTHER
8,250.00	50.00		5.00			

ACCOUNT NUMBER BR | ACCOUNT | T* | IE

CUSIP NUMBER

NET AMOUNT	TRADE DATE	SETTLEMENT DATE
8,305.00	03/16/00	03/17/00

YOU	INVESTMENT DESCRIPTION		
SOLD 10	CALL DLQ DELL COMPUTER STK PX 45 EXP 04/22/00 S/D 03/17/00 CLOSE UNSOLICITED	MKT	SYMBOL
PRICE: 9 1/4		04	DLQ DI

PRINCIPAL AMOUNT	COMMISSION/ SERVICE CHARGE	ACCRUED INTEREST	TRANSACTION FEE	CERTIFICATE FEE	S.E.C. FEE	OTHER
9,250.00	100.00		5.00		.31	

ACCOUNT NUMBER BR | ACCOUNT | T* | IE

CUSIP NUMBER

NET AMOUNT	TRADE DATE	SETTLEMENT DATE
9,144.69	03/16/00	03/17/00

Split Play #5

Company:	Dell Computer	
Last Split Date:	03/08/99	
Open:	$4,930.00	04/17/00
Close:	$5,444.81	04/17/00
Profit:	$514.81	
Monthly %:	313%	

Action: *Set a GTC for 1/2 point; I got a better fill than expected.*

CONFIRMATION
OF TRANSACTION

Nondeposit investment products are not insured by the FDIC, are not deposits or other obligations of or guaranteed by Association or its affiliates, and involve investment risks, including possible loss of the principal amount invested. Bank Certificates of Deposit are FDIC insured up to $100,000 per institution.

MILES NELSON
DARLENE NELSON

INVESTMENT EXECUTIVE NAME & TELEPHONE NUMBER

BRANCH OFFICE SERVICING YOUR ACCOUNT

YOU	INVESTMENT DESCRIPTION	MKT	SYMBOL
BOUGHT 10	CALL DLQ DELL COMPUTER STK PX 45 EXP 05/20/00 S/D 04/18/00 OPEN UNSOLICITED	04	DLQ EI
PRICE: 4 7/8			

PRINCIPAL AMOUNT	COMMISSION/ SERVICE CHARGE	ACCRUED INTEREST	TRANSACTION FEE	CERTIFICATE FEE	S.E.C. FEE	OTHER
4,875.00	50.00		5.00			

ACCOUNT NUMBER BR | ACCOUNT | T* — IE

CUSIP NUMBER

NET AMOUNT	TRADE DATE	SETTLEMENT DATE
4,930.00	04/17/00	04/18/00

YOU	INVESTMENT DESCRIPTION	MKT	SYMBOL
SOLD 10	CALL DLQ DELL COMPUTER STK PX 45 EXP 05/20/00 S/D 04/18/00 CLOSE UNSOLICITED	04	ORQ AP
PRICE: 5 1/2			

PRINCIPAL AMOUNT	COMMISSION/ SERVICE CHARGE	ACCRUED INTEREST	TRANSACTION FEE	CERTIFICATE FEE	S.E.C. FEE	OTHER
5,500.00	50.00		5.00		.19	

ACCOUNT NUMBER BR | ACCOUNT | T* — IE

CUSIP NUMBER

NET AMOUNT	TRADE DATE	SETTLEMENT DATE
5,444.81	04/17/00	04/18/00

12

Putting The Pieces Together

This chapter took me far more time to complete than I had expected—there is still so much to be covered. I have already discussed the five phases and how to play them, and some of the necessary skills for success. Anything after the five plays might seem anti-climactic, but I believe you will find what follows is valuable and exciting—more than just a recap.

Investor Psychology

In the Bible, Paul talks about looking through rose-colored glasses, meaning that people tend to color life the way they want it to look. Why is it that ten different people can have the same experience and each will have a different version of what happened? We all have a specific focus in life that causes us to see what we expect to see. We seem to do the same with books we read, courses we take, and audiotapes we listen to, and even in the stock market. We can't help it; it's part of human nature. This focus will ultimately lead people to success or failure in life's opportunities.

My son is a great example. When he gets up in the morning, he has a specific routine. Each school morning he goes into the dining room, turns on the TV, grabs a bowl and pours himself some cereal. Then he heads to the fridge and grabs the milk. If anything goes wrong with the schedule he looks like he just struck out in the ninth inning. If he misses any part of the morning routine, he has a hard time getting through his day. If I want to find out how many times the family ran out of milk, all I have to do is grab his school performance record. On the days that we ran out of milk he receives an F on cooperation, participation and completion. In contrast, on the days his routine proceeds as expected he performs wonderfully at school and home.

I see my son in the faces of people every day. Did they miss their morning cup of coffee? Was their favorite parking space taken? Did someone borrow their stapler without permission, or was the kitchen out of Pop Tarts? Each day people have experiences that cause emotional reactions, good and bad.

Emotion Is A Powerful Force

The same is true for the stock market. In fact, emotion is the greatest moving force in the world of finance. While facts and figures allow us to predict general trends, emotions drive overriding swings in the price of a stock. If you want to see raw emotion in full force, go to the Chicago Board Options Exchange (CBOE) and watch the waves of calm and excitement that pass through the room. There are moments when people are drifting off to sleep at their terminals, yet a few seconds later they can't scream loud enough.

These never-ending tides of peace and turmoil are like the waves breaking on the Hawaiian coast. At times, the water is almost silent and then the tide moves in, the waves get larger, and the sound becomes deafening. A while later peace returns to the sand and the quiet erases all memory of the recent turmoil.

When the stock market opens for business, the opposing teams enter the field—some call them the bulls and the bears. Both sides want to score. The crowd gets excited and yells, wave after wave of excitement passes around the stands. When the market closes, brokers tally up the damage and issue their margin calls. Investors drink a toast to their victory or lick the wounds of their defeat. Both are already thinking about the next morning and the next opportunity to capture the golden ring.

The stock and options exchanges are constantly being swept by emotion. If you ever have the opportunity to go to the CBOE, take it. You will be able to see the emotional waves that sweep through trading pits when news or other events causes increased trading volume. It's absolutely fantastic, better than being on the 50-yard line at the Super Bowl!

Fear And Greed

Of all the emotions portrayed in the market, fear and greed seem to be the strongest. The problem is that when people are controlled by their emotions, they usually make the worst decisions, selling when stocks are at their lowest and buying when prices are at their peak. Of course, no one intentionally loses money, but that is exactly what happens to investors that are controlled by fear and greed. Good planning is the best way to save on taxes and the only way to preserve your capital in the market.

I took an investing course taught by Steve Wirrick that covered the basics of stock options investing. In that class, Steve talked about investor sentiment, particularly the tendency of people to be sucked into the "group." As people read the news or watch a business program they can get all wrapped up in current events, and then their emotions take over and start controlling their trades. When that happens, the investor becomes a member of the "group" that is buying and selling at the wrong time.

I watch out for feelings like "I sold too soon," or "Why didn't I get into that stock last night?" If I get those feelings, I know that it's time to go take a shower. I am no longer objective. If you make trading decisions based on the fear of loss, you will get caught every time.

Stocks don't climb in a straight line, they look more like a lightning bolt making a jagged climb into new territory. When stocks hit new highs, they can climb a little more, then like a mountain climber, they often need a rest; they back off and take a breath, while the rest of the world catches up.

It is important to develop a trading style that will prevent emotions from clouding your decisions. In order to win the battle, you need to know who the players are and what part they play in the game. When you understand the patterns of the game and the plays that match those patterns, you can use the formulas that win the game.

The Prayer Meeting That Moved Markets

I am going to tell you another story to illustrate how emotional the stock market is. This story is an example only—it is not intended to be a political comment or to endorse or demean any specific person, belief, or thing.

Set It Up

In July of 1998, stock markets around the world started getting nervous. Asian financial problems were becoming a big concern and Japan's situation was declining. The largest banks in Japan were nearing collapse. On the morning of July 20, 1998, the U.S. got a wake up call—world markets were knocking on Wall Street's door. The Dow Jones Industrial Average (DOW) fell 47 points. This alone is not a large movement—there are many days that the DOW moves up or down 50 to 100 points—but world markets were spinning out of control and U.S. investors were concerned.

The world situation got scarier and, over the next 10 days, the DOW dropped more than 500 points. Investors were fearful and looking for opportunities to pull their money out of the market. Each time stocks rose, another rash of selling occurred driving them down further. Market commentators were declaring the beginning of a bear market.

August 4, 1998 marked a major turn of events. Ralph Acampora, Chief Technical Analyst at Prudential Securities, stated that the bear market had arrived and that stocks would fall. The DOW had already fallen from its July 1998 highs of 9300+ to under 8,900 on August 3rd. Then on August 4th, the DOW was already down 150 points for the day when Acampora made his devastating press release. Within minutes, the DOW plummeted, and by day's end the bears had scored a 300-point victory.

Each day world markets reported falling stock prices. By the end of August, Russia was defaulting on loans—their stock market had lost more than 90% of its value and the country was on the verge of bankruptcy. This caused other countries to take large losses of their own. Brazil was headed for disaster, Japan was in terrible shape, and China was getting grumpy. Analysts claimed that these events confirmed the beginning of the Bear Market of 1998. Each day the DOW sank further and news hosts were interviewing gloom and doom prophets foretelling the end of the financial world. All eyes were on the markets as people watched their life savings crumble. If Russia went bankrupt, some claimed that it would cause world collapse and if Brazil did not get their financial situation under control, the damage could cause collapse of U.S. markets, not to mention Japan and other struggling countries. It looked like the bubble had burst worldwide and the pessimists would be proven correct.

By the end of August the DOW had hit 7,400 and bottomed out. Doomsayers were predicting another 5% to 50% fall of stock prices. Others were claiming that the bear market could last five years, while Wade Cook and other optimists said that conditions indicated it was a great time to get into the market. Cook said the DOW had hit support at 7,400 and had held that mark a number of times.

What Happened?

On September 12, 1998, Miles was in bed watching CNBC and looking for opportunities to profit from the market volatility. The DOW was falling hard; it had already lost 50 points when CNBC did a live broadcast of President Clinton speaking to a group of 106 religious leaders at a breakfast prayer meeting.

As Mr. Clinton stood, the DOW fell 15 points. Within five minutes, the market was down 100 points, falling fast. At the exact moment that President Clinton made a public apology for his immoral actions and asked for forgiveness, the DOW stopped falling. The President's speech continued and the market started to climb. By the end of Clinton's speech, the DOW was headed into positive territory, and by the end of the day the DOW had gained 167 points. From a bottom of more than 100 points down, to a closing increase of 167 points, President Clinton's speech made almost a 300-point difference in the DOW.

What does all of this mean? Investors can be very emotional and may use their feelings as a decision-making tool. Professionals agree that feelings need to stay in the desk drawer when making investment decisions. To make a decision you need to use logic and knowledge. However, you can use emotions as an indicator of the market's trend. Think of the market as a large field with hundreds of wild animals—if a threat enters the field, all animals head to the opposite end of the grassland. By the same token, if food appears, all of the animals will head in that direction. The moral of my story is that when you see emotions taking hold of the market, you can predict what is likely to happen and profit by using that knowledge to your advantage.

Analysts And Market Makers

As I have just illustrated, analysts have a substantial effect. Some can move individual stocks and others sway whole markets. At times outspoken analysts are called "axe men" because when they speak financial heads roll. As you get familiar with the companies and sectors that are your favorite targets, you will begin to notice the analysts and brokerage houses that can sway prices. As you move through your day you might hear part of a news report. Walking past a television: "Ralph Acamp..." is all you hear. Those few syllables could be enough to tell you, "I better check this out, it could be important!"

Practice Trading (Paper Trading)

Recently, my six-year-old taught us a wonderful lesson. We had been scanning charts using TeleChart2000™ and he selected a few stocks that were part of his name—B, BR, Y, CE. After writing down the symbol of the stocks he chose, he said to my husband, "Call your broker and buy my stocks." Miles told him we didn't have any money left and that we couldn't call the broker.

Bryce said, "But dad, they only cost forty-eighty thousand dollars."

Again Miles told him that we would have to wait, because the family had already invested everything in the brokerage account.

Bryce jumped up and said, "I'll be right back." We heard things falling in his room, boxes being moved and other mysterious noises. A few moments later Bryce returned with a big smile and handed Miles a pile of money that he had taken out of all of the games in his room saying, "Here dad, you can use this." To him, the pretend money was just as real as the money in my brokerage account. All he wanted to do was get the stock; it didn't matter what kind of money he used.

What I learned from Bryce that day is the value of treating practice trades (paper trades) with the same excitement as the real thing. Paper trades are just as important as real trades—success depends on how much you practice. Here are a few points to understand about practice trading.

- First, learn how to practice a strategy perfectly before you ever put real money into it. Why would anyone want to put real money into a technique before they work out the bugs?
- Second, continue practicing even when doing real trades. If you quit doing deals when money is tied up, you quit learning. Knowledge is money.
- Third, if market conditions change and you have not mastered the new condition, go back to practice trading before risking real money. Keep your hard-earned cash for winning deals.

When you want to learn a new technique, it is critical that you practice before you ever risk a penny of your hard-earned money. This is usually called paper trading or Simutrading™. I like to call it practice trading. The concept is simple: practice trading to perfect your success rate before you risk real money. Select a stock, get a price quote, and make a purchase choice. Confirm the practice purchase by getting a second quote, to confirm that you got filled at the desired price. After the trade is opened, set two exits: a GTC and a stop-loss. Follow the stock until it reaches your exit point, and then get another quote to confirm the exit price. Follow a practice trade all the way though to see if you lost or made money. You are practicing in order to learn from your mistakes.

In order for practice trading to be effective, you must treat each transaction as if it was made with real money. You need to give it the same energy, importance and attention. If you do lackluster practice trades, you will not really be sure of the results. When Bryce came out of his room with that pile of pretend money, I got a clear picture of how practice trading should be approached.

Using Practice Money

Years ago I heard a phrase "Practice makes perfect." Then Miles said a very wise person taught him, "Perfect practice makes perfect." If you practice something wrong, you will not do any better when you try the real thing. To assure your success, you need to practice until you get consistently successful results. Then, and only then, should you attempt the real thing.

The stock market presents a model opportunity for investors to practice before acting. It is simple to get price quotes and to track the progress of specific stocks or sectors. You will be able to test a concept before you ever try it with real cash.

Step By Step Rules For Practice Trades

Here are the steps to be sure that your practice trades are effective:

1. Determine how much money will be allocated to the trade.
2. Contact the broker and get a quote.
3. Make a purchase decision.
4. Confirm with the broker that the price target was reached.
5. Record the transaction in a logbook.
6. Set a GTC and stop-loss.

7. Follow the stock until the exit point is reached.
8. Close the transaction by getting a quote from the broker. Record the results.
9. See how you did, and learn from it for future plays.

Practice Trading That Hurts

I have seen many people practice trade and claim fantastic success. Then when they start using real money their success ratio drops and they lose cash—lots of it! For some reason when they do paper trades they can't lose, but when they convert the action to the real thing they can't win. What are they doing differently? Maybe nothing. Maybe that's the problem. Maybe they are suffering from one of the "Top Five Loser Habits."

The Top Five Loser Habits

1. No Pressure. As they follow the paper trade they do not feel any emotional pressure because it's "just pretend." There is nothing really at stake.
2. No Accountability. They throw out the silly trades saying, "I didn't really mean to do that one." It's like cheating at solitaire; since there is no accountability it's easy to look under cards and give yourself an extra turn. If you do that with practice trades, you are setting yourself up for massive failure when you do a real trade.

   Anyone can have success if they only count the winners. If you want your practice trades to be useful you must track every decision and account for them. Learn from the losers. They can be your best teachers.
3. No budget. I find that when people paper trade they don't have any budget concerns, so they make unrealistic paper purchases. It's easy to practice trade five million dollars, but if you only have $5,000 of real money, stay in that price range. Things have a totally different appearance when you have to live within your means—no "credit cards" here.
4. No real time. Some people do day trades, using a 20-minute tape delay, but they are responding to news, pagers and other real time events. If you are paper trading short-term trades (under 72 hours) you have to use real

time quotes. They are free on the Internet and with full service brokers. Even if you have to pay your broker $50 for a few months of quotes, it's a better deal than losing your $5,000!

To locate free quotes on the Internet, use the search function in your browser. Look under "Free real time quotes." There are plenty to choose from.

5. No consistency. Some people will paper trade all kinds of different formulas and strategies. Practice trades must be disciplined and focused. Keep the different formulas and trading strategies separate and account for each one separately to track your degree of mastery.

Professionals know that the amount of money you can make during the next 60 days is insignificant compared to what you can earn for the next year. Take the time to correctly learn these techniques.

Go back to number three for a moment. I want to stress proper budgeting again because it's the most common mistake in practice trading. If you are going to be working with $10,000 then you need to paper trade using $10,000 in pretend money. If you will be using $100,000, then do the same on paper. If you also want to trade larger portfolios on paper, go ahead, but it's important to keep the two records separate. My experience is that when you set a limitation on how much money can be used, you start to get a much clearer picture of what the formulas and techniques really require for success.

In review, some of the most important aspects of practice trading are:

- Budget—Use a specified amount of money.
- Track—Keep a record of all trades.
- Account—Be accountable for all decisions.

There is an excellent book that teaches you how to papertrade by David Hebert titled "On Track Investing, A Guide To Simulation Trading." *Go buy it today!*

When you are ready to dive into the market, please use the same habits that you did while doing the practice trades. What I find is people can do great when they practice, but when real money is involved, they handle things much differently because of the emotion they feel when using real money. If you know someone else that is doing practice trades, swap notes, learn together, and account to each other. This can keep both of you more realistic.

Once you have success on paper then transferring that success to real trading depends on your ability to keep emotions out of your decisions. After all, practice trader and real trader are essentially the same thing; the paper just looks different.

When To Do The Real Thing

How do you know when you are ready to start investing for real? I suggest that you practice for 60 days or a minimum of 15 successful trades for each specific technique that you are practicing. When you have 10 consecutive profitable trades, you are getting warm. If you have nine profitable trades and one loser, keep trying.

Even after getting to the point of doing the real thing, keep practice trading. I still do practice trades each day. I do five or more real and practice trades every day. Think about it—do you think Michael Jordan, the world's best basketball player, ever practiced? You bet! Probably more than anyone else. He was the best because he kept practicing, even when he was on top!

Laws And Rules of Engagement

When you enter the Wall Street battlefield, be ready. Like all combats, there are laws and rules of engagement.

The Law of Abundance

Miles and I once attended a personal development course facilitated by Brian Klemmer. He reminded us that there is a never-ending supply of resources. Every day tons of minerals fall from the sky. The earth is constantly being showered with enough radiation and heat to power every home in the planet for a year, and every day more minerals and energy flow to mother earth.

Yes, I know that there are plenty of scientists claiming that the world population is using up everything and we are all going to starve if we don't stop our ever increasing consumption of ______ (fill in the blank). But people will adapt.They always have.

Please do not get sidetracked in a philosophical debate about this last statement.The point I am making is that there are thousands of companies in the stock market. Every day some of them go up in value, even when the market takes major dips. You will always be presented with opportunities to earn money. You don't have to panic and try to milk every penny out of every deal. All you need to do is make a profit on your trades and over time you will have everything you want. If you get into a deal late or exit too soon, it's okay. There will be another deal tomorrow.

The Batman Syndrome

Human nature is a curious thing. People do a few good trades and they feel invincible, like Batman. Then they start cutting corners.They become less selective in trades, drop a few steps, accept greater risks. Then, heaven forbid, they decide to venture out into uncharted territory and try new/untested techniques and formulas. After a few months, they start seeing their good trades get thinner and their bad trades get fatter. Eventually they can't seem to pick a good stock even if their life depended on it. What has happened? Human nature is what happened.

When I am teaching a Wall Street Workshop™ I get to see the full range of experiences. (See the Appendix for a list of stock market classes taught by Darlene Nelson.) I've had many students come up to me on a break and tell me, "At first I had great success, then something happened and I started losing money. What do you think I should do?" I tell them that they need to go back to the basics and start over. If they had success, they will be able to have it again. I find that going back to the original formulas after each trade allows me to examine my success and make sure that I am staying on track.

If you want to feel like Batman, you need to earn enough money so that you can hire a special effects team to help you. Until then, keep the cape in the closet.

It's OKAY To Walk Away

This may seem like a silly statement, but I'll say it anyway—it's OKAY to walk away. That means you do not have to invest anything this time, today, or even this week. That is a difficult concept for people who are accustomed to putting money in a savings account. When I started investing in the stock market, I had the misconception that I had to have my money invested at all times. I knew that the local bank would only pay me interest when my money was placed in an interest bearing account.

With this background, I had the urgent desire to keep my money working at all times. I thought, "How can I earn money if I don't own anything?" When I closed a transaction, I immediately wanted to jump into another trade. It was hard to sleep at night if my money was just sitting in the brokerage account. I felt like a seven-year-old with birthday cash burning a hole in my pocket; I had to spend it as soon as possible.

With an unstoppable urge to get my money working for me, I would select another trade and jump in with both feet. Then, later that day I would review the plays of the day and my stomach would get a sinking feeling. Why did I do that? That was a stupid play. And that night I would still have trouble sleeping.

The truth is, you do not need to direct your money in order to have it working. It is working anyway! When funds are placed in a brokerage account they are swept into a money market fund and interest is calculated. At the end of the accounting period your statement will include a line that shows how much your brokerage account earned. Of course it isn't a big rate of return, but it beats losing the money on a bad deal.

I actually look for reasons to walk away from a deal! I prefer to pass on good opportunities and keep my money in the bank for great opportunities. Then when screamer deals come across my desk, I can go for it! A few successful trades will accumulate more money than a string of poor trades. If there are no good deals today, I go to bed happy knowing that I'll have more to play with tomorrow. It does not take long to have fantastic returns if you just take your time. I know this sounds like a paradox, but it's true.

Don't get me wrong, I am not suggesting that you look at opportunities and pass them up just because they aren't windfalls. I have plenty of little trades that return $100 here and $500 there. I pass on plays that are questionable. If it does not look like a sure play, I wait for a better one.

How Superheroes Save Money

Every professional trader knows one big secret about stop-losses: use them, or lose those dollars! By setting your pre-determined loss, you are making a choice of how far you will let a stock fall before you get out. Professionals have learned to become non-emotional about stop-losses. Had people used stop-losses in the summer of 1998, they would have had most of their stock holdings sold before the market took a major nosedive. Then they could have gotten back in when the market changed directions. Many people doubled their holdings during the month of October 1998; the profits were fantastic.

When News Breaks—The Deal Is OFF!

As you are playing the stock market game you have to know when to say, "The deal is off!" There is so much to this subject that I should write another book, but I'll share a few situations that are specific to stock split plays.

If news develops, all bets are off. If the news is bad, the play can go bad. How significant is news? Will it affect earnings, change the company, or damage the sector?

If the company releases an earnings warning or a bad financial report—run, don't walk—to change your trade. If another stock in the sector has really bad news it will affect your company too! Keep your eyes open and listen to news that warns investors of problems. If you are climbing the face of a volcano and it starts to smoke, get your asbestos pants on and start running. It might be necessary to get out of the deal, wait for things to hit bottom, and then get back in.

There Will Be Another Bus

I was downtown waiting for a bus. I stepped away from the stop for a moment and when I turned around, I saw the diesel blowing behind my bus! In a panic I was ready to run in hopes of catching it at the next stop. Then I heard someone say, "Don't worry sweetie, there will be another bus coming soon."

The same goes for the stock market; there is always another fantastic play waiting to be discovered. I have learned that what looks like the opportunity of a lifetime today is just another deal tomorrow. Don't get suckered into thinking that you have to catch an event because you don't want to miss out. There will always be more.

Professionals Check Their Sources

Professionals always check their sources before a single penny is invested. They want to make sure that the resource is accurate and reliable. If someone gives you a tip, ask where it came from. Ask yourself, "Does it fit my investment program? Is it worth the risk?"

When a professional investor learns a new formula or skill, they confirm first and act second. They know that acting without confirmation is a surefire way to lose money. Rumors are free, and you get what you pay for. If the rumor is reported on the news wire it could be worth a dollar. If the rumor is from the shoe shine gal at the airport, she might have just shined the CEO's shoes or she might not have. If it comes from the guy at the deli counter, someone could be taking you to lunch!

Be especially careful when gathering information from the Internet. Only use reliable sources, because there is a 99.99% potential for deception. Chat rooms are particularly suspect since there is no accountability.

Unfortunately, it is common for people to use the Internet to disseminate incorrect information for personal gain. It's actually pretty easy to buy a stock that has limited float, start a rumor, and sell when others are buying. Of course you would have to look behind your back for the SEC's fraud division.

The Law Of Compound Earnings

What happens if you wait 60 days before you start using the techniques in this book? What happens if it takes you six months of practice before you risk your hard-earned money? Will you really miss something important?

If you assume that you can already earn 12% a year in your accounts, that's 1% a month. What happens if you do practice trades and are able to improve your performance to 20% a year, 1.67% a month? Or, after a little more practice you start earning 5% to 20% a month? Look at the chart, the difference in earnings is fantastic. After a few months, the higher rates of return shoot off the chart. What happens if you wait a few months? You will probably do better, because you are likely to have fewer losses, better returns and more success. Take the time to practice—you will increase your profits!

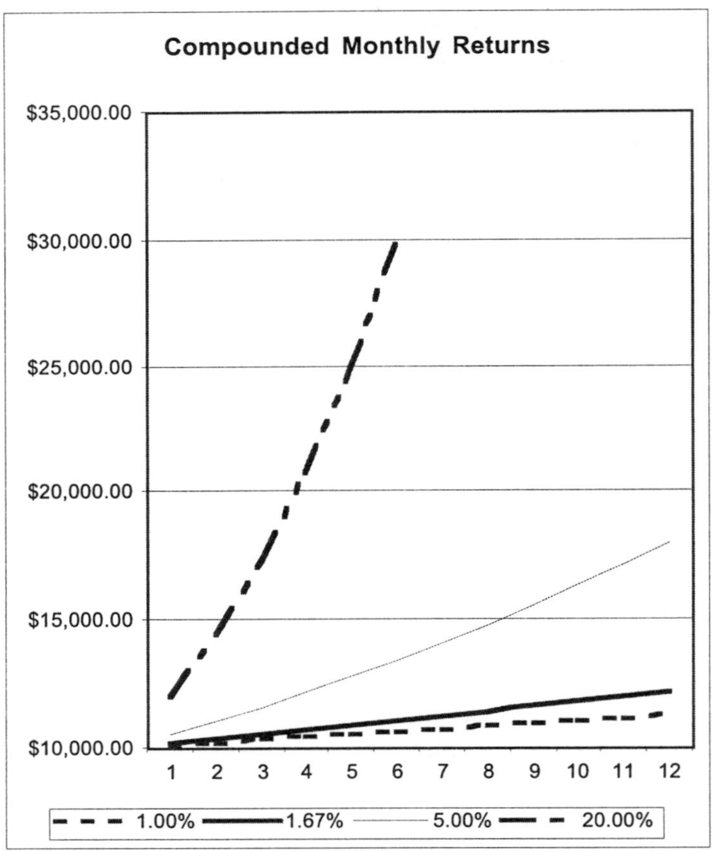

No Emotions In Decisions

When people get too caught up in daily news and the fluctuations in stock prices, they can become emotional and lose their ability to make wise decisions. The story that follows reads like a joke, but it is ice cold reality! Plenty of people are sucked into the emotion of the market and soon find themselves lying broken on the floor.

This is a typical series of conversations and actions that occur in many homes around the country. Sam and Suzy Saver have an account at Harrison Hot Springs Brokers, and they make investment choices during dinner.

Sam says to his wife, "Honey, it looks like IBM is almost at an all-time high. Everyone says that it is going to back off a little, but if we can hang on for another day we might make a few more dollars. I know that we should sell now, but I really want to get our account up to $20,000 by the end of the year." The next morning the stock starts to move up and Sam says to himself, "I was right, it's moving up higher than I expected—maybe it will go up even further." During his lunch break he calls his broker and buys another 50 shares.

That night Suzy says, "You sold our 45 shares of IBM today right? It hit the price we thought it would."

Sam responds, "Not yet I think it will go up even more, so at lunch time I called the broker and got another 50 shares." Suzy looks upset and hands Sam the evening paper. To Sam's horror, IBM fell $5 in the last 10 minutes of the market. The next morning, Sam calls his broker. IBM was already another $4 lower than when the market opened. He yells, "Sell! Sell all of the IBM that we have... please." The broker repeats the order and hits the send button. Within 10 minutes of market open, Sam has sold his 95 shares of IBM at the low of the day. That night Sam is devastated to discover that IBM bottomed out five minutes after he sold, and climbed for the rest of the day and by market close, had hit an all-time high.

The next morning Sam calls his broker and makes a purchase of 95 shares of IBM. The broker says, "Sam, they are at an all-time high and volume is thin, are you sure you want to do this?" Sam is still stinging from the memory of selling his shares of IBM too soon. All he can think about is the money that he could have earned, had he held on just one more day. He tells the broker to get the shares as soon as possible. The broker enters an order to purchase 95 shares of IBM at the market price. A few minutes later Sam has his 95 shares of IBM back, at the highest price of the day.

That night Sam reads the evening news. Shortly after market close, five different brokerage firms released news of IBM being downgraded. The next morning Sam watches the morning financial news and IBM has been falling all night in after-hours trading. The lady on the TV says, "IBM is expected to open down at least six dollars." Sam calls his broker again, he screams into the phone, "Sell the IBM, fast!" A few minutes later the market opens, Sam's order is the first one filled. He sells his stock at the lowest price of the day.

This story may seem like an overstatement, but I know too many people that have made investment choices in a manner very similar to Sam and Suzy. People are constantly allowing emotion, fear and greed to control their investment success.

Many analogies can be gleaned from this story. The most important are:

- Don't let greed make your investment decisions.
- Don't let the fear of loss make your choices.
- Don't get in if the stock is at a high, on thinning volume.
- Make your buy and sell decisions when you can think clearly.
- Don't use market orders—use limit orders.
- Avoid buying during the first 30 minutes or last 15 minutes of the day.

The last item can be debated. Some people claim that the opening price is set by emotional investors, and closing prices are determined by seasoned traders. In many cases, the opening price is the high or low of the day. If you want to sell, you might find the best price by selling at market open if the stock is opening high.

Only Captains Go Down With The Ship

When the Titanic was floundering, its captain issued the famous words, "Women and children first." Among all of the sad things that happened on the Titanic, the worst was an ongoing sense of denial. People refused to believe that the ship was sinking, they refused to believe that help was too far away, and they refused to believe that their half-full lifeboats could help those other victims in the freezing waters. How does the story of the Titanic relate to investing? Look at its lessons.

I have watched people get into a trade, realize that they've made a mistake, and go into immediate denial. They get depressed, yes, but decide to stay in the deal, hoping that divine providence will shine down on them and rescue their money. Say an option position started out costing $3,500. When they realize their error, the investment is worth $2,500. A few days later it's worth $1,100. There is a surge in interest and the investment moves up to $1,600. Over the next few days it falls back into a new trading range below $1,000. A few weeks are left before options expire and the contract value drops to $850, $750, $725, $675, $650. Life comes back and the options jump up to $850, $900, $1,000. Then it falls prey to the support and resistance lines and drops to $600. The last week things get really depressing: $500, $400, $300, $250, $200, $150, $100, $50, $0.

If you make a mistake, fix it or get out. Rotten deals only get worse. For every miracle there are 19 dead ends. Looking at the above example, the poor captain of the $3,500 investment Titanic could have gotten out with $2,500, or at the $1,600 surge, or any of the other surges. If you realize you made an error, you might need to adjust your thinking and look for the best opportunity to make a graceful exit. Don't go down with the ship!

Explanations And Terminology

Bulls and Bears. The terms Bulls and Bears are used to describe the battle waged every day in the market.The Bulls expect stock prices to go higher and Bears expect prices to go lower. If a stock closes lower than the day before people say the Bears won the battle. Conversely, if a stock closes higher than the prior day the Bulls claim victory.

Bear Market. A "bear market" occurs when those who expect prices to fall (bears) are more numerous than those who expect prices to rise (bulls).When either expectation is strong enough and has enough followers, it creates a self-fulfilling prophecy.

13

Bonus Plays And Tools

As you are playing the five stock split phases, there may be other opportunities to generate cash-flow. That's right, there are more ways to profit from stock splits. I've covered the five major stock split plays and now I'll introduce you to some minor plays.

These are techniques that I wish someone had made clear when I first started playing the market.

Buy On Rumor, Sell Before Fact

"Buy on rumor and sell before fact" describes a technique that takes advantage of rumors and predicted future events. Of course there is a common term in the industry called "buy on rumor sell on fact," but I think that saying gets people in trouble because they end up selling too late. Read on and I'll explain what I mean.

A stock may climb in value three to ten days before a rumored or potential event. Because of rumor, excited investors want to strengthen their position. As they seek to obtain additional interest, there are more buyers than sellers, creating high demand and increased prices. As the event gets closer, the pressure increases and so does the stock price.

When the event actually happens, rumor is replaced by facts. At that moment many investors are happy with their profits and decide to lighten their holdings. As the facts are understood, the high expectations of investors run into the reality of cold hard numbers. In many cases it's like cold water on a hot face—a shock. As sellers rush to the market dumping their shares, it creates a surplus of sell orders and not enough buyers, so the stock will drop in value. How far it drops depends on many factors. Observe the pullback by looking at recent resistance and support lines. Each one of these points usually has a handful of buyers with pending orders. When the price drops to a level that has enough willing buyers, the stock stabilizes.

A great way to use the rumor/fact effect is to watch the masses. Once they make a clear indication of their expectations, the stock or market will make a strong move in the expected direction. Acquire a position that will increase in value as the masses get excited. Then, on the eve of the fact, pull the plug on your trade, getting out with a profit. This means that you have missed some of the initial movement and part of the ending movement, but you protected your capital and now have the opportunity to take advantage of other rumors.

Be careful—if there is too much emotion in the market you may not get enough warning when the masses change direction. A stock can be climbing at a terrific rate and seconds later another rumor breaks out and the stock falls so fast there is no way out until it hits support and the dust settles.

How do I mix this concept with stock split plays? Pick your play, either 1, 2, 3, 4, or 5. Each play is based on investors expecting that the stock price is going to increase. You can watch for the price-moving effects of rumor and jump on for the ride. Always be careful to use self-protecting tools like stop-losses and logic.

FYI: The exit point is not a clearly defined moment. In some cases, a stock can fall back early, especially in stocks that have had very fast, large increases.

The Sympathy Play

Although this is not an actual formula, I want to discuss the effect of sympathy on the value of a stock. If a particular stock is moving up in value, other stocks in that business sector or industry group also tend to move in the same direction—up or down. This is called a sympathy move.

It is much like my 6-year-old son, Bryce. A few days ago his older brother Marin was sick. I gave "big brother" lots of attention, special drinks, food in bed, TV all day long, and Marin didn't even have to pick up after himself. The next morning Bryce said, "I don't feel good Mommy. Marin made me sick." Of course Bryce was perfectly healthy, but the benefits of being sick were so good, he had to be sick at any cost.

Investors jump on exciting stocks, pushing the entire industry group up or down in value. If a company declares a stock split, not only will they have a surge in attention, but many other companies in the same industry will get a "bounce" out of the announcement. This is particularly true when one of the top three companies in a group releases news; it can create a tidal wave that sucks the other companies in the same direction.

Sympathy moves are particularly powerful when tracking stock split announcements. When split announcements are made, watch the other companies in the sector. Within a short time you will usually see some of the other companies declaring stock splits. It almost becomes "last one in the pool is a rotten egg."

Again, although this is not a formula, it is information you can use to make a profit, either by riding sympathy moves or using it to identify potential companies for Phase 1, "before the announcement" plays.

The Earnings Game

When it comes time for a company to report earnings, be wary. If the investment community thinks that the company is going to have better than projected earnings, the stock will move up as the earnings date gets closer. If the stock is expected to perform poorly, the price will fall as the earnings report date nears.

This play is very simple; look at what the masses expect and take advantage of their emotions. As you get closer to the earnings date, be ready to pull the plug if the stock moves in the wrong direction. This is a perfect time to use tight stop-loss settings.

Holding positions through an earnings announcement is very dangerous. The saying "Buy on rumor and sell before fact" plays out rapidly in the stock market. Before an earnings announcement there might be a run-up in stock values, but when the announcement happens, the rumor ends and cold hard facts calm the fire.

Even an unbelievable earnings announcement can still be a disaster. I can think of 10 companies, big ones, that had great earnings announcements and their stock went down the next day anyway! In spite of great earnings, a company can miss the street "whisper" number or some analyst's projection of what the company might report. To see the street numbers, whisper numbers and other estimates, go to the Internet. There are many different sources with this information. (I love www.briefing.com.)

Be careful of "sympathy" influence. Watch the big three companies in the sector or industry; when they release earnings, all companies in that group could be affected by the news. Of course, if you have an extra long-term position, say ten years or more, you might not care about the ups and downs caused by earnings announcements.

To recap, playing the pre-earnings run-up can be a wonderful way to generate profits. Play the event like it is a Stock Split Play #1, make sure that your stop-loss controls are in place, and get out before the actual announcement. One other caution: some companies get done with their reports early and they are impatient, so they announce a day early. It's rare, but be prepared.

If a stock split is expected to be announced at the same time as earnings, take advantage of the run-up, but escape before the event!

FYI: Whisper numbers are the "rumored" figures that the "street" is expecting a company to announce, a number usually higher than analyst expectations. A company may meet the earnings expectation and still miss the "whisper" amount.

The Date Of Record Or Recording Date

When it comes to dividends, the recording date is critical because the holder of the stock on that date will receive the dividend. However, if the dividend is stock, the only date of concern is the split date; you have to hold a position before the actual split in order to benefit. The owner of the stock or option benefits from the stock split on the date that the split actually occurs. Many investors are confused about the date of record. To be safe, they buy the stock three or four days before the recording event. That way they can assure participation in the split.

However, here is a way to earn a little more money. Although there is no legal or logical reason to be concerned about the date of record in a stock split event, traders can use it to make money. If you look at the charts of many stock splits, there is a mini run-up in stock prices during the four to five day period before the date of record. There is usually a small selling time for one to three days after the date of record. You can play this run-up and the fall back. It's almost like free money, because it happens a lot! After this non-event, you can get back in when the pullback is over.

It's a fun little game that should only be played with in-the-money options, because you need a high delta to have the play be profitable. I am talking about only a one to five dollar movement in the stock price. If there is only $1 in stock movement, you could end up with 25¢ to 50¢ in option movement. With enough contracts or a high enough delta, that modest movement could spell c-a-s-h. Practice this perfectly first!

Play this like Phase 4, the split-date play (a short-term play).

Let me to tell you a little more about the date of record as it applies to stock split companies. This date is actually an internal event at the company that has little or no effect on the shareholders. The Date of Record, or Recording Date, is the day when the accountant makes a list of the shareholders, so that the stock split can be made. If I were to sell my shares the day after the date of record it will have no benefit or disadvantage to me as a shareholder. Of course, you will usually see a dip in share prices on the day after the Date of Record or Recording Date.

Play The Shareholder Meeting

If the company is having a shareholder meeting that includes a request to approve an increase in the number of authorized shares, there is almost always a run-up before the meeting. Play this like Stock Split Phase 4. Shareholders almost always approve the increase in the number of authorized shares, so this can feel almost like free money. This play works even if a stock split has already been announced!

Self Preservation Tools

There are a few points that I need to go over to assure that I have covered all of the bases.

The Earnings Trap

I repeat, holding a position through an earnings announcement is a dangerous play. It's a win-lose-lose opportunity. In other words, you are far more likely to lose than win. Prior to an earnings announcement, a stock can experience a sharp increase in value. When the earnings numbers are released, reality sets in and investors usually sell. This can cause a sharp decrease in the value of a stock. I have found that holding a position through an earnings announcement is worse than risky; it's almost a guaranteed disaster.

If you absolutely have to go through the earnings announcement, be safe and have a long-term position so you can ride out a dip. If the current option has less than four months left, roll out to a longer-term option. Otherwise, get out of the deal entirely. Why not pull out of your position, wait for a dip, and get back in at a nice discount?

Gumpism: "My Momma always said, 'you gotta take your lumps before they stick in your throat and choke you.'" Meaning: if a play has gone bad, take your lumps (losses) early, before they get worse.

The Announcement With Earnings Gamble

What if the company is strong and they are expected to make a stock split announcement with the earnings? Chances are the stock has already increased in anticipation of the event. The earnings report and any stock split announcement will only be a confirmation of the price run-up. There is rarely a continued run after the announcement unless there is a market uptrend, investors are buying regardless of price, and your company comes out with a big, positive earnings surprise.

I have seen that 80% of stocks take a dive after they announce earnings, 15% stay unchanged, and 5% have a short-lived rocket ride. Why play when you have a one in 20 chance of winning? To make the law of averages work for you, the winning trades will have to produce $20 and the losing trades cost you only $1. Look at the market, the stocks you play and reality. Do you really think that an earnings announcement is going to result in a $20 jump in your stock? As far as I'm concerned, it's not worth the risk.

Roll Out/Roll Up For Profits

To "rollup" means to keep the same expiration date, but exchange your current options for ones with higher strike prices. For example, if you have options with a $75 strike price, you might roll up to an $80 or $85 strike price.

As the event draws near, look at the option. Is it two or more strike prices in the money? You can lighten your risk by making a quick change in your position. Do this by purchasing another option that is at the money or slightly in the money with the same expiration date. Right after getting the less expensive options, sell your original options, keeping the net profits from the difference in the option prices.

Rollup Example

Strike (Same Month)	Value	Action
$75	*$7 1/2*	*Sell*
$80	*$3 3/4*	*Buy*

The stock is at $81 1/2

Look at this example of moving from a $75 strike price to a $80 strike price. The stock is currently at $81 1/2. The $75 options might be worth $7 1/2 and the $80s could have a value of $3 3/4. When you roll up, you keep the difference between $7 1/2 and $3 3/4, which is $3.75 times the number of contracts, less commissions.

It's important to avoid the temptation of letting both ride (the $80 strike and $75 strike) because that is usually greed talking. If you want to double your investment that's fine, but if you want to roll up, stick to the plan.

To "rollout" means keeping the option strike price the same, but moving the contract term out one or more months. Buy options that have the same strike price, but a longer life, and sell the original options. This transaction costs money because the options you are purchasing have more time value, which makes the premium higher.

This technique works great when you want to stay in a deal for another month or two because either the stock is performing well, or it has not moved as far as you need. By rolling out, you are increasing the total investment, and it is only wise if you have a strong assurance that the stock will perform as expected. This type of play is common while you are in Phase 5 and you are riding the stock to higher levels. Or when you are in a Phase 1 run-up and the anticipated announcement date has changed.

Rollout Example

Month (Same Strike)	Value	Action
September 70c	*$3 3/4*	*Sell*
October 70c	*$7 1/2*	*Buy*

The stock is at $71 1/2

Be cautious if you are tempted to roll out simply to delay the acknowledgement that the play has failed to perform. If bad news has crushed the value of the stock, or other events have made the play a rotten deal, it's almost always better to take the loss and move on rather than allow the bleeding to continue.

Choose One Or Two Formulas For Success

I have presented five major and five minor formulas for profiting from stock splits. If I were starting out today, I would choose one formula and master it. Then I would add a second. I have found that most highly successful investors focus their energy on only one or two formulas. They study, practice, apply, study, practice, apply, et cetera. When I was starting, I don't think I could have effectively handled more than two techniques, even if I worked 10 hours a day.

Pick a winner: study, practice, apply, study. Follow those four steps and you will be able to pick winners over and over and over if, and only if, you select one or two formulas to master as a starting point.

In addition to choosing just one or two formulas, top investors go a step further and get to know a small group of companies that they use repeatedly for profits. Using options and the other techniques in this book, you can pick a few of your favorite companies and milk them all the way to the bank.

There is no reason to divide your energies by trying to take on the entire investment world at the same time. The most successful investors know how to control excitement and they stay within the limits of their chosen trading style. My suggestion is that you select one or two of these formulas and focus your energy. By learning one or two techniques, you should never run out of opportunities or profit potential. I have spoken to three highly successful stock market investors this month who are only playing one stock split phase—all are doing extremely well.

How to milk the market: pick a few strong companies. Get to know their heartbeat. Learn what makes them tick. What events cause stock changes? Who controls what, when, and how? After a few months you will be able to milk that company stock over and over again for wonderful profits.

Let's face it, when you look at the stocks of over 28,000 public companies in the U.S., plus another 20,000 stocks from worldwide corporations, you will never run out of profit opportunities. Successful investors learn to look for specific investment indicators. They know, often from hard experience that if they divide their energy they will get overwhelmed and lose. Of course, experienced investors have a big bag of tricks, but they select from that repertoire a few techniques or formulas for their investment focus. I love to play stock splits. More than 90% of my trades are based on stock splits. I don't have time to waste, so I concentrate on plays that fit my lifestyle and leave the other plays to someone else.

Applying Knowledge

Knowledge is money, but only if you apply it correctly!

Keep A Record

I find that keeping a clear record of my trades gives me a tool to learn from my mistakes and successes. In that record I track the purchases and sales, but I also record other important pieces of information. I note news events, stock prices, and things that have an effect on the market. I keep copies of options chains, daily charts, important quotes, company filings, et cetera.

I do not spend hours writing a journal; I use my computer and a cardboard box. If I see an important news event, I cut it out of the newspaper or magazine and throw it in the box. If I see something on the Internet, I just send myself an e-mail message with the news article attached. I may sound like a pack rat, but it doesn't have to create a mess.

The power of information is that history tends to repeat itself. When I come up on changes in the market, I can look back at similar times and see how the market was reacting.

Sell Options—Time Is On Your Side

To put it bluntly, it is almost always better to open a position by selling an option than it is to purchase an option. I have not discussed selling calls or selling puts as a trading method. However, some readers already know how to sell calls and puts (naked or covered).

When you purchase an option, time works against you and the stock must move quickly in the right direction if you are going to profit before the option expires. Purchasing an option (put or call) only provides a one in three chance of success. By selling a put or call, time is on your side because the stock can stay flat and you still get to keep the money. That makes for a two in three chance of profit.

The reason I am bringing up selling puts and calls is to introduce the idea that there are advanced techniques available that can enhance the concepts and formulas presented in this book. Purchasing calls is only the beginning—there is so much more! There is magic in using LEAPS for long-term accumulation. Selling puts can capture tremendous returns, and spreads are wonderful.

If you already have a firm grasp on these investment methods, you will probably see how to apply them to stock splits.

I wish there was more time and space to cover these concepts, but I guess I'll have to write another book or a few special reports. I have written a special report that will show you how to profit from LEAPS. It's called "Poolside Investing with LEAPS" (look in the Appendix).

What's Safer—Buying Stock Or Options?

Some people get very concerned when the words "safety" and "stock option" are used in the same paragraph. I could get in real trouble with this concept if I were selling you an investment, but I am not selling anything other than education. You are the person who makes the decisions and you control your risk!

If you purchase a stock for $150 and an option for $25, which has less risk? If the stock goes into the toilet, losing $110 in value, your option can become worthless, but the stock never expires, so hope lives on. However, knowing that the option has a limited life, people tend to sell sooner and act faster. This means the money can be put back into service, earning profits in another deal while the stock sits in the freezer waiting for a miracle. Which is safer? Neither! Both can be a blessing or a nightmare.

Consider this. You purchase an option for $25, leaving $125 that can be put into other deals. If you are concerned about the options loss of value, spend a little more money and get a six-month, nine-month, or even a twelve-month option. Look at the stock—if it is in a general uptrend, it should continue in that direction. If your option lasts long enough, your risk is minimal. However, if the stock should suffer a reversal and head into a long-term downtrend, you can be happy when the stock hits $40 and you only lose your $25 option premium. You can thank providence that you kept most of your money for other plays.

Don't Forget To Cancel Old Orders

If you are using discount, deep discount and Internet brokers you need to cancel old orders before you enter new ones. If you have a pending order on a stock or option it must be canceled before another order can be entered. For example, say you own an option worth $20 and you have a $15 stop-loss. You get up in the morning and discover that the option has zoomed to $27. You call the Broker and say, "Sell my option for $27 please." With pride and satisfaction you hang up the phone having locked in a $7 profit.

But wait! If the stop-loss order is not canceled, you could end up with some challenges.

- First, your $27 sell order could be canceled, because another order is still pending.
- Second, you could get filled at $27, and if the option falls below $15 your original stop-loss could trigger and you sell the same options a second time! If you get filled twice, you will now have sold options for $27 and $15. That means you have sold an uncovered or "naked" position for $15. If the stock starts climbing you are at risk!

  If you have a stop-loss or GTC order, remind the broker that you need to cancel the old order before the new order is entered. If you use deep discount or an Internet brokerage, you need to remember to cancel those orders. If you need to find a new stockbroker, see my special report in the Appendix called "Finding a Great Stock Broker."

Swimming Lessons

This last story will let me end this book in style! I hope it stays in your memory forever. It can be a resource to help protect your assets and assure your success.

When Miles was about five years old he wanted to learn how to swim. His mom called the local pool and found out about lessons. They went to register and Miles was ready to jump into the pool that moment. His mom had to grab him to keep him from running right into the deep end with shoes, shirt, pants, coat and all.

They struggled a bit until Miles calmed down enough to hear his mom talk. To his dismay, he learned that the lessons didn't even start until the following week. Waiting was miserable for both Miles and his mother. He thought about those lessons every waking moment. He wanted to practice as much as possible, so he could show his teacher that he was going to be a good swimmer. He begged his mom to let him take a bath three or four times a day. Finally she taught him how to run the bath himself, so she could get things done around the house.

The first day of lessons arrived. Miles got his swimsuit on while he was still home. He darted to the car and ran in place trying to make time move faster. When they got to the pool his mom had to grab him again, and restrain him from running to the water. They made their way to the pool. When in the pool area Miles wanted to head for the deep end because all of the big kids were there. "Little kids go to the shallow end, Miles," his mom said.

Even the teacher wouldn't let him into the water right away; the kids had to practice on deck first! Agony, pain and tears—Miles thought he'd never get to swim. Finally after what seemed like months (it was only two minutes), the boys and girls were ushered to the edge of the pool. Miles could not hold back any longer—he ran to the edge and plunged into the water. It was too deep and he was too skinny; he immediately sank to the bottom of the pool like a wet boot!

The teacher pulled Miles off the bottom and put him on the deck. Funny thing is, even as he was choking and gagging, Miles wanted to get back in. The other kids watched the entire thing and were scared stiff—they wouldn't get near the pool.

After that first lesson was over, Miles's mother had a heart-to-heart talk with him. She explained that he would become a great swimmer if he would listen to his teachers and take the classes. He would learn better and get to the deep end faster if he was willing to practice what he learned and was patient. Miles did what his mom said and he became a wonderful swimmer. He entered competitions, became a professional instructor, was a lifeguard, and even managed his own swimming school for a few years. He got to the deep end and more, by taking the classes, step by step, and practicing what he learned.

The Deep End

Many adults act the same way about investing. They are ready to head into the deep end before they learn how to float. Unfortunately, most are on their own in the stock market and many drown before they get any help. The stock market is not forgiving or patient—either you know what you are doing or you lose your money. Period.

I promise you that the people who have the greatest success applying the principals in this book are those who take the time to practice before they ever get near the water. At first these formulas may seem simple, because they are, but then people discover that there are hidden nuances, which can only be learned with practice and experience.

It's okay to say no today–there will be another chance of a lifetime tomorrow!

Let me tell you what will likely happen. As you start practice trading it will get hard to keep practicing, because some trades will work well, and you could say to yourself, "This stock is too good an opportunity. Something like this only comes once in a lifetime. I have got to do this trade with real money." Don't get sucked in and drown in a sea of red. Take the time to go to the shallow end and start out slow. Practice trading first. It's okay to say no—there will be another chance of a lifetime tomorrow!

Experience Is A Great Teacher

If you want a good education you can get it by attending the school of hard knocks or by learning from someone else's mistakes. Education is expensive, but don't put it off; you will pay for it either way. I know many very successful investors who continue to improve their skills, constantly taking classes and seminars, reading books and magazines, doing everything they can to improve their knowledge. Knowledge, in this case, can be translated into cash. Experience is a great teacher, especially if it is someone else's experience!

In closing, I'd like to share a quote:

> ***"Unlike the Lord, the market does not FORGIVE those who do not know what they do."***

It is rumored to have come from Warren Buffett, one of the savviest investors in the world.

As you use the information in this book, both Miles and I wish you success, huge profits and fun playing stock splits. We hope that you will choose to take a small percentage of your profits and use the money to benefit a good cause or organization.

Best wishes,
Darlene and Miles Nelson

Explanations And Terminology

Lighten A Position. To lighten a position means to sell shares or reduce the investment.

Strengthen A Position. Strengthen a position means to purchase additional shares, investing more money.

Appendix

Supplemental Information

Throughout this book I have talked about various stock price charts and information resources that I use when making decisions about my investments. To help you in your research, I have listed these items in the next few pages, along with instructions on how I like to use and interpret them.

Key Components

The following is a listing of some of the key stock component lists, or indices. These lists are continually referred to by news agencies and market professionals.

- DJ-15—Dow Jones 15 Utility Component Stocks
- DJ-20—Dow Jones 20 Transportation Component Stocks
- DJ-30—Dow Jones 30 Industrial Component Stocks
- S&P 100—Standard and Poor's 100 Component Stocks
- S&P 500—Standard and Poor's 500 Component Stocks
- NASDAQ-100—A listing of the 100 top companies in the NASDAQ

There are other lists, however, I am constantly finding that most of the stock split plays that catch my eye are stocks listed in one or more of the above lists. In fact, when I look at the S&P 500, I usually play the stocks that rank in the top 30%, based on volume.

LEAPS®

LEAPS = Long-term Equity AnticiPation Securities.

LEAPS are just like other options except they have very long expiration periods counted in years. In most cases, you can purchase LEAPS and have time on your side, because you can have an extremely long time for the stock to perform as you expect before the option expires.

Look at a ten-year chart for the stock you like. What has been the average annual movement? Has the stock been in a general uptrend for that time? I get very excited if I see that the stock has done a two-for-one stock split every one to three years, because that means the stock has doubled in value over that time period. Imagine purchasing a LEAPS option and holding it over that time. The option value will increase, providing the stock continues its upward trend. Talk about fun; you control large amounts of stock for small amounts of cash!

If you want to get information on LEAPS, the CBOE has tons of resource information at www.cboe.com or call 1-800-OPTIONS. Or visit the NASDAQ-AMEX exchange by logging to www.nasdaq-amex.com.

The EDGAR Database

The EDGAR Database is accessed by logging onto the SEC's Internet site at www.sec.gov.

Then simply follow the screens. When I wrote this book, the database was accessed in this manner:

Log to SEC	*"www.sec.gov"*
Select	*"EDGAR Database"*
Select	*"Search the EDGAR Database"*
Select	*"Quick Forms Lookup"*
Choose	*Using "Customized Forms Selection" choose which company and report you are seeking.*

The EDGAR database system is not ticker symbol friendly. When searching, try using the first few characters of the company's name. For example, GTW would be found by entering "Gate," because GTW is the ticker symbol for "Gateway."

This system is free, but it is not fast or the most up-to-date. There are pay services with more features, but they do cost money. You can find the pay services on the Internet.

Stock Price Chart Styles

Each stock price chart style has its own benefits and disadvantages. What follows is an extremely brief tutorial in the different stock price chart styles used.

Line Charts

Line charts are plotted using the closing price for each period or day. These points are connected using a line, so the line represents the closing price, without any indication of the daily trading range (highest and lowest prices). Line charts can be plotted using daily, weekly, monthly prices, et cetera.

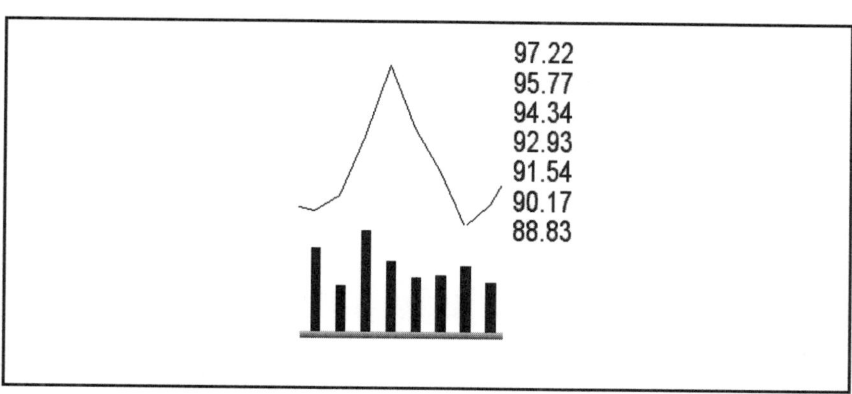

High-Low-Close Charts

This style of chart has a vertical bar that shows the trading range for the day. The top of the line is the highest price, the bottom is the lowest. The closing price is indicated by a small horizontal line pointing to the right. A single bar can represent a single day, an entire week, month, year, et cetera.

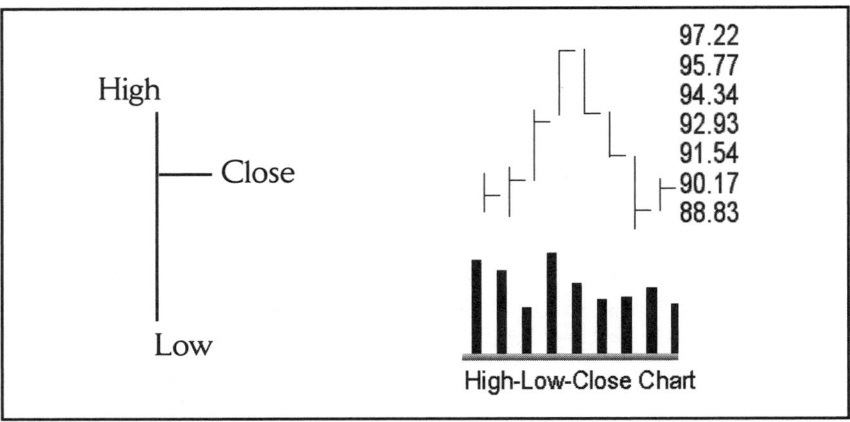

High-Low-Close Chart

Open-High-Low-Close Charts

A vertical bar shows the trading range for the period. The top of the bar is the highest price, the bottom of the bar represents the lowest price. A small horizontal line to the left indicates the opening price and the right hand horizontal line indicates the closing price. Each bar can represent a day, week, month, et cetera.

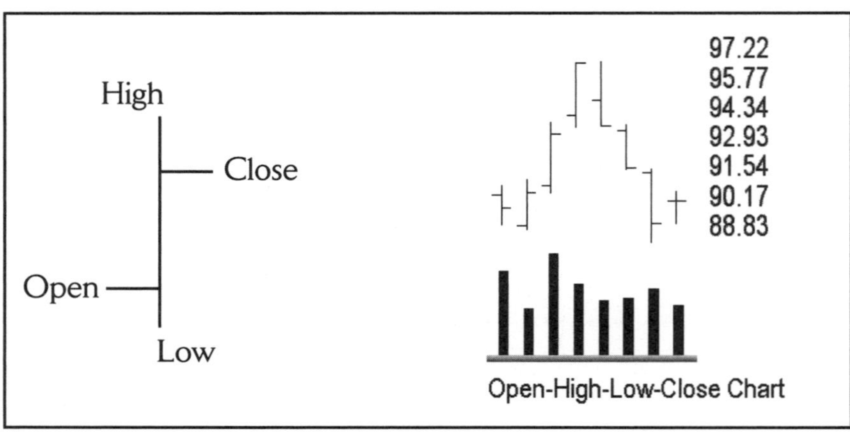

Open-High-Low-Close Chart

Candlestick Charts

Candlestick charts are also called "Japanese Candlesticks" because the charting style originated in Japan. Candlesticks are similar to the open-high-low-close chart. Instead of using lines, a box is used to indicate the trading range. The line above or below the main body of the box it is called a "wick." The wick shows the highest and lowest prices. The box portion of the candlestick shows the opening and closing prices. If the candlestick is open or clear, the bottom of the box is the opening price and the top is the closing price. If the box is filled in or solid, the top part of the box is the opening price and the bottom is the closing price. Each candlestick can represent a day, week, month, et cetera.

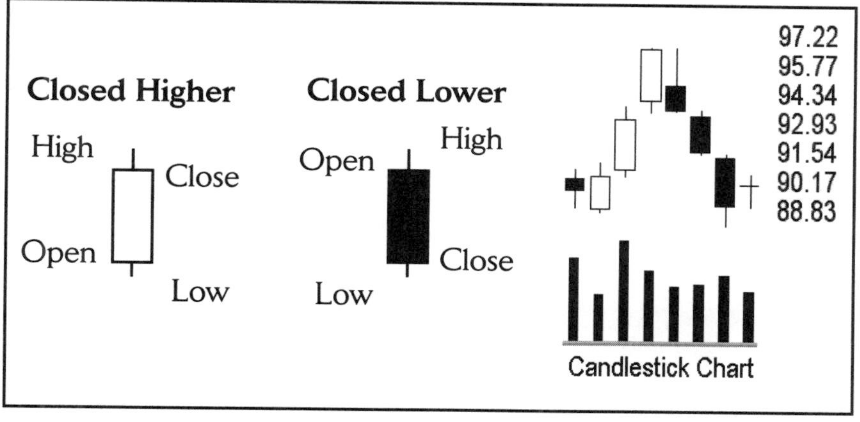

Adjusted and Unadjusted Splits

There are two ways to show stock splits in charts: "unadjusted" and "adjusted." If the chart is unadjusted for splits you will see a big drop on the split. This makes finding splits easy, but it makes all other charting functions a mess. In order for trendlines, support lines, et cetera, to show up correctly, the chart must be adjusted. By adjusting the chart, trendlines appear correctly. When a chart is adjusted in this book, I have added a symbol (⌂) so you can see where the split occurred.

See the following page for examples of adjusted and unadjusted stock split charts.

Adjusted

Unadjusted

Using Research And Information Services

When I'm home, I love to play with my kids, talk to my husband and watch TV. I don't really enjoy looking at stock charts, research notes and a computer screen for hours on end; I don't have the time or the desire. I've found that there is a much faster method of finding the stocks I want to play for my next profit. I use professional research services. They have teams of eggheads whose brainpower can light up a small city and who love to look at technical indicators and financial reports. They read the *Wall Street Journal* in the morning and study 10-Q filings at night. They love to do research and I love to spend time with my family. For me, they're a great deal!

The truth is, there are over 28,000 possible companies to profit by. The most efficient and cheapest way to sort them out is by using high quality information services. By high quality information services, I don't mean then next bigwig CNBC analyst with his buy and sell recommendations, or the stock picker hour with its favorite stocks. What I do is use professional research services for specific research and then I sort out the details and make my own decisions.

It all breaks down to efficiency. I choose the research services that look for specific things. They provide a report that I can scan for companies that meet my requirements. After finding a few dozen companies, I look at the charts, check out the fundamentals, look at news reports, the sector, then I make the final decision.

My Favorite Tools

We are often asked, "How did you learn? Where did you find out about that? How did you figure it out?" All of those questions can be handled by providing one answer: we study the market with a passion. Here is a list of our favorite tools that I use daily:

- I.Q. Pager™ notification service
- A PCS Phone or Cellular Phone
- Internet connection
- Wealth Information Network™ (W.I.N.™)
- Other Online Services
- Real Time Quotes and News Services
- Stock Split Research Service

- SEC Filings—Real Time Research
- The SEC Edgar database
- TC-2000© (Telechart-2000©, by Worden Brothers, Inc.)
- The Value Line Investment Survey

Most of these services cost money. Each service pays for itself with a constant flow of profitable trades. Without them we would have far less time for our family, fewer executed trades and probably far more losses.

Comment about real-time charts–be careful! People can actually lower their success rate when they use real-time charts. By watching the moment-by-moment movements of a stock, people tend to get sucked into the market emotion. Once they are trapped in the ongoing emotions of the market, making good decisions becomes more difficult. I use real-time charts so I can take advantage of the best entrance and exit opportunities. However, I resist sitting in front of the computer all day long–it's too easy for me to lose my perspective.

Free Research And Services

There are also great tools available for free on the Internet, which include quotes, news releases, simple charts and more. There are also tons of free research services and stock picking systems. Just go to any web search engine and they will have stock services boldly displayed. Just keep in mind that you get what you pay for!

Research services can bring fame and fortune to the sellers of the service. However, the consumer can get hurt by stock-of-the-month recommendations. A word of caution, or more strongly, a word of warning. You are virtually guaranteed a loss if you take any research service and purchase the stocks or investments they recommend. I'm not saying their advice is poor; I'm saying that each one of us is personally responsible for our own money. If you let someone else manage your finances, someone who does not care as much about the results as you do, then your risk is greater. Research services are valuable as a source of leads or investment possibilities, but you still need to do the final research and make investment choices based on your own objectives, abilities and needs. Buying is only the first step. The most profitable step is selling.

When it comes to research, "quality" is the word of the day. Price is not always the best indicator, but free is a dead giveaway. Free services are usually supported by the advertisers. The time to become concerned is when the advertisers are the products being promoted in the newsletter or on the website. That's right. Some research services, newsletters and companies are paid directly by the products they are promoting. This presents a scary conflict of interest. Kind of like the lonely husband when his wife asks how she looks. Of course he's going to say, "You look great honey!"

Caution! Warning! Be Careful!

Pay close attention to how the newsletter or information service is supported. If they are inexpensive as compared to other services of the same type, there is something wrong. In addition, if there is no disclosure statement, contact the publisher and ask them if they receive compensation from any of the companies mentioned in their report.

To make my point, the following is an excerpt from a recent news brief filed by SEC.

> "Recently the SEC filed suit against 44 stock promoters in the very first Internet Securities Fraud Sweep. Washington, D.C., October 28, 1998 'Following an unprecedented nationwide sweep, the SEC today announced the filing of 23 actions against 44 individuals and companies across the countries for committing fraud over the internet and deceiving investors around the world.'"
>
> [www.sec.com, Investor Alerts, "Investment Fraud and Abuse Travel to Cyberspace (File name: cyberfr.htm), REVISED October 1998"]

The basis of the lawsuit was that 23 promoters had recommended stocks as great investment opportunities and failed to disclose adequately that they were paid substantial sums, by the investment companies, to promote the investments. In one particular case, a promoter had been paid more than one million dollars to promote a stock! This was a case where the only person who made money on the stock was the person promoting it!

Additional Tools From The Authors

Special Reports

Subject: Stock split education

- The Rules
- The Basics
- The Mini-Play Book
- Upgrading Your Accountant
- Poolside Investing with LEAPS
- How to Find a Great Stock Broker

Education Classes

- Successful Stock Split Secrets—1½ hour class
- Stock Split Secrets—All day class
- Poolside Investing—2 day boot camp

If you want to purchase these products, or attend a class, please call 1-800-872-7411.

We Want To Hear From You

We would love to hear from you. Do you have an experience in the market that others would benefit from? Write us and tell us your story—good or bad, win or lose. We cannot write back, but we may want to use your story in future publications or articles. Please include your full name and contact information. Send your correspondence to:

Stock Split Secrets Stories
c/o Lighthouse Publishing Group, Inc.
14675 Interurban Avenue South
Seattle, WA 98168-4664
Fax: (206) 901-3170
lighthouse@wadecook.com

When we quote stories we usually give first name, last initial, and state of origin of the person doing the submission. If you want us to keep your name confidential, please tell us.

Appendix

Available Resources

The following books, videos, and audiocassettes have been reviewed by the Stock Market Institute of Learning, Inc.™, Lighthouse Publishing Group, Inc., or Gold Leaf Press staff and are suggested as reading and resource material for continuing education in financial planning, and real estate and stock market trading. Because new ideas and techniques come along and laws change, we're always updating our catalog.

To order a copy of our current catalog,
please write or call us at:

Stock Market Institute of Learning, Inc.™
14675 Interurban Avenue South
Seattle, Washington 98168-4664
1-800-872-7411

Or, visit us on our web sites at:
www.wadecook.com
www.lighthousebooks.com

Also, we would love to hear your comments on our products and services, as well as your testimonials on how these products have benefited you. We look forward to hearing from you!

AUDIOCASSETTES/CDS

Zero To Zillions™

Presented by Wade B. Cook

A powerful four-album, 16-cassette audio workshop on Wall Street-understanding the stock market game, playing it successfully, and retiring rich. Learn 11 powerful investment strategies to avoid pitfalls and losses. Learn to catch "day-trippers," how to "bottom fish," write covered calls, and to possibly double your money in one week on options on stock split companies. Wade "Meter Drop" Cook can teach you how he makes fantastic annual returns. Each album comes with a workbook, and the entire workshop includes a free bonus video called "Dynamic Dollars," 90 minutes of instruction on how all the strategies can be integrated, giving actual examples of what kinds of returns are possible so you can play the market successfully. A must for every savvy, would-be investor.

The Financial Fortress Home Study Course

Presented by Wade B. Cook

This eight-part series is the last word in entity structuring. It goes far beyond mere financial planning or estate planning. It helps you structure your business and your affairs so that you can avoid the majority of taxes, retire rich, escape lawsuits, bequeath your assets to your heirs without government interference, and, in short—bomb proof your entire estate. There are six audiocassette seminars on tape, an entity structuring video, and a full kit of documents.

Red Light, Green Light™

Presented by Wade B. Cook

This is the ultimate on making timely trades. As CEO of a publicly traded company, Wade Cook discovered a quarterly pattern of stock price behavior that corresponds with corporate new reports. Since most companies file their reports about the same time, many stocks would move accordingly.

If you're playing options, those price movements—or lack thereof—have a dramatic effect on your returns. The Red Light, Green Light course shows you how to recognize and use this information to make more money and avoid losing trades. This "news/no news" discovery is exhilarating!

BOOKS

Wall Street Money Machine, Volume 1

By Wade B. Cook

A revised and updated version of the New York Times Business Best Seller, ***Wall Street Money Machine, Volume 1*** contains the best strategies for wealth enhancement and cash flow creation you'll find anywhere. Wade Cook describes his favorite strategies for generating cash flow through the stock market: rolling stocks, proxy investing, covered calls, and many more. It's a great introduction for creating wealth using the Wade Cook formulas.

Wall Street Money Machine, Volume 2: Stock Market Miracles

By Wade B. Cook

Finally, a book by an author that understands what the average investor needs: knowing when to sell. The information in this book will give you the ability to make money using real tried-and-true techniques. No special knowledge required, no strings attached. These tools can help you secure real wealth. Thanks to Wade Cook, financial miracles happen every day for thousands of students who are applying what they learned from this book. Buy and read ***Wall Street Money Machine, Volume 2: Stock Market Miracles*** today and see what happens in your life.

Wall Street Money Machine, Volume 3: Bulls & Bears

(formerly titled *Bear Market Baloney*)

By Wade B. Cook

A timelier book wouldn't be possible. Wade's predictions came true while the book was at press! Don't miss this insightful look into what makes bull and bear markets and how to make exponential returns in any market.

Wall Street Money Machine, Volume 4: Safety 1st Investing

By Wade B. Cook

Over two decades of research and experience have culminated in Wade Cook's book, ***Safety 1st Investing***. In it you will learn how to "preserve and grow your asset base as you build an ever-increasing income stream," by utilizing cash flow strategies designed for low risk with good cash flow, including: writing in-the-money calls, bull call spreads, bull put spreads, index plays, and index spreads.

On Track Investing

By David R. Hebert

On Track Investing is the instruction book for novice stock market investors or anyone wanting to practice investment strategies without risking actual cash.The Simutrade™ System helps you originate good trades, perfect your timing, and check your open trades against your personal criteria.There are Simutrade™ Worksheets and step-by-step guides for 10 strategies. ***On Track Investing*** helps you develop a step-by-step map of what exactly you're going to do and how you're going to accomplish it.

Rolling Stocks

By Gregory Witt

Rolling Stocks shows you the simplest and most powerful strategy for profiting from the ups and downs of the stock market.You'll learn how to find rolling stocks, get in smoothly at the right price, and time your exit.You will learn to recognize the patterns of rolling stocks and how to make the most money from these strategies. Apply rolling stocks principles to improve your trading options and fortify your portfolio.

Sleeping Like A Baby

By John C. Hudelson

Perhaps the most predominant reason people don't invest in the stock market is fear. ***Sleeping Like A Baby*** removes the fear from investing and gives you the confidence and knowledge to invest wisely, safely, and profitably. You'll learn how to build a high quality portfolio and plan for your future and let your investments follow. Begin to invest as early as possible, and use proper asset allocation and diversification to reduce risk.

Brilliant Deductions

By Wade B. Cook

Do you want to make the most of the money you earn? Do you want to have solid tax havens and ways to reduce the taxes you pay? This book is for you! Learn how to get rich in spite of the updated tax laws. See new tax credits, year-end maneuvers, and methods for transferring and controlling your entities. Structure yourself and your family for tax savings and liability protection.

The Secret Millionaire Guide To Nevada Corporations

By John V. Childers, Jr.

What does it mean to be a secret millionaire? In ***The Secret Millionaire Guide To Nevada Corporations***, attorney John V. Childers, Jr. outlines exactly how you can use some of the secret, extraordinary business tactics used by many of today's super-wealthy to protect your assets from the ravages of lawsuits and other destroyers using Nevada Corporations. You'll understand why the state of Nevada has become the preferred jurisdiction for those desiring to establish corporations and how to utilize Nevada Corporations for your financial benefit.

Wealth 101

By Wade B. Cook

This incredible book presents 101 strategies for wealth creation and protection that you can't afford to miss. Front to back, it is packed full of tips to supercharge your financial health. If you need to generate more cash flow, this book shows you how through several various avenues. If you are already wealthy, this book will show you strategy upon strategy for minimizing your tax liability and increasing your peace of mind through liability protection.

A+

By Wade B. Cook

A+ is a collection of wisdom, thoughts, and principles of success, which can help you make millions—even billions—of dollars and live an A+ life. If you want to live a successful life, you need great role models to follow. For years, Wade Cook's life has been a quest to find successful characteristics of his role models and implement them in his own life. In *A+*, Wade will encourage you to find and incorporate the most successful principles and characteristics of success in your life, too. Don't spend another day living less than an A+ life!

Business Buy The Bible

By Wade B. Cook

Inspired by the Creator, the Bible truly is the authority for running the business of life. Throughout ***Business Buy The Bible***, you are provided with practical advice that helps you apply God's word to saving, spending and investing, and how you can control debt instead of being controlled by it. You'll also learn how to use God's principles in your daily business activities and prosper.

Don't Set Goals (The Old Way)

By Wade B. Cook

Don't Set Goals (The Old Way) will teach you to be a goal-getter, not just a goal-setter. You'll learn that achieving goals is the result of prioritizing and acting. ***Don't Set Goals (The Old Way)*** shows you how taking action and "paying the price" is more important than simply making the decision to do something. Don't just set goals. Go out and get your goals, go where you want to go!

Wade Cook's Power Quotes, Volume 1

By Wade B. Cook

Wade Cook's Power Quotes, Volume 1 is full of motivational and inspirational quotes. Wade Cook continually asks his students, "To whom are you listening?" He knows that if you get your advice and inspiration from successful people, you'll become successful yourself. He compiled ***Wade Cook's Power Quotes, Volume 1*** to provide you with a millionaire-on-call when you need advice.

VIDEOS

180° Cash Turnaround Video

By Wade B. Cook

Now you know how to make money in any market—up, down, or sideways; if it's moving, you can profit on it! Now spread that knowledge by sharing the 180° Cash Flow Turnaround Seminar on video with your friends, family and co-workers. If you are tired of trying to explain what you are doing in the market, it just takes 180 minutes to turn their stock market thinking around by watching America's premier stock market educator and best selling author Wade B. Cook!

The Wall Street Workshop™ Video Series

By Wade B. Cook

If you can't make it to the Wall Street Workshop™ soon, get a head start with these videos. Ten albums containing 11 hours of intense instruction on rolling stocks, options on stock split companies, writing covered calls, and eight other tested and proven strategies designed to help you increase the value of your investments. By learning, reviewing, and implementing the strategies taught here, you will gain the knowledge and the confidence to take control of your investments, and get your money to work hard for you.

The Next Step™ Video Series

By Team Wall Street

The advanced version of the Wall Street Workshop™—full of Wade Cook's power-packed strategies, this is not a duplicate of the Wall Street Workshop™, but an important partner. The methods taught in this seminar will supercharge the strategies taught in the Wall Street Workshop™ and teach you even more ways to make more money! In The Next Step, you'll learn how to find the stocks to fit the formulas through technical analysis, fundamentals, home trading tools, and more.

Spread & Butter™

Spread & Butter™ is Wade Cook's tremendously popular one-day seminar on video. Filmed in early 1999, this home study course is a live taping of Wade himself teaching his favorite cash flow spread strategies. You will learn everything from basic bull put and bull call spreads to index spreads and calendar spreads, and how to use each effectively.

CLASSES OFFERED

Wealth U™

Wealth U™ combines the most powerful, practical and pragmatic training and tools available from Stock Market Institute of Learning, Inc.™. Our education can and does change people's lives, but we have discovered that often newer students are unsure what classes they need most in order to gain the skills necessary for creating, building and protecting net worth.

Wealth U™ is the answer: a comprehensive yet flexible program of core courses, services and tools rolled into one cost-effective package. Wealth U™ is based on a two-fold vision of financial freedom. The key to this vision is in understanding both how to increase income and assets and then how to protect that wealth from the challenges of our economic system. Wealth U™ includes everything you need in order to learn, practice and successfully implement our wealth strategies and reach your dreams!

The Wall Street Workshop™

Presented by Wade B. Cook and Team Wall Street

Once you learn the Wade Cook way of trading stocks and options, your time will belong to you again. The Wade Cook way is not really that different from the strategies the wealthy have used for years. However, it is vastly different than what your typical stockbroker or financial writer will suggest. They want you to turn your money over to a mutual fund manager, broker, or financial planner on the theory that these people know better than you how to take care of your investments.

We believe that no one will take better care of your money than you. Treating the stock market as a business means keeping control of your money, getting educated about how the market works and how to make it work for you. It means making your own decisions, choosing your own investments, and putting the focus on selling.

After attending the Wall Street Workshop™ and applying Wade Cook's system of "Study, Practice, Understand, then Do," you'll be well on your way to achieving your financial goals. You too, like thousands of other Wall Street Workshop™ graduates, could be making more money than you ever imagined in the stock market —money you can reinvest for more cash flow, or pull out of your brokerage account and spend tomorrow. With a job-free income from the stock market, a life of freedom awaits you and your family. Start your cash flow education today!

Business Entity Skills Training (B.E.S.T.™)

Presented by Wade B. Cook and Team Wall Street

This one-day seminar is dedicated to teaching new and experienced traders how to do exactly that. You'll learn how to use legal entities such as Nevada Corporations, Family Limited Partnerships and Living Trusts. People who are creating wealth through the cash-flow strategies taught in the Wall Street Workshop™ need education on how to protect themselves and their loved ones from the three primary destroyers of financial freedom: lawsuits, income taxes, and death taxes.

Scheduled to follow most Wall Street Workshops™, B.E.S.T.™ is designed to give an overview of basic business entities and correct entity structuring in a one-day format. Your introduction to the world of business entities awaits—it's the B.E.S.T.!

The Next Step Workshop

Presented by Wade B. Cook and Team Wall Street

Continuing quality education is the key to success, and Stock Market Institute of Learning, Inc. is dedicated to making that education available to you at every step of your journey to financial freedom. The Next Step™ covers 14 topics that will let you multiply your returns and dramatically cut losses while you trade the basic Wall Street Workshop™ strategies, plus advanced strategies including puts, spreads and combos.

The information you obtain from this course will dramatically expand your market and financial horizons. By the time you finish the first half of Day One, you'll be too excited to eat! You will learn how to ride the market all directions, and make money consistently. You will hear how you can limit your risk and harness maximum profits in trade after trade.

Youth Wall Street Workshop

Presented by Team Wall Street

Wade Cook has made a personal commitment to empower the youth of today with desire and knowledge to be self-sufficient. Now you too can make a personal commitment to your youth by sending them to the Youth Wall Street Workshop and start your own family dynasty in the process! This workshop demonstrates the power and money-making potential of the stock market strategies of the Wall Street Workshop™. The pace is geared to the students, with time devoted to vocabulary, principles and concepts that may be new to them.

If you're considering the Wall Street Workshop™ for the first time, take advantage of our free Youth Wall Street Workshop promotion and bring a son, daughter, or grandchild with you (ages 13 to 18, student, living at home). Help make your children financially secure in the future by giving them the helping hand in life we all wish we had received.

Financial Clinic

Presented by Wade Cook and Team Wall Street

People from all over are making money–lots of money–in the stock market using the proven strategies taught by Wade Cook. Is trading in the stock market for you? Please accept our invitation to come hear for yourself about the amazing money-making strategies we teach. Our Financial Clinic is designed to help you understand how you can learn these proven stock market strategies. In two and one-half short hours you will be introduced to some of the 11 proven strategies we teach at the Wall Street Workshop™. Discover for yourself how they work and how you can use them in your life to get the things you want for you and your family. Come to this introductory event and see what we have to offer. Then make the decision yourself!

Executive Retreat

Presented by Wade B. Cook and Team Wall Street

The Executive Retreat™ instructors are business entity specialists. This hands-on workshop teaches how to set up, manage, and maintain corporations to maximize efficiency and impact your bottom line. Incorporation is a powerful tool for protecting wealth from frivolous lawsuits and over-taxation. This is a unique opportunity for small corporations to network and share information.

Wealth Institute

Presented by Wade B. Cook and Team Wall Street

During the three days of the Wealth Institute™, we propose to take you on a journey. The directions will be given in simple, understandable language. Fair warning, though—if you take this journey with us, you may never be the same. Your view of the world of finance will be broader, and your understanding of that world will be deepened and improved.

Our journey will take you into the world of entities, step by step—explaining who should incorporate, why, and most importantly, how. You will learn about the many tax and other benefits available to corporations. We will teach you the structure and strategies of trusts, limited partnerships, and pensions to maximize your net wealth and minimize your tax burdens. We will also look at the importance of and methods for creating positive cash flow.

There is simply no other course available anywhere like the Wealth Institute™. If you want to harness the awesome power of legal entities for yourself or your business, the Wealth Institute™ is for you. Typical education is about specialization, focusing on the minute details. At the Wealth Institute™, you'll learn about connections and synergies. You'll discover not just how entities work, but how they work together.

Fortify Your Income

The Fortify Your Income™ seminar (FYI™) is designed to be a refresher course, an additional kick-start to help you use your new knowledge. Our students learn tremendous things at our more basic workshops, but without fortification, their interest often wanes (especially if some of their trades don't go as planned). On the other hand, there are students who become excellent traders and want to give something back by sharing what got them to that point. Whether you are a novice or a seasoned trader, FYI will provide access to knowledge, problems, and solutions to help you face the world of trading head on.

SUPPORT

SUPPORT is designed to be a one-year continuing education program with six one-day events focused on enhancing your knowledge is specific areas. One of the keys to successful trading is to find a strategy and system that fits your personality, available time, money resources, and risk tolerance. There's no better way to design and implement a personal system than to study several until you identify the one that clicks with your lifestyle and trading goals.

SUPPORT is designed as continuing education for graduates of the Wall Street Workshop™ and others who are interested in specialized training in specific strategies. Students can purchase SUPPORT classes separately or pay a low package price for the right to attend multiple classes of your choosing. Focus on one or two favorite strategies or instructors, or explore several to find the right style for your personality and goals!

Semper Financial

Semper Financial Conventions are for everyone! You don't need a financial degree or thousands of dollars to get started making money in the stock market. Anyone who is interested in a brighter financial future for themselves, their spouse, children, friends, church or business associates can come learn these simple cash-flow techniques and formulas in a powerful three-day multi-seminar format.

You owe it to yourself to attend a Semper Financial Investors Educational Convention. Never has there been a more exciting way to continue your education or to inexpensively introduce friends and family to stock market strategies for financial freedom!

Wealth Information Network™ (W.I.N.™)

This subscription Internet service provides you with the latest financial formulas and updated entity structuring strategies. New, timely information is entered Monday through Friday, sometimes four or five times a day. Wade Cook and his Team Wall Street staff write for W.I.N.™, giving you updates on their own current stock plays, companies who announced earnings, companies who announced stock splits, and the latest trends in the market.

W.I.N.™ is also divided into categories according to specific strategies and contains archives of all our trades so you can view our history. If you are just getting started in the stock market, this is a great way to follow people who are doubling some of their money every $2^1/_2$ to 4 months. If you are experienced already, it's the way to confirm your research with others who are generating wealth through the stock market.

IQ Pager™

This is a system which beeps you as events and announcements are made on Wall Street. With IQ Pager™, you'll receive information about events like major stock split announcements, earnings surprises, important mergers and acquisitions, judgements or court decisions involving big companies, important bankruptcy announcements, big winners and losers, and disasters. If you're getting your financial information from the evening news, you're getting it too late. The key to the stock market is timing. Especially when you're trading in options, you need up-to-the-minute (or second) information. You cannot afford to sit at a computer all day looking for news or wait for your broker to call. IQ Pager™ is the ideal partner to the Wealth Information Network™ (W.I.N.™).

EXPLANATIONS Newsletter

In the wild and crazy stock market game, *EXPLANATIONS* Newsletter will keep you on your toes! Every month you'll receive coaching, instruction and encouragement with engaging articles designed to bring your trading skills to a higher level. Learn new twists on Wade's 13 basic strategies, find out about beneficial research tools, read reviews on the latest investment products and services, and get detailed answers to your trading questions. With *EXPLANATIONS*, you'll learn to be your own best asset in the stock market game and stay on track to a rapidly growing portfolio! Continue your education as an investor and subscribe today!

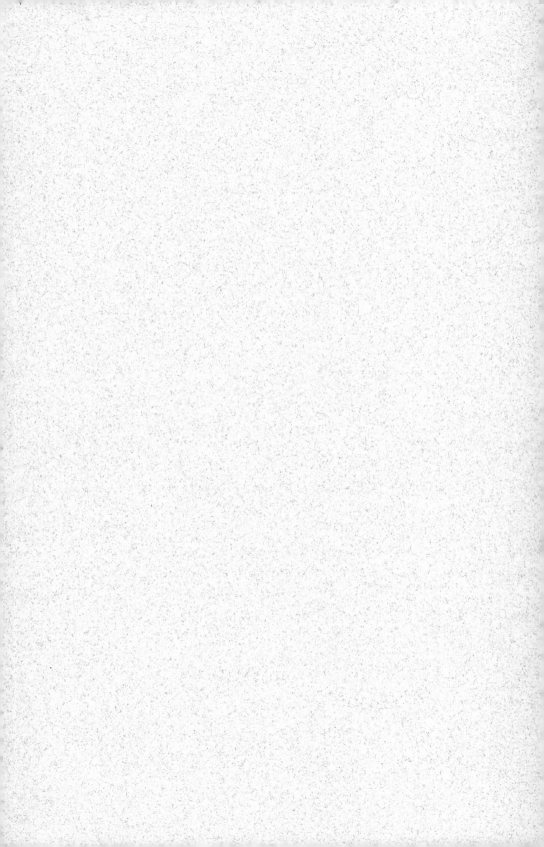